YESTERDAY'S JUNK TOMORROW'S ANTIQUES

Yesterday's Junk Tomorrow's Antiques

John Bedford
Revised and updated by James Mackay

MACDONALD AND JANE'S · LONDON

This edition first published in 1977 by
Macdonald and Jane's Publishers Limited,
Paulton House, 8 Shepherdess Walk, London, N.1

ISBN 0 356 08429 9

Made and printed in Great Britain by
Thomson Litho Ltd,
East Kilbride, Scotland

INTRODUCTION

I first became interested in collecting as a teenager, browsing around the stalls of Glasgow's Barrowland on Saturday afternoons in the 1950s. A few years later, in 1961, I came to work in London and discovered the delights of the street markets of Lisson Grove, Portobello Road and Camden Passage. These markets seemed to grow up around a nucleus of permanent junk-shops and breakers' yards. Another of my favourite haunts was a junkshop *par excellence*, the Treasure Trove in Birmingham. My indispensable *vade mecum* was a handy little volume, just published that year, entitled *Looking in Junk Shops* whose author, John Bedford, had just the right knack of introducing beginners like myself to a bewildering multitude of subjects in a chatty, downbeat manner–often highly entertaining, sometimes provocative and opinionated, always informative, and, above all, bubbling over with intense enthusiasm for collecting so that one was liable to infection. You might dip into the book for some information on fans and easily become sidetracked to firebacks and thus fall into an entirely new obsession. Such are the occupational hazards of the natural collector–and John Bedford's remarkable facility for switching from furniture to glass, from silver to textiles and ceramics, must have aggravated many a bad case like myself.

The success of *Looking in Junk Shops* led to a sequel a year later. *More Looking in Junk Shops* was followed in 1969 by *Still Looking for Junk*. Many of the subjects discussed in the first volume had by that time graduated to the antique shop and some had even been elevated to the august premises of the West End auction houses. Conversely, there were many new collectables which had scarcely (if at all) been considered in the 1950s. Distance lends enchantment, and by the late 'sixties collectors were beginning to turn an appreciative eye on Art Deco and a number of more ephemeral subjects.

The junk shops themselves were changing rapidly. In the 'sixties antique shops proliferated like Chinese restaurants and the traditional junk yard was fast disappearing. One can sense something of these changes in the last of the three volumes but progress–if it can be called that–did not stop there. Today there *are* no junk shops and yesterday's tat has become today's much sought-after collectable. The in-built obsolescence which our modern consumer society has encouraged has, in turn, given rise to the instant antique, where objects from yesterday–let alone the day before yesterday–have acquired antiquarian interest already.

In the introduction to *Still Looking for Junk* John Bedford sensed that the time criterion of antiques was moving forward at an alarming rate. By that time Art Deco had become the newest junk style of them all. Now Art Deco has graduated to the salerooms of Sotheby and Christie and collectors have moved on to the Art Moderne of the 'thirties, the Utility of the war years and now the 'Contemporary' of the 'fifties, of the Festival of Britain, the Korean War and the Truman-Eisenhower era.

And now the junk shops are themselves a thing of the past, their place taken by posh antique shops and that phenomenon of the 'seventies–the antique supermarket, lacking the *al fresco* atmosphere of the old street barrows. Even the Portobello Road and the 'new' Caledonian market in Bermondsey no longer have the informal character that John Bedford knew so well and loved. Gone are the totters who would sell you choice Vickers Britannia metal teapots at a scrap value of 'five bob an ounce'. Even the money isn't the same any more!

Much of what John Bedford wrote between 1961 and 1969, however, is still perfectly valid today. Long experience born of many years of making happy discoveries by chance in the unlikeliest places, learning the hard way, profiting by his mistakes and acquiring a 'nose' or a 'flair' for all manner of objects–these were distilled into the text of these three books. It has now been my pleasant task to amalgamate these books, revising and up-dating the text where necessary but retaining the essential matter which is still as relevant today as when John Bedford first set it down on paper years ago.

The articles have been arranged in alphabetical order and you can follow up related subjects by watching for the words in SMALL CAPITALS. This book is intended as no more than an introduction to a vast number of subjects and anyone wishing to pursue a particular line further is directed to the Reading List at the end.

A few remarks about the author himself may not be out of place. John Bedford was the *nom de plume* of George Douglas Hillyar, born in Dover in 1907. He went to sea as a captain's boy in the Merchant Navy at the age of fifteen. He visited many countries all round the world and then left the navy to become a reporter for the trade magazine *Syren & Shipping* based in London. He married in 1938 and lived on a farm near Ivinghoe Beacon in Buckinghamshire. Later he moved to Hurstpierpoint in Sussex and enlisted in the Royal Navy in 1942; he was commissioned and served on the Arctic convoys. Demobilised in 1946, he took a post as farm bailiff at Roch in Pembrokeshire, but re-entered journalism three years later when he became Advertising Representative on *World Review* published by Hulton's Press. Subsequently he became Advertising Manager of *The Farmer's Weekly*. In 1953 he began writing short articles on antiques for the home section of that paper under the name of Jane Douglas, scouring the antique and junk shops of the West Country for suitable material. This led to the first of the *Junk* books, which he wrote under the name of John Bedford. The last nine years of his life were exceedingly prolific. The sequels on junk were followed by *Horse Brasses, Talking about Teapots, The Collecting Man* and *London's Burning*, and a series on Collectors' pieces which ran from *Wedgwood* (1964) to *Victorian Prints* (1969). He also wrote numerous articles for the antique collecting magazines. He was engaged on a *Dictionary of Silver* when he died in 1970.

And finally I would just reiterate what John Bedford himself wrote, in his Introduction to *Still Looking for Junk*: '...when collecting or buying for decoration, do not only buy because you think you are getting a bargain; buy because you like and want a thing–and it will always be a bargain.'

James A. Mackay
Dumfries, March, 1977

Adams Pottery

One of the pleasant things about potters is the way they go on existing: sometimes for several hundred years. This means that you can have fun looking at their current products as well as their antique ones: and, considering the pleasure given us by the old wares, I hope my readers are sometimes decent enough to buy a plate or two of the new, and thus keep the potters happy and prosperous. (I remember getting a rather reproachful look at Worcester once when I suggested that mid-Victorian painted and gilt plates could sometimes be bought more cheaply than the current production.)

Adams is a name which has been connected with potting in Staffordshire since Elizabethan days, and probably before. Today, in their showroom, you can see not only reproductions of some of their own earlier designs–notably for the American market–but, what is more interesting, adaptations of designs in a modern idiom. It can be fun to put these alongside their predecessors.

Adams were early in the field with Staffordshire printed earthenware, using an attractive and distinctive cobalt blue: and if all those printed with American views have long since disappeared, so too have most of the English views, especially those of places around London. In their borders, they especially favoured bluebells.

But the various branches of the family have also had a hand in other wares of renown. Their jasper ware was more violet than Wedgwood's, and the reliefs freer in treatment; their black basaltes are worth looking for, and so is a fine caneware with coloured reliefs. Similar stoneware jugs to those made by Turner are sometimes found with the name impressed on the bottom and also in silver mounts: there are also some very attractive unglazed teapots faintly reminiscent of Castleford, with reliefs and sliding lids. Adams 'granite' ware is hard to find, being made for hard use rather than the cabinet.

Albarello

A vase shape–usually a slightly waisted cylinder–of great antiquity, but offering interesting possibilities in its more recent forms.

Throughout the eighteenth century it was overshadowed by Chinese and classical shapes; but, despair not, for this gets you out of the expensive period and lands you neatly among the mid- and late-Victorians, who, looking around the museums for ideas, found the flat surface of the *albarello* ideal for painting on, with colours or in lustre.

A Faenza albarello-shaped apothecary jar

Look for *albarelli*, therefore, among the varied wares of DOULTON and Minton, especially their MAJOLICA; and among the products of such firms as BEARDMORE of Fenton, who evidently thought it a Greek form, since they used it in their 'Athenian' range, giving it a touch of contemporary ART NOUVEAU. A more homely and pastoral use was made of it by these potters for a series called 'A Bit of the Old Country'. Another fruitful field might be the coloured and iridescent glazed wares of Bernard Moore and the LANCASTRIAN POTTERY.

The *albarello* first appeared in Syrian and Persian pottery of the twelfth century as a receptacle for drugs and medicines–*el barani*, they were called, and this gives us the derivation of the name. The *mudejars*, or Moorish potters of Spain, brought it to that country when they conquered it; and they introduced the shape to Italy in the fine iridescent Hispano-Moresque wares they exported thither through Majorca. The *maiolica* (hence the name) potters of Faenza and elsewhere found that its dished sides offered an admirable surface for their painting–and the apothecaries liked it because the dished side made it easy to grasp when taking it down from their shelves.

If you find any of these exalted kinds of *albarelli* in the junk shops for a few pounds, pay up and bear them silently and swiftly away.

Amber

Worth mentioning because it is so often confused with ambergris, a waxy substance which comes from sperm whales.

True amber is called a semi-precious 'stone', though in point of fact it is not a stone at all but a fossilized resin, found in long-buried forests of fir-trees. Most of it comes from such an ancient forest which lies under the waters of the Baltic. It isn't always amber-coloured: sometimes you find it almost black, while there are also varieties in brown and orange shades.

Plain strings of amber beads were highly popular wear during the Aesthetic craze of the 'nineties, and amber pipes are seen often enough. Amber beads of a more streamlined form were fashionable in the ART DECO period of the 'twenties, and it may also be found in various objects from bangles to babies' teething rings. Curio hunters like to find pieces in which flies and other insects have been entrapped for centuries.

Apostle Jugs

A smearglazed stoneware apostle jug, made by Charles Meigh, c. 1848 (City Museum and Art Gallery, Stoke-on-Trent)

These relief-decorated jugs in fine stoneware, together with stablemates like Minster jugs, are–according to the way you look at them–either Victorian vulgarity or rather fun. They typify a whole class of pottery which the mid-Victorians were very proud of, and bought in huge quantities.

The Apostle jugs are straight out of the Gothic Revival, and show a frieze of the apostles standing in niches with pointed arches. The chief maker was Charles Meigh of the Old Hall, Hanley, who also produced many other designs in this moulded ware, in classical as well as Gothic styles. So too did many other potters, including Samuel Alcock, some of whose efforts showed the relief figures in white against a coloured ground. Another whole class features the running plant decorations so beloved of that period, with or without colour.

Here is a field where comparatively little systematic collecting seems to have been done so far. But anyone interested should not have any particular difficulty in finding their way, for not only did these makers usually impress their names on the wares, but sometimes also (or instead of) gave them the useful registry marks which enable you not only to date the piece accurately but also to identify the maker from the Patent Office records now preserved in the Victoria and Albert Museum.

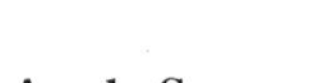

Apple Scoops

The earliest examples were made mostly from the shank bones of sheep, the knuckle forming a nicely classical voluted handle–a feature which must have appealed to the Romans, who seem to have been the first to use them to core English apples.

Some are the work of the whittler, the exponent of CHIP CARVING rather than professional wood-carving; others are as finely worked as ivory, and indeed they may sometimes be found in this material. Some have dates, usually from the eighteenth century; and like LACE BOBBINS they often served to convey a tender message to ladies–though the moment chosen here would be when they were about to bake an apple pie.

Later examples may be found in silver, Sheffield plate, brass or steel and many of these metallic scoops and corers also had patent compartments for nutmeg and spices. The wide range of decorative styles found on these scoops affords considerable scope for the collector looking for small objects that are still reasonably priced.

Argyles

These devices ensured that dukes obtained their gravy hot and free from fatty scum. The invention of a Duke of Argyll, who had long suffered from the distances between kitchen and dining-room at Inveraray, it consists of a metal pot with a hollow chamber which can be filled with hot water. The spout for the gravy generally starts at the foot of the pot and comes up level with the top. Those in silver and Sheffield plate are as expensive as other articles in these materials, but there are occasionally to be found examples in ELECTRO-PLATE from the second half of the nineteenth century.

Late 18th-century silver argyle

Art Deco

This term was coined by Bevis Hillier to describe the jazzy, geometric styles of the 'twenties and 'thirties. It is derived in a shortened form from the great Paris exhibition of decorative arts (*arts décoratifs*) held in 1925. Much of the junk that is still available belongs to this period, and the collector who can discern the distinctive lines of Art Deco amid a jumble of otherwise worthless objects can often pick up a handsome bargain.

To recognize it in its various forms–and combinations of forms–Mr Hillier suggests that you look not only at ART NOUVEAU, but also at the ARTS AND CRAFTS MOVEMENT, the industrial ideas of the Bauhaus, at the Russian Ballet of the 'twenties, at the pre-Columbian art of the Aztecs and Mayas, at ancient Egyptian art (popularized by the discovery of Tutankhamen's tomb in 1922) and the various other 'contemporary' movements of the inter-war period–all intermingled in a way which seemed rather horrifying not so long ago, but now...?

This was a period when new materials were being explored, when bakelite and other early forms of plastic were being applied to jewellery and objects of *vertu*, when stainless steel and chrome-plate were applied to furniture and household articles, when gadgets associated with electricity and the new-fangled wonder of radio-inspired designers, unfettered by any preconceived ideas or traditions. Generally speaking, the gaudy, sometimes garish, colours of the 'twenties became more muted in the 'thirties and emphasis shifted from decoration of surfaces to plain, streamlined forms which foreshadowed the utility styles of the war years and the 'contemporary' fashions of the 'fifties.

A racing-car china teapot, c. 1925

A suite of Norwegian Art Deco birchwood furniture: severe functionalism tempered by traditional Norse motifs (Christies, South Kensington)

Art Nouveau

This style gets its name from a shop called 'L'Art Nouveau' which was opened in Paris in 1895 by a German art dealer called Samuel Bing–and this French expression meaning simply 'new art' became fashionable in Britain at the turn of the century, though oddly enough, the French themselves preferred to call it 'le Style Anglais'–the English style, since much of the decorative art in this genre was imported from Britain! In Italy it gets the name 'Stile Liberty', after the shop in London's Regent Street which–up to date then as always–sold furnishing suited to it. In Germany it is known

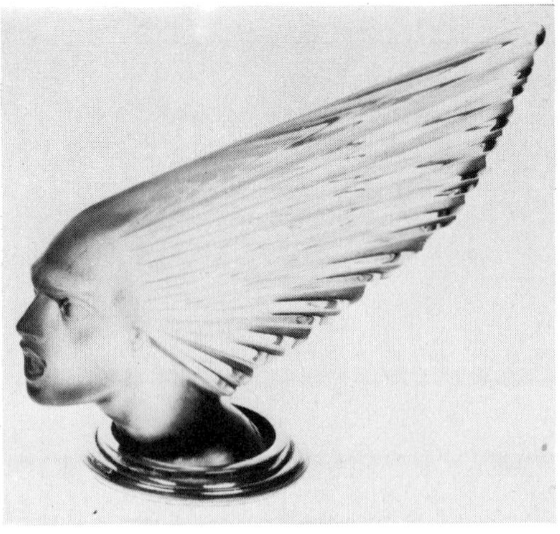

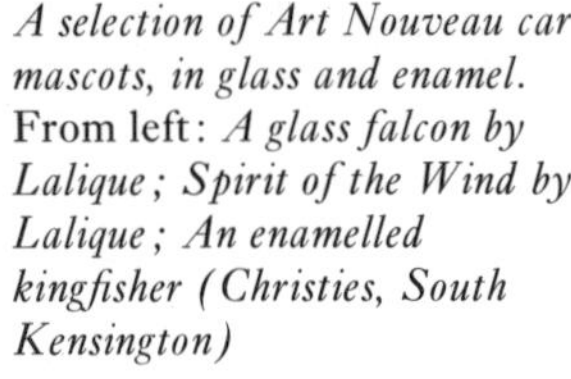

A selection of Art Nouveau car mascots, in glass and enamel. From left: *A glass falcon by Lalique; Spirit of the Wind by Lalique; An enamelled kingfisher (Christies, South Kensington)*

Above: *Art Nouveau inkwell.* Right: *Two Tiffany-style lamps of the 1910 period,* from left, *antique bronze mount, and characteristic tulip and lily-pad features (The Tiffany Shop, Christopher Wray's Lighting Emporium)*

as 'Jugendstil', after an art magazine called *Jugend* (Youth).

Not so long ago it was fashionable to decry the sagging curves and boneless wonders which typify Art Nouveau, but more recent critics have tended to rhapsodize about its ethereal beauty and sinuous lines typical, as one writer has put it, 'of the lengthening spiral of cigarette smoke'. In Britain it is seen in glass, in pottery–particularly LANCASTRIAN and DOULTON–in hammered metal ornaments, in hand-made jewellery using enamels and glass paste on copper or pewter, in the book illustrations of MackMurdo, Crane and Kate Greenaway, in the household furniture, fabrics and light fittings of Charles Rennie Mackintosh, Herbert McNair and the Macdonald Sisters. The universality of the style is evident in the favrile glass of Tiffany in America and the iridescent glassware of Lötz in Austria, in the delicate colours and subtle textures of the glass produced by Lalique and Gallé in France; it is to be found in the lithographic POSTERS of Alfons Mucha, Grasset and Cheret in France, in the textile designs of

Gustav Klimt, in the cutlery of Henry Van de Velde and the furniture of Majorelle in France and Horta in Belgium, in the textile designs of Hoffmann, Olbricht and Kolo Moser and in the furniture of Pankok and Riemerschmid.

Though Art Nouveau has been fashionable for some years now, there are still many examples of the style which are relatively unconsidered. I particularly like the vases, centre-pieces and inkwells in moulded and cast pewter, some of the majolica vases and tiles with raised decoration, and some fine needlework screens.

Arts and Crafts Movement

In the last few years there has been an enormous revival of interest in the work of William Morris and his followers, who were undoubtedly one of the mainsprings of ART NOUVEAU, itself one of the begetters of the latest style to come back into fashion, ART DECO.

The beautiful work of Morris and his disciples, which helped to free late-Victorian art from its clutter and tawdry fussiness, is now eagerly sought by private buyers and museums, and has even become the subject of exhibitions and erudite treatises. The works of Morris himself, and designers such as C. F. A. Voysey, C. R. Ashbee and Christopher Dresser, in CHINTZ, WALLPAPER and the applied arts generally, of William De Morgan in TILES, of Walter Crane and L. F. Day in graphic design, of W. A. S. Benson in metalwork and jewellery, and of James Powell in glassware, languished for many years unloved and largely unbought. Now these items are major collector's pieces, but there are still numerous examples of similar work by less well-known artists and craftsmen. It is worth noting that because the products of the Arts and Crafts Movement were more subtle than those of the succeeding Art Nouveau style, they have tended often to be overlooked and consequently are still reasonably plentiful at not too inflated prices.

Below left: *A corner of the dining-room in the artist Derek Hill's home in Co. Donegal. Art Nouveau glass and Palissy ware are arranged on the mantelpiece above De Morgan tiles, against a background of original Morris & Co. wallpaper (By courtesy of Derek Hill and* Country Life.
Below: *Section of a pair of curtains designed by William Morris (Christies, South Kensington)*

Ault Faience

Look carefully for this hitherto neglected ware before it all disappears. The revival of interest stems largely from the sale of Victorian and Edwardian Decorative Art, held in no less a place than the Great Rooms of Messrs Christie, Manson and Woods in the summer of 1968: need one say more?

It is the work of William Ault of Swadlincote, South Derbyshire, following his shortlived partnership with Henry Tooth in the production of BRETBY WARE. Ault's own wares seem to have followed the LINTHORPE glaze techniques, which he doubtless learned from Henry Tooth at Bretby.

Ault himself had begun his career at the Foley works in Longton and then at Church Gresley, one of the homes of the famous BARGE TEAPOT which, of course, used heavy brown 'rockingham' glazes. The art historian Blacker met him about the year 1910, when the potter was nearly seventy, and found that the splendid colour glazes used on his wares, splashed, striated and broken, were due to his own experimentation and supervision of the formulae.

Ault Faience vase

Like Tooth he made a great many large pedestals and pots, as well as various grotesque ornaments which do not seem to have been identified; and with them he won the highest award at the Chicago Columbian Exposition in 1893. Some vases from his pottery bearing the initials C. J. A. are painted with butterflies and flowers and plants in a somewhat ART NOUVEAU manner: they are the work of his daughter Clarissa J. Ault.

The word 'faience' is here used not in the true sense of tin-glazed earthenware, but, like MAJOLICA, to denote the Victorian lead-glazed kind.

Ball-in-Ball

How on earth, you ask, can anyone put a carved ivory ball inside another carved ivory ball which is inside yet another carved ivory ball . . . and so on, sometimes up to twenty of them diminishing in size and all capable of being moved around in their prisons?

These objects, often beautifully carved, have a long history, and are still being made in the East. Making them, although very laborious, is not all that difficult. The carver takes a solid block of ivory and shapes it into a sphere. Then he drills holes at intervals around it down to a certain depth, cuts away with a side cutting tool until he has released one of the balls, then cuts through another layer in the same way, all the time working his carving into the hollow spheres. I believe they actually start with the smallest ball first.

The ball-in-ball, sometimes called Devil's ball, was a popular feature of the CHESSMEN from Canton and other Oriental export centres.

Bamboo

Bamboo hall stand and pot stand

Nobody can poke about for long in old furniture stores without coming across specimens of the bamboo furniture which the Victorians were so fond of around the time of the Jubilees (1887–1897). For such apparently tender stuff it is surprising how well it has hung together. Obviously inspired by that late Victorian penchant for *Japonaiserie*, the bamboo was usually combined with other canes, wicker or dried grasses: it took the form of high overmantels fitted with many small shelves and mirrors; of hat and umbrella stands and other sorts of hall furniture; of many kinds of little tables, of music canterburies, trays, picture frames, brackets, lamp-standards and even Chesterfield settees upholstered–just to mix things up–with 'Djijm Kelims'.

Bamboo furniture made its debut in the western world after Japan was opened up to western trade from 1853 onwards. Following the highly successful Japanese Exhibitions, held in Paris and London in the 1870s, bamboo furniture became something of a craze. The earliest bamboo furniture sold at Liberty's (1875) was

A pair of 18th-century chinoiserie bamboo chairs (Aspreys)

imported from Japan, but within five years demand had far outstripped supply and thenceforward the bulk of bamboo furniture was made in Europe. The London suppliers would not only furnish a whole room for you, but would make the pieces especially to fit your circumstances: they would even mount your own embroidery on bamboo screens.

Being so fragile, most of the pieces one sees are somewhat battered, and would, I suppose, be expensive to repair by anything except amateur labour. But if people should decide they want it–and one has seen far less likely revivals–I daresay this can be remedied in the twinkling of a dealer's eye.

Barge Teapots

These huge brown teapots, often with a minature replica of themselves on the lid, belong to a family of wares which chiefly hail from around Burton-on-Trent. There are gallon and half-gallon teapots, jugs and also large mugs called 'clouts'. I have one of the latter labelled 'M. E. Neal, Honington, 1895', so if any reader can claim descent, they may have it in return for more information. People still living in the area recall some of the small, one-man potteries like that of 'Bossy' Mason, a jovial soul by all accounts, who lived at a village called Jacks-in-the-Hole, near Midway; his name is often to be found on the pots. They get the name 'barge' pots because they were popular with the canal-boat people passing through. I don't know when production ceased, but the last person to sell them, apparently, was a Mrs Anne Bonas, of High Street, Masham, who died about 1931. The latest date I have seen on a pot is 1914. Around Burton, these are called 'Rockingham' wares, after the brown glaze, but as the 'clouts' do not seem to be known there I suspect that at least some of the pieces were made elsewhere, perhaps in Staffordshire. An interesting line of research for a Midlander?

A 'Barge' teapot

Barometers

A long lifetime can be spent tapping the glasses of barometers without getting any useful result, probably because few people understand how or why the thing works–and anyway prefer to look upon it as a pleasant piece of wall furniture, like a DELFTWARE plate or a COPPER warming pan.

They can be made to work, of course, if you take them to one of the scientific

A Georgian stick barometer (Christies, South Kensington)

instruments people–and also find out how to read them. But even so I would much prefer a mercury one to the usual aneroid type. My favourite is old Admiral Fitzroy's model, patented in the 'eighties, where you have the column of mercury in front of your eyes (no nonsense about pretending it's a clock) and a storm glass and thermometer thrown in, all in that rather delightful 'Victorian scientific' style.

But if we are talking about furniture, there are some very handsome pieces about, considered *as* furniture. The early 'stick' barometers, which are simply cases for a vertical column, have some fine workmanship, especially in inlay work, and consequently make their price. But the more modest wheel or 'banjo' barometers of the last century show first-rate cabinet-making, and are well worth the money for this alone.

Barum Ware

Royalty were patrons of the slipware pottery made in late Victorian and Edwardian times by Charles H. Brannam at the still existing, and still family-controlled pottery at Barnstaple, North Devon.

Potting has been going on there since the seventeenth century, and Brannam's father had worked the Northwalk pottery, making pots and pans for the local trade. The son, profiting by ideas learned at the local school of art, began his own reign at the pottery by developing the local tradition of '*sgraffito* or incised decoration on a white slip over the local brown clay.

Below: *A Barum Ware jug with slip decoration, dated 1894*

This pleasant revival of an old country tradition took the eye of the London dealers Howell & James, who marketed the wares so successfully that by 1885 it was bought by Queen Victoria herself. From then on he developed coloured slips, sometimes in high relief covered with a lead glaze, and soon Barum Ware (after the Roman name for the town) found its way into the catalogue of Liberty's, then the principal fount of fashion in applied art.

Brannam seems to have thrown the vessels himself, and usually signed or initialled them, as did decorators like J. Dewdney.

Basaltes

One of the less expensive of the early wares. The relative unpopularity of basaltes today is due, I feel, to the fact that people sometimes overlook what black basaltes can do when accompanied, say, by cornflower blue or a fiery orange.

Wedgwood Basaltes, an urn, an amphora and a teapot (Christies, South Kensington)

You have here a black pottery whose blackness is not even relieved by a glaze, as it is in what has become known as Jackfield Ware. On the other hand, it carried some superb relief decoration, and if you like the neo-classical styles popularized by its inventor, Josiah Wedgwood, you will admire the shapes of the vases and other ornaments, boxes, table wares and busts.

Wedgwood named his discovery after the famous black basaltic rocks of the Giant's Causeway in Northern Ireland, but many other potters cashed in on 'Egyptian Black', as it was popularly called.

Sometimes they decorated it with encaustic ('baked on'), in the style of Greek pottery. But it seems to me that if you are going to have something black, you might as well go the whole hog. Try a few pieces on that white-painted shelf.

Battam Ware

The Victorian era was a great time for the revival or imitation of ancient styles. One of them was called the 'Etruscan'–due to the mistaken idea, current since Josiah Wedgwood's day, that the Greco-Roman styles revealed by the excavations at Pompeii and Herculaneum in the mid-eighteenth century had something to do with the vanished civilization of Etruria. The name was given by Wedgwood to the new pottery village where he made wares in this style.

By the time of the 1851 exhibition, the 'Etruscan' was wildly popular, and in one corner of the great glass and iron building a decorator named Thomas Battam built as his exhibit an Etruscan tomb, showing a cave packed with funeral pots.

There were vases, sometimes huge, in which the Greco-Roman designs were left in the terra cotta body and painted round in black. The classical subjects followed those of Dillwyn & Co. of Swansea but in fact are to be traced back to Wedgwood himself.

A four-foot vase in this style made by F. and R. Pratt of Fenton was bought by Prince Albert, the Prince Consort.

Beadwork

Beads and bugles (these latter are the long tube-shaped ones) have been made of glass

A mid 17th-century beadwork picture (Christies, South Kensington)

in imitation of JEWELLERY since the times of Ancient Egypt, and have been in demand for rosaries and necklaces ever since.

They have also been worked into all manner of EMBROIDERY. Still to be found very reasonably priced nowadays are all those little items like bracelets, hair ornaments, brooches and other forms of costume JEWELLERY; also handbags, purses, table mats, work tidies and boxes, stocking or miser purses, book covers, baskets, spectacle covers and other small articles. Beads have also been worked on chair seats and covers, screens, footstool covers, tea cosies and a host of similar domestic items. Beadwork pictures chiefly show landscapes and animal subjects, worked on a silk or satin foundation: these are getting pricey, if in good condition.

Some beads are so tiny that the hole is too small for the needle; these were sewn on with a special thread. There are also pieces decorated with the eighteenth- and early nineteenth-century cut-steel beads mentioned under JEWELLERY. Gilt metal was also used.

One of the nice things about collecting old beadwork is that if you are a needlewoman and take the trouble to learn old methods and styles, damaged pieces can be repaired at home. You could also go a little further and sell it back to the trade: they couldn't possibly get the work done any more cheaply than you do it yourself.

Beardmore Pottery

Another of the art potteries thriving around the turn of the century was Frank Beardmore & Company of Fenton, Staffordshire.

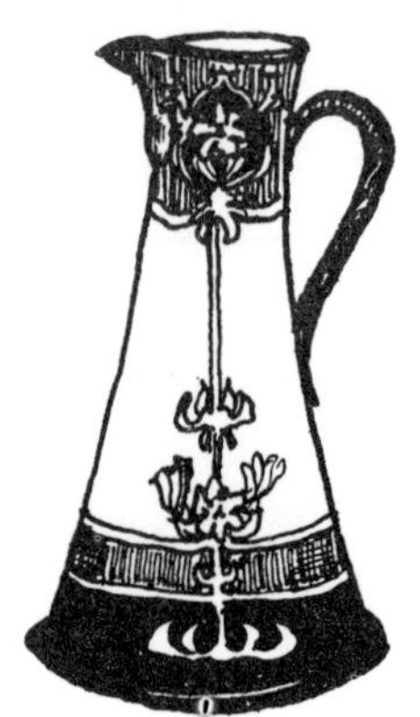

Jug in Beardmore's Sutherland Art Ware

They worked the Sutherland Pottery there from 1903 till 1914, but they were inheritors of some earlier concerns, notably Hume and Christie (1894–1902): they seem also to have brought some of the patterns and shapes of the once flourishing firm of W. Brownfield and Son (1850–92), makers of an excellent bone china: this concern petered out in the short-lived Brownfield Guild Pottery.

Beardmore's thus had one eye firmly fixed on the past, and expressed it in their coloured 'Athenian' art ware, which revives a mid-Victorian obsession: there is an infidel ALBARELLO among all the Greek shapes. To encourage customers to buy this ware they quoted Ruskin in their catalogue: 'The Greeks have been the origin not only of all broad, mighty and calm conception, but of all that is divided, delicate and tremulous.'

Another series of this kind was 'Basaltine', where figures are seen against a fine dull black body on Greek shapes.

Of more interest today perhaps is their 'Sutherland Art Ware', for many of the designs were by Kate Greenaway, whose simple outline drawings and flat colours are held by some to be one of the mainsprings of the ARTS AND CRAFTS MOVEMENT. For those who liked something rather less way out, these potters produced another series, with cottages under giant elms and quiet streams with punts, called 'A Bit of the Old Country'.

Where the firm does not give its full name in a stamp mark, the initials are used.

Bear Jugs

We no longer bait bears, but we can still buy bear-baiting jugs. They take the form of a bear sitting up on its haunches, hugging a dog to its furry breast. Attendants took them round, filled with ale, at bear-baiting tourneys.

Great rarities now, and only to be found in the big sales, are the ones made in early Staffordshire salt-glaze, and so also are those in Nottingham ware covered with clay chips to imitate the animal's fur. But there are rather later ones in earthenware covered with a brown slip, and there are also quite a few in nineteenth-century

BROWNWARE. Bear-baiting would have died out long before they were made so they must have been among the items made at that time to entrap collectors of the eighteenth-century ware.

Some bear jugs were adapted to current affairs: one well-known model dates itself fairly closely by showing, instead of a dog, a figure of Napoleon being crushed by a Russian bear. There is also another quite different case where the dog is actually attached to the bear's stomach and becomes a spout.

Bedroom Crockery

Now is the time–while they are still reasonably cheap–to sort over all those hitherto despised items which, like hand wash-stands, were banished when modern plumbing appeared. If you have not already discovered it for yourself, you may be astonished to know what junk shops can provide in the way of admirably shaped and decorated ewers and basins, shaving mugs, footbaths, soap dishes and even slop pails. I saw one of the latter, with beautiful gilded *Chinoiseries* and loaded with flowers, hanging from a balcony in Chelsea not so long ago. There is even another article in this family to be found *under* the junk-shop tables; and if you balk at bringing one of these into the lounge I would remind you that Queen Marie Antoinette's chamber pot, exquisitely mounted as a vase with a boy on top, is one of the cherished possessions of a house belonging to the National Trust.

A fine matching set of Victorian toilet china, made c. 1860 for Mr Lea of Lea and Perrins (The Dyson Perrins Museum of Royal Worcester Porcelain)

Nobody need be surprised, of course, to find good-quality pottery in this department, for all the best Victorian potters–Minton's and Wedgwood's among them–were in the trade, and gave of their best in it.

While still in the bedroom, it is worth taking another look at all those dressing-table sets, with trays, candlesticks, trinket boxes and powder pots. A Worcester style popular early in the century, with flowers and gilding on fawn-tinted china, is already in the shop windows.

Bed Steps

When beds stood higher off the floor than they do now–and if the statisticians are right we were all shorter then–it was handy to have something to help you climb into your fragrant sheets, nicely aired with the WARMING PAN. For this job came the set of bed steps–which nowadays one finds handier for getting books off the top shelf in a library. Some models include a night-stool or commode.

Bellarmines

A 17th-century bellarmine (S. H. Cole)

These are the familiar globular bottles in brown mottled stoneware, with long narrow necks, the fronts marked with the mask of a bearded man. They originally came to Britain, along with Rhenish wine and RUMMERS, under the name of Cologne ware, but they were also made by the English potters of the seventeenth century, like Dwight of Fulham.

They have for long borne the name of Cardinal Roberto Bellarmino, said to have been a rigorous persecutor of Protestants in the Low Countries during the Spanish occupation in the seventeenth century. A 'gallonier' contained a gallon, a 'pottle pot' two quarts, a 'pot' a quart, and a 'little pot' a pint.

How unpleasant or pleasant a person Bellarmino might have been you can discover for yourself by reading the biography of him (published in 1960). Actually, the jugs named after him were made long before he was born; they seem, in fact, to have descended from similar bottles bearing the masks of lions and other animals. So here, it seems, we have a case of a character getting his name attached to something which already existed.

An even odder fact about them is that they have been found buried in ditches containing nasty and spooky things like cloth hearts pierced with pins, fingernail parings, human hair and other appurtenances of witchcraft.

Bells

If you want to be posh you call them *tintinnabula*, so collecting them makes you a tintinnabulist.

This is one of those fields of collecting which don't make themselves apparent until you see an actual collection. But when you think that bells and gongs have been used in all ages all over the world for everything from fire engines to Buddhist shrines you can see what scope there is. (A gong, by the way, is something you hit with a hammer or other instrument: a bell has its own clapper–if it hasn't lost it.)

If you want to take your tintinnabulism seriously, of course, you need a yard, not a house. For, leaving aside the odd Indian temple bell brought back as a memento of service with the British Raj, there are always ships' bells at Admiralty and merchant service break-up sales, old railway bells, school bells (there'll be more of these as they pull down village schools) and those fire bells that used to thrill us as the fire engine raced through the town. All these can make a grand noise, as can the brass or bronze gongs from the East, not all of them as mighty as the one at the beginning of the old Rank films, but still capable of sending delicious throbbing reverberations round the district if you chose to call in some friends for a party.

Passing from the great crashers down to the tiny tinklers, the ones most frequently seen are the little brass call bells for the table, often with crinolined ladies whose legs are acting as clappers. There are other figures as well, including the Apostles, but here many are being made again, and if you want to be sure of having old ones you must inform yourself about BRASS.

Also in this metal are the horse bells, in tiers, some of them arranged as chords, used in association with HORSE BRASSES. There are cow and wether bells, dancers' bells, hand-ringing bells of the sort used to give concerts in village pubs, kitchen bells ripped out of old houses. There are also those call bells which once stood on shop counters–you reached up and banged the nob on the top when you wanted someone to come and sell you a pennyworth of sweets.

As to materials, the big ones, of course, are in bell metal, an alloy of copper and tin. Then, apart from brass, they come in such metals as antimony, silver, gold. You can even find them in china (GOSS included them in his armorial range), in porcelain (there is a carillon of Meissen ones somewhere in Germany), and of course, you will have seen many of the blue or red NAILSEA ones.

Benares Ware

What has become, one wonders, of all the old Benares brassware which Anglo-Indians or globe-trotting tourists once brought home? One sees a little of it about, but not nearly as much as might have been expected.

Finest of all, naturally, is the early ware made before the setting-in of self-conscious catering for the tourist trade. It gave us, in a metal as brilliant as gold, cauldrons, pots, bowls, snuffers, salvers, betel-nut cutters, goblets, flower holders, all with beautifully chased and embossed designs, often using a frosted background effect. But the later work is much less brilliant and suffers from overcrowding and monotonous ornamentation.

A Benares brass tray with scalloped edge

This is as good a place as any, however, to call attention to the wonderful range of shapes in Indian metalwork vessels. There is the long necked *Surahi*, or water vessel, with a stopper; also the *Lota*, a slightly flattened globular drinking vessel with a turned-out rim—a shape made continuously for two thousand years. No room to illustrate or describe the many others, such as the *Galubdani*, for sprinkling water at religious ceremonies, the *Bandan*, a case for holding betel-nut leaves, the *Bivala*, a metal cup, and the bell-shaped *Hukka* (or Hookah) bowl.

Bentwood

Still to be found tucked away in unconsidered corners are chairs, tables, hatstands and other articles of bent beechwood, elm and birch. A young German furniture maker, who seems to have been as far ahead of his time as Christopher Dresser in England, intrigued the crowds at the Great Exhibition of 1851 with examples of this furniture.

Bentwood settee

Michael Thonet, a native of the pleasant Rhineland resort of Boppard, conceived the idea that wood could be steamed into the same kind of pliable forms as steel, and thus make a cheaper, lighter and yet stronger article than the conventional cabinet makers could. It was, in fact, engineering in wood: and the inventor was asked by Prince Metternich to move to Vienna and set up there a large factory from which bentwood articles could be sent out all over the world.

For the better part of a century, these cheap pieces of furniture were to be found in every café, waiting room, school or office, and a few decades ago they began to be thrown out or relegated to an outhouse. Nowadays the more complicated types, offering a beautiful flowing line, are much sought after, and are even imitated by modern designers. The bentwood of Thonet inspired the Bauhaus designers to experiment with tubular steel in the 'twenties, though this ultra-modern style did not win widespread acceptance till after the Second World War.

If you can find one of those old bentwood armchairs, treasure it for your old age; and note that nobody ever designed a more comfortable rocker than Michael Thonet.

Berlin Woolwork

I suppose you could call this another of our PICTURES WITHOUT PAINT, although primarily it was used for decorating furniture. Nevertheless, it is often used in framed pictures.

The process was very much like that used in the wool rugs that are made today. To make Berlin woolwork you bought a ready-made design, in colour on squared paper,

Berlin Woolwork firescreen, c. 1850

and each square of the design called for a stitch of embroidery. Pieces made of it are full of colour–or rather *were*: they are often faded now. The name is derived from the fact that the original printed designs hailed from Berlin; though latterly similar prints were produced in Britain and America.

One finds all kinds of designs in Berlin woolwork. Perhaps the most popular one of all showed very colourful red and green parrots, and today these are very much sought after. There are also bouquets of flowers, groups of children, landscapes and often biblical scenes.

Bickers

Collectors of the odder kind of drinking vessel may have sometimes come across small straight-sided vessels shaped like a bucket with two of the staves coming above the rim and forming a pair of handles. The usual name for this kind of vessel is a bicker, but it is also sometimes called a cap or cappy–'better a timmer cap o' ma ain than a siller cap that's borrowed'.

These little vessels of Scottish origin are most cleverly made. They are usually of different kinds of wood–perhaps sycamore or alder steeped in the peat bogs to colour it to a dark brown. The staves fit into each other with five wooden 'feathers', as the craftsmen called them, so that although they are made totally dry, without any kind of fixative, they are completely watertight. Each stave is grooved horizontally on the inside near the base to take the bottom, and the whole assembly is banded with a willow band.

In some very fine specimens there are two bottoms separated by a space in which there is a pea, so that you can rattle the bicker when you want it filled up again.

Bidri Work

Not so frequently found as it once was, like old BENARES WARE, this handsome variety of damascening is made in Bihar, Hyderabad and other Indian craft centres. Ash trays, hukka bowls, spittoons, cups, plates, tumblers, flower vases, cake stands, small boxes and even teapots are found in this fine 'silver and black' ware, as well as the set of household utensils customary as a bride's dowry in Hyderabad. Salvers, boxes, cigarette cases and decorative articles are also made in this manner in Pakistan to this day.

The alloy is similar to pewter, being of zinc, copper, lead and tin. After inlaying the decorative work in silver, the piece is turned jet black by a chemical solution, after which the silver is polished so that it shows up against the black background.

Anyone having fine pieces of old Bidri work, with fine floral decoration, is to be envied, for this kind of craftsmanship, even if it continues, will become more expensive to find as time goes on.

Biedermeier

Biedermeier sofa, c. 1825

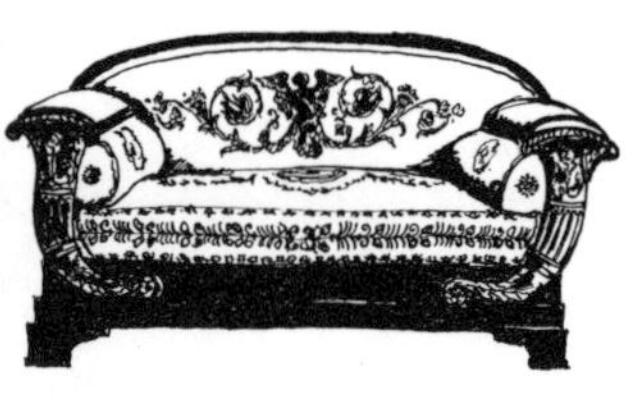

You will hear this word used of a style seen mainly in Germany, but having strong echoes in the France of Louis Philippe (1830–48)–and more than a hint of the early Victoriana left behind you at home.

To recognize Biedermeier you think of French Empire, make it simpler and more ponderous, with the classical motifs sometimes turned into realistic ones; also a general homeliness which makes you think of MEERSCHAUM pipes, smoking caps and bourgeois prosperity. Cherry and birch were used, but mainly mahogany.

Its period was roughly 1825 to 1860, and its name comes from a pair of popular magazine characters of the day, Biedermann and Bummelmaier, who portrayed the

Philistine bourgeois types.

As you might expect from its period Biedermeier furniture was superbly made: and if you put exactly the right piece in exactly the right place, you may be surprised at its effectiveness in reconciling the apparently irreconcilable.

Bird Cages

When the Victorians sang their heart-rending ditties–as folk still do in the pubs off the Mile End Road–about being only a bird in a gilded cage, they were doubtless thinking of the magnificent brass affairs which stood on their parlour tables.

From a shop catalogue of the day one sees that they had the offer of plenty of them; sometimes small and round, sometimes large and square or octagonal: either way they had those peculiarly 'different' lines which the modern manufacturer is too efficient to be able to produce–and which for us constitutes the period charm. The cages, with their gilding, their cut ruby glass surrounds, their wire trapezes, their little golden bells, are much admired and desired today: you can, if you look hard, find them domed, 'wagon-shaped', and sometimes even grander–like the 'Crystal Palace Aviary', in polished mahogany and tinned wire offered by Harrods in 1900 for 38s. 6d. (£1.92$\frac{1}{2}$).

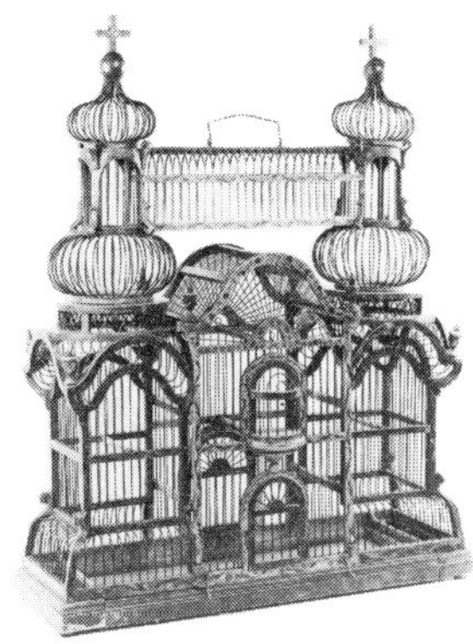

A painted, late 18th-century, Russian-style birdcage (Christies, South Kensington)

For those who like to be sure that their bird will sing there are cages already supplied with a bird whose native woodnotes wild come from a small reed organ, carefully hidden away below decks: the songster, perched upon a wire bush above the papier mâché floor, seems to be pouring out his profuse strains of unpremeditated art entirely on his Tod Sloan. Many ingenious cages of this sort survive, and their number has been increased with the help of modern manufacturers. The decorators love them, especially if they have clients for Victorian Louis decor of whatever number. Further notions along these lines are indicated under MUSICAL BOXES.

Bird Call

A small pottery whistle in the shape of a bird. You blow through the tail, and in some cases, by wiggling the fingers you can achieve the two-noted cuckoo call.

Sometimes the bird is found in a group, perching on a fence with her fledglings all around her. Sometimes she is built into a mug handle, a delight for children (and maybe the origin of 'wetting one's whistle').

Sometimes she is just a little bird of very ordinary clay, in which guise she has been found built into chimneys, to keep away hobgoblins and other things that go boomp in the night.

A 16th-century bird call or whistle (The Museum of London)

Biscuit Figures

Browse among any gathering of pottery figures and you will come across some which look like small pieces of white stone sculpture–which is what they were intended to do.

These figures are in *bisque* or biscuit porcelain–an odd name, for whereas most other porcelain is baked twice, this is not. Perhaps it occurred to someone that the unglazed texture was not unlike that of the baker's biscuit.

At all events, *bisque* saw the light of our world for the first time in the middle of the eighteenth century, at first in France and then in England, and especially at Derby. Around 1840 it had a tremendous revival in the form of PARIAN WARE which remained popular through much of Victoria's reign. It is still made today in one form or another.

When a subject has as long a history as this, however–and many charming designs date back to the earliest days–it is interesting to go back to beginnings. In this case it was at the court of Louis XV of France, whose friend and counsellor Madame de Pompadour, having been given the running of the Royal porcelain factory, had decided to move it from Vincennes to Sèvres, where she could more easily direct its activities.

At this time the establishment was producing the lovely soft-paste porcelain of the English Chelsea and Bow type; and Jean-Jacques Bachelier, the art director, had recently introduced *bisque* as a material which made possible a much greater delicacy of modelling.

When the Pompadour invited Etienne-Maurice Falconet, sculptor to the King, to take over the direction of the modelling at Sèvres, it was natural that his thoughts should turn to using this material for miniature versions of the kind of subject that he was used to carving in stone. It was also natural that he should have taken many of these subjects from the paintings of François Boucher, who was painter to the King at the time. And since they both lived in the age of the rococo, it was even more natural that these subjects should have expressed the prettiness, gaiety and charming wantonness of that mood.

They particularly went in for children subjects–for example, cupids or the little persons in the fables of La Fontaine; and so we have a whole range called *Enfants Boucher* or *Enfants Falconet*. There were often couples–'The Little Vintner' and 'The Little Harvester'–but perhaps the most famous figure of all was one we now call Psyche. On her first appearance in 1761 she was called *Une petite fille qui cache l'arc de l'Amour*, or 'A little girl who hides Cupid's bow', the companion figure being indeed without his bow and looking very annoyed about it.

It is sometimes suggested that the original of this subject was a certain Marie-Anne Collot, who would have been about thirteen at the time; who married and was deserted by Falconet's brutish painter son; who afterwards lived with Falconet for the rest of his life, nursing him through total paralysis; and who lived long enough to see the head of the Princesse de Lamballe carried on a pike below her windows during the Revolution.

No *bisque* is so fine in grain and so delicate to the touch as the *pâte tendre* of these early days: and the hardpaste porcelain which succeeded it in the French and other Continental factories was stonier in tone, and seemed to invite the untender severities of the Neo-classical age which followed the rococo.

Only at Nidervillier and Lunéville, in the *terre de Lorraine* used by Paul-Louis Cyflée, is anything like the old feeling to be found; and it is interesting to see that when the William Duesburys (father and son) of Derby took up *bisque* figure making, they used several of Cyflée's model subjects, especially the famous one of a cobbler whistling to his caged bird. The Derby paste had a fine 'smear' glaze, which is very pleasant to the touch and the modelling is always very well done, particularly in the early days.

If you like the subjects in the coloured stipple prints of Angelica Kauffmann and Francesco Bartolozzi–the bacchantes, cupids and virgins–you will find them here in three dimensions in a very fine material which Parian never quite matched, however hard it tried. And if you cannot afford originals, remember the excellent reproductions *chez* SAMSON OF PARIS.

Black Jacks

Although we still find leather the finest stuff for keeping our feet dry-shod, we do not at first think of it as a container for liquids. We did not always think so. A seventeenth-century rhyme scorns the tankard, flagon, bottle or jug, saying:

'For when they are broken or full of cracks,
Then must one fly to the brave black jacks.'

Black Jacks were rather large leather jugs, sometimes over eighteen inches in height, with loop handles and usually a metal rim, and they often come up at clearance sales of old farms, old houses, and inns. There were also bottles (the 'lether bottel' of the song), and pots or tankards with silver rims, sometimes mounted with crests or initials of the former owners.

I have a 'black jack' of my own which is modern and not really of leather, but of some form of plastic. I found it among several dozen others in a lot of surplus army stores and it was evidently used for handling acid. Still, it is big, jug-shaped, nice to handle, cost me a mere half-a-crown (12½p), and you should see what it does for marigolds.

Blanket Chests

What we nowadays call a blanket chest is a long low box, just fitting the end of a bed. There is sometimes a drawer at the foot, perhaps for linen, perhaps for clothes. After the chair and the bench and the table this must have been a basic piece of furniture; and it blossoms in surprising ways, for example as the Italian CREDENZA.

The oldest of them are in oak, sometimes plain, sometimes richly carved; but I have seen some well-made panelled ones in painted whitewood, no doubt run up by conscientious local craftsmen in Victorian times or later.

I mention them because they are still about, they have nice proportions, are not even now outrageously dear, and make a fine feature for a hall.

Victorian blanket chest with drawers

Boiserie

Persons with a decorative speculating eye have for some time past been looking for these carved wooden panels, which were perhaps once part of larger pieces of furniture or were built into the walls of rooms which have long since been demolished.

Some of them are a great deal older than one might at first imagine, for the motifs used in decoration–the shells of the Louis XIV era, the trophies, bouquets and cupids of Louis XV–are sometimes original and not necessarily nineteenth-century revivals: in fact these later carvers seem to have preferred the Renaissance styles in which some of the finest of this wood carving was done–the linenfold variety for example.

Here is another good reason for keeping in close touch with those great treasure hunters, the breakers-up of old houses.

Wooden panel from a chest front carved with diamond and tulip motifs (17th century)

Bonbonnières

A bonbonnière is a little box, usually in enamels or precious metals, in which are carried bonbons, cachous or comfits. You used one when you lived in the eighteenth century to give fragrance to the breath, or perhaps simply as something to offer round, like a cigarette case.

The box was often round: those in Battersea or Bilston enamels are well beyond our reach, but there are attractive Limoges and Birmingham enamels, and some of these are still in production. There are also tortoiseshell ones, sometimes ornamented with PIQUÉ work. They also come in pottery and porcelain and in Wedgwood jasper ware.

What were these 'comfits'? Apparently such delicacies as coriander and caraway seeds, cloves and other spices, sugared and coloured up attractively. Sometimes, instead of being put in a box, they would be in a tiny tray or basket held out to you by porcelain children or shepherdesses.

Bone Carving

If we like intricate, and sometimes quite beautiful, carving we must not overlook bone, that humble relative of IVORY–which is only a form of elephant bone anyway, although of course with quite special qualities of hardness, translucency when thin, of soft tones and of taking a beautiful polish.

But carvers used bone usually because it was all they had to hand. Perhaps the best-known examples of bone carving are the ship models made by French prisoners of war during the Napoleonic Wars, but these were the result of a centuries-old tradition of bone carving carried on by the seamen of St Malo and Dieppe. Intricately worked bone ship models, with rigging of human hair and metal parts wrought from the gold earrings worn by the French sailors, are now exceedingly rare and have long since passed beyond the level of the junk shops, but there are many other sorts of things. I can recall a beautiful games box, its sides inset with pictures of coloured landscapes and flowers, these pictures being behind glass. There were dominoes, of course, but also to my surprise a complete set of playing cards made of flat pieces of bone.

Another item at a sale was a working model of a guillotine, with soldiers standing over the victim, whose head was cut off neatly by a tortoiseshell blade. More cheerful was a working SPINNING WHEEL, with two women working it.

I notice that the seaside gift shops have burgeoned forth with thin bone carvings of some delicacy, but showing signs of mechanical work. Should one suspect Hong Kong, where the BALL-IN-BALL is still made?

Booth's Silicon China

Teapot in Booth's Worcester

Anyone who is fond of the shapes and styles of early Worcester, and does not mind having them in fine Victorian earthenware rather than eighteenth-century soft-paste porcelain, might look out for pieces of Booth's Silicon China, made at Tunstall from about 1900.

Here are the perforated baskets and plates, the flower vases, tea wares, leaf-shaped dishes, coffee pots and the rest, with rose peonies, exotic birds in gay plumage and all the other felicities of Dr Wall's reign on Severnside. Although one of the marks bears the date 1750, this is (one hopes) intended to mark the pattern rather than the date of manufacture, but in any case the firm's name is there as well–when it hasn't been removed by some enterprising dealer.

Boots and Shoes

I know a lady who has a most wonderful collection of boots and shoes–not real ones but miniatures of glass, china, earthenware, silver, pewter, wood and brass. Except for the porcelain ones they are not very expensive items, for most of them were made as novelties to be sold very cheaply, or perhaps as containers for perfume or snuff.

What I find interesting about them, however, is the different styles and types of footwear they show to have been used over the past couple of centuries–some of them so charming that one wonders they have never been revived. Ladies' high-laced boots of about the mid-nineteenth century show the tooling in the leather: little slippers in spatter glass have trimming in clear glass, slippers in opaque glass are often cased with coloured glass to show patterns sewn on.

A continental silver vesta case in the shape of a boot; boots were a popular form for small bibelots in the 19th century (Christies, South Kensington)

There are babies' bootees, men's jackboots, moccasins, dancing shoes, shoes with skates. As to use, apart from those already mentioned, you can find little boots in the shape of RUMMERS–very popular in hunt clubs for drinking toasts 'in a lady's shoe'. There are shoe and boot ink bottles, thimble holders, match containers, ash trays, salt and pepper pots, Vaseline jars, flower-holders, spoon-holders, lamps and wall-pockets. Some of these, though originally sold as containers of something, often carried the something in a bottle which fitted into the shoe or boot, but which has now been lost. Look for registry marks on glass slippers: this will lead to date and manufacturer.

Still in the shops today, of course, are the modern Dutch 'delftware' bottles, and if you are a real collector you won't despise these: what you throw away today your grandchildren will eagerly collect tomorrow. Where, for example, are all those lovely small shoe bottles and boxes in Victorian bone china, with beautiful hand painting, made for *your* grandmother?

But china and glass is only the beginning of your shoe shop. Pewter, wood and silver ones, with pincushions in the top, are still about; there are enamel boxes and bottles too. This is another of those quests which can be pursued on your foreign holiday, for overseas you will find a whole lot more styles, from Turkish slippers to Dutch clogs.

Bottle Gardens

People are beginning to notice how very handsome are some of the big stoneware jars and glass carboys. And as many of these are being superseded by plastic containers, these big pots have begun to appear in the junk shops.

There's no need to wait for that, of course. A visit to Doulton's or one of the other manufacturers of chemical stoneware might open your eyes very much to the fine shapes and textures of these things, and how their very size and coarseness flatters the delicacy of your flowers and plants. I've no doubt at all that one day these things will be as seriously collected as salt-glazed stoneware or slipware is today.

As for the glass carboys, these are being used as miniature gardens. You may know that there is such a thing as a Wardian case–a glass affair, used for transporting plant specimens alive from one place to another. The carboy garden is a development of this idea; you put in some finely sifted soil, also some seeds of ferns and other plants, and providing you water them regularly and let them see the sun they will flourish like the green bay tree.

Brass

There are two things to be said in favour of collecting brass. One is that your best bargains will generally be found in such a shocking state that after you've got them home and put in a little elbow grease on them, they seem to be worth at least twice as much as you've paid for them.

The other is that if you boggle at the idea of regular cleaning, you can buy a form of lacquer which keeps them bright. Having said which, let me tell you that I know at least two collectors who would rather die than lay a glistening coating over the subtle glow of brass. Though never known to help with the smallest household chores (brass collectors are generally men) they will sit for hours indoors in the brightest weather,

Below left: *Brass hanging lamp by The Century Guild (William Morris Gallery).*
Below: *George III brass trivet (Christies, South Kensington)*

Brass letter rack

neglecting their lawns, their meals and (if they dared) their jobs while they fondle and polish their treasures.

But what to collect? I think you have first to make up your mind if you are interested in 'genuine' brass–or rather what you mean by that term. Brass, which in its modern sense is an alloy of two parts copper to one part zinc, seems not to have been made in England until late Elizabethan days, and it is worth noting that when Shakespeare said:

'When sometimes lofty towers I see down-raz'd
And brass eternal slave to mortal rage'

he was talking about bronze, which didn't pick up its own name until about the middle of the eighteenth century. So here we have a curious example of an old product giving up its name to a new one, and taking another name for itself. Some etymologist collector may one day tell us where both these names come from, for the *Oxford Dictionary* doesn't seem to know.

Anyway, if you want old brass, you must learn to distinguish between the earlier alloys and the way they are worked, i.e. whether the piece was cast or hammered out of latten, the name given when the metal came in the form of sheets.

Not, perhaps, surprisingly, dealers seem to know a lot less about metals than they do about china or glass, though of course they are well aware of its scrap value, which is often used as the basic yardstick of price. After that they look at workmanship, apparent age, curiosity or what not.

But if you study the subject at all, you will be well ahead of most of them except the specialist dealers, of which there are several among the members of the British Antique Dealers' Association. With these, of course, you will be the humble learner, and must treat them respectfully, as if they were your family solicitors.

Again, what to collect? Well, there are all those miniature ornaments, such as tiny brass stools and fenders, which Birmingham is still making industriously. There are BUTTONS and small brass DOOR KNOCKERS, which are also being made again. I like shape in all things, and there is a graceful water jug which is worth its position in any home; there are also helmet-shaped coal scuttles, andirons and other FIREPLACE FURNITURE.

Lifting your eyes from the fireplace to the cottage mantelpiece, there are those quite fascinating brass and other metal ornaments stamped out in the shape of figures, like horses, peacocks, shepherds. Sometimes you will find groups, like 'the goose that laid the golden egg', and then there are numerous kinds of PLAQUES.

Apart from brass figures do not overlook those amusing DOOR PORTERS, or the little tobacco tampers which go right back to the beginning of pipe smoking in Britain. Their business end is flat and small enough to press down the burning tobacco, but the other end can be in the shape of almost anything, from a king's head to a lady's leg.

Then there is the whole range of Oriental and African brass which will take you into the realms of legend, ritual and religion and can keep you interested for several lifetimes. Here it is not so much a question of antiquity as of their intrinsic interest, for many of these pieces are being made still for their original purpose.

I must confess that I'd never really looked very closely at such things until one day when I chanced to be in a little bric-à-brac shop gazing round at a depressing assortment of Victorian china. Suddenly I saw a small brass group consisting of a very much elongated negro shooting a spear from a bow, with a dog attached to his leg. The pair seemed only that moment to have stepped out of a bush and were about to knock down a buck. As I didn't buy brass at the time, I went out without buying, but that hunter and his dog haunted me for days. Eventually I phoned the dealer in a panic (I had to ring the police to find out his name) and sent him the thirty shillings (now £1.50) he wanted.

When the group arrived, of course, I desperately wanted to know all about it (see what I mean about collecting?). By poking about in places like the British Museum and that wonderful Pitt Rivers Museum at Oxford, I found that the group came from Dahomey, in West Africa, and had been made by a process known as *cire perdue* or 'lost wax'. With this, a model is made in wax, which is then coated with fire-resisting clay. When fired the wax melts and runs out, leaving a hollow mould into which the molten brass or bronze is poured. Thus, every piece made by this process is unique and unrepeatable. But there are many different subjects–chiefs walking in procession, mothers calling their children, men rowing in canoes. As I say, they're still being made, but I don't find that this worries me for here we're not collecting antiques, or things made in imitation of them, but little works of art illustrating the customs and habits of human beings–than which, of course, there is nothing more exciting.

In a similar field there are those fascinating little gold weights from Ashanti: they're tiny brass figures in all sorts of grotesque and comic forms used as scales in the gold dust trade of West Africa. These you will see more often in museums than the Dahomey figure, and I've yet to find my first one in a junk shop. But keep on looking!

Bretby Ware

Here is another of those late Victorian potteries whose wares are now becoming highly desirable and which have moved into the Sotheby and Christie class. It was a second flowering of the talent of that potting non-potter Henry Tooth of LINTHORPE, when, at first in partnership with William Ault in 1833, he established the Bretby Art Pottery at Woodville, in South Derbyshire. The two men fought like cocks on the same dunghill, however, and Ault moved away a few miles to establish his own pottery at Swadlincote renowned for its AULT FAIENCE.

Vase imitating the effect of wood and metal, in Bretby Art Ware

You may recognize Bretby ware in large pedestals, pots, umbrella stands and the like, with the coloured glazes developed so successfully at Linthorpe; but also by a new line in which Tooth followed the favourite Victorian pastime of making pottery look like any and every other kind of material. There was 'copperette' ware, which looked like hammered copper, also imitations of bronze and bamboo; ash trays in the form of a leaf carrying walnuts and nut-crackers, biscuits, fruit and suchlike, not to mention reels of cotton, thimble and scissors, or corkscrew, cork and lemon. There were also some rather engaging little figures.

Another product of the Bretby Pottery which has found a new market is the large colour-glazed stork or swan which once sat in the windows of dairies, holding eggs between its wings.

Britannia Metal

Now that both silver and Sheffield plate are very much a rich man's quarry, quite a few of us have been looking at what is to be found in Britannia metal. One of the discoveries one makes is that table wares made in it have some extraordinarily fine and simple shapes; another is that its sheen, rather like that of pewter, can appeal to one as much as silver–unless the silver is very old.

Britannia metal teapot

PEWTER is discussed elsewhere, and when you pick up a piece of Britannia metal and ask the dealer what it is, nine times out of ten he will tell you that it *is* pewter. He is very nearly right, for it is an alloy of tin, antimony and copper, differing only from the usual pewter alloy by having no lead in it. The dealer's criterion is that he gets about the same price for both as scrap.

Britannia metal emerged in the late eighteenth century when John Vickers started using an early version of it under the name of Vickers Metal, or White Metal, for pieces in the styles of Sheffield plate. Up to the time of the invention of ELECTRO-PLATE,

Britannia metal appeared wearing its own skin, which was a passable imitation of silver; but time took off this sheen and the pieces would settle down to the quiet grey glow of pewter. This did not suit the Victorians very well, for they wanted their guests to think they really could afford silver, so upon the invention of electro-plate in the eighteen-forties, many articles of Britannia metal were put through this process and given a coating of silver. They can be spotted by the letters EPBM (electro-plated Britannia metal) on the base. But an enormous amount of the metal must have been sent out just as it was, for this is what one finds nowadays. On the other hand, much of it, if not sold as scrap, is being sent by dealers to the platers where, after acquiring a hard cold silver coat, it goes to the flashy shops in seaside resorts. The word Sheffield, a number, and perhaps the name of a maker like Dixon, lead some people wrongly to infer that it may be Sheffield plate.

British Plate

This was a development of SHEFFIELD PLATE and had the advantage that its core was not of copper, but of a silver-coloured alloy which did not show through when the silver coating became worn. Its manufacturers often hopefully stamped it with devices intended to pass off as silver hallmarks.

The alloy was known as GERMAN SILVER from its place of origin, and it included copper, zinc and nickel. Articles made of British plate followed the styles of Sheffield plate, but were sometimes given solid silver mounts. Occasionally pieces may be found which bear the letters EPGS (electro-plated German silver), instead of the more usual EPNS (electro-plated nickel silver), the alloy used in ELECTRO-PLATE which eventually superseded it.

Brocs à Cidre

One of the shapes that the peripatetic junk-shop haunter may find in Europe, especially in Northern and North-Western France, is a rather elaborate jug used for carrying cider. The locals in Normandy, Picardy and Brittany have been using these jugs for a good many centuries, and in fact they still make and use them.

The finest of them are closed with a lid of pewter or silver, which is attached by a kind of ring to the handle of the jug, and has a thumb button for lifting it. The older ones, made from about 1720 onward, were obviously greatly treasured; they were dated, and probably made to order, because like some of our own pottery in Britain they often had a special inscription. They might have a portrait of a young man and woman and the date of their wedding. The predominant colour is blue, mainly blue guipure.

An Art Nouveau bronze figure (Christies, South Kensington)

Bronzes (and things like them)

Figures, groups and other objects cast in bronze were unjustly neglected not so very long ago–unless, of course, they happened to come from the Italian Renaissance or Ancient China. A dealer friend used to tell me that this was due to the fact that 'they ain't got no colour, which is what the woman wants, and what's the good of trying to please men in this business?'

Unlike the *cire perdue* process which I mentioned under BRASS, the majority of the small bronzes which you will find in the shops nowadays were produced by sand-casting–a much more economical process which enabled the bronze-founder to repeat the edition an infinite number of times. Small *bronzes d'edition* were exceedingly popular with the rising bourgeoisie of Europe but they lost ground at the turn of the century when more artistic figures of dancing girls in swirling, diaphanous veils in the spirit of ART NOUVEAU came into fashion. They, in turn, gave way to the bronzes of the 'twenties which often incorporated portions of carved ivory. The figures of this period consisted mainly of girls–dancing, performing athletic feats or simply looking coy and arch in the best 'twenties manner. These bronze and ivory figures went out of favour shortly before the Second World War. Nowadays, all these obsolete kinds of bronze have been restored to popularity. First to enjoy a revival were the bronze figures and groups of animals and equestrian statuettes by the so-called Animalier School of French sculptors, and as they rose dramatically in price in the late 'sixties, collectors turned to the Art Nouveau females of Raoul Larche and Laporte-Blairsy–and now it is the turn of the bronze and ivory figures of Chiparus, Preiss and Zack to go through the roof pricewise.

But there is still quite a number of metal figures available and these will probably be the next to catch the eye of the collecting public in a big way. Figures in spelter, a cheaper, more leaden version of bronze, and even the aluminium figures of the interwar years, are worth considering. Up to now there has been little interest in electrotyped figures (distinguishable from cast bronze by their relative lightness and hollow, 'tinny' sound), but now is the time to give them a second glance.

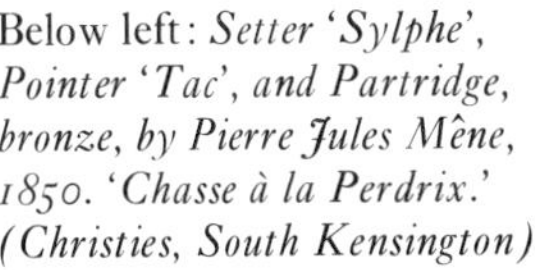
Below left: *Setter 'Sylphe', Pointer 'Tac', and Partridge, bronze, by Pierre Jules Mêne, 1850. 'Chasse à la Perdrix.' (Christies, South Kensington)*

A brown saltglaze tobacco jar, Staffordshire, early 19th century (City Museum and Art Gallery, Stoke-on-Trent)

Brownware

Collectors with a taste for the unusual rather than the conventionally pretty have long been putting together the many different sorts of things made in what seems nowadays to be generally known as Brownware, or salt-glazed brown stoneware.

You may recognize it in the famous HUNTING JUGS and mugs, puzzle jugs with their baffling spouts and holes, cylindrical jugs called 'canettes', two-handled posset pots and LOVING CUPS, CANDLESTICKS, tea kettles, TOBACCO JARS, decorative twisted tobacco pipes after the manner of NAILSEA, BEAR JUGS, TOBY JUGS, 'windmill' jugs, but most of all the astonishing range of spirit bottles.

In buff, brown or deep chocolate stoneware of an immense hardness, with carvings or impressed designs and showing scarcely any marks of time however old they are, these pieces were so popular with collectors in late Victorian days that the potters of the day obliged with replicas of what they had made a hundred years before. Today, therefore, in the absence of a mark, it is often very difficult to trace a piece not only to a maker but to a century. However, no true collector has ever been put off by a consideration like this, so here is the quarry for those who like detective work, as well as

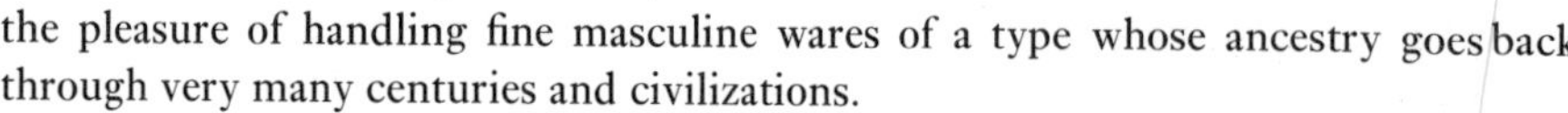

the pleasure of handling fine masculine wares of a type whose ancestry goes back through very many centuries and civilizations.

Buckles

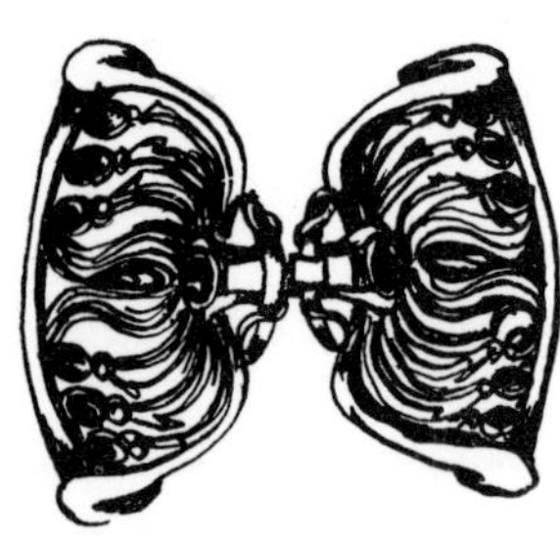

Art Nouveau buckle

There are certain collecting subjects where pennies and pounds may be made to go a long way provided one is prepared to go to some trouble about displaying them.

Such a subject, I suggest, is the buckle. First imagine that you have on your wall a large picture frame, empty but for a stretch of coloured velvet, satin or some coarse-woven material, set back a little from the glass.

This is your cabinet: you now go out and collect buckles of all kinds and shapes and arrange them, carefully and harmoniously on the coloured background: you then seal up the back with brown paper.

Now for the buckles. One has to think of them as articles of jewellery–costume jewellery if you like–worn at waist, knee and foot. They have been used for belts and girdles, of course, ever since these articles were worn: but there is hardly room here to tell this long story.

Shoe buckles seem first to have become fashionable articles of wear about the time of Charles II–Samuel Pepys records in his *Diary* for January 22, 1659–60 that 'This day I began to put buckles on my shoes which I have bought yesterday from Mr Wotton.' By the time of Beau Nash fashion called for 'huge buckles'–Lady Mary Wortley Montagu's son was described as being 'worth £2,500 in buttons and buckles'.

After a hundred years, at the end of the eighteenth century, they suddenly went out of fashion. It is therefore in that period that one seeks the finest and more ornate kinds, perhaps encrusted with stones–although mostly paste. But there also of silver, pewter, enamel, MOTHER OF PEARL, Wedgwood cameos set in steel, pinchbeck, tinplate and even blackened iron.

In Victorian times one looks for belt buckles, often designed *en suite* with brooches or diadems, of gilt or silver filigree, beads, jet or clusters of pearls. Toward the end of the century there appear fine buckles of the fashionable chased or oxidized silver; others were made up of coiled serpents, butterflies or portrait heads; also large paste buckles, made at the back of the dress.

You can, of course, buy for purely decorative reasons, to complete your framed picture: but you may also find yourself with an interesting little museum of styles and materials.

Buttons

I never thought buttons could be of any particular interest until one day in the Caledonian Market I came across a whole lot of them marked with different crests. I was told they were livery buttons, made for the household servants of the great ones of other days. Some of them were very handsome affairs, either in silver or gilt, and there are many collectors whose delight and interest it is to get sets together and identify the person or family owning the crest–which, of course, can be done by turning up heraldry reference books.

A late 18th-century jasper hunt button. The bas-relief horse is one of a number of horse studies originally modelled by George Stubbs for Wedgwood (Wedgwood)

Since then I've realized that there are many other kinds of buttons to be collected. Apart from naval and military ones, there are those worn by engine drivers, guards and other personnel of all the old railway companies, fire-brigades, shipping lines, police forces, prison services, security organizations–the list is endless.

In craftsmanship it is difficult to find anything better than the sporting buttons–hunt buttons struck with the name of the hunt and a fox mask; shooting and cock-fighting clubs had theirs as well.

So far as materials are concerned, there are the early silk and stuff ones, purely for ornament, while afterwards they come in BRASS, tin, PEWTER, COPPER, gold, silver, IVORY, glass, HORN, tortoiseshell, BONE. China ones were a speciality of Minton's while Wedgwood made them in jasper ware.

Cachepot

It literally 'hides a pot', so that the plant or the flowers in it seem to be growing in a (usually) porcelain container. In Italy you would describe it as a *copro vaso* and in Germany as a *Topfhüll.*

As with the CASOLETTE, here is a subject which you can collect in most styles of the past 250 years. In porcelain you might start by looking at Vincennes and Sèvres and then come down through all the Continental and English factories, stepping on to the collecting ladder wherever you fancy–or can afford to.

A pair of variegated creamware cachepots and stands made by Wedgwood (Christies, South Kensington)

Cadogan Teapot

This peculiar peach-shaped teapot, which comes in all sizes from miniature to giant, and is usually covered with a brown glaze, has no lid, and therefore must be filled from the bottom, through a tube which goes up inside the pot itself. It is said to be named after a Lady Cadogan of the eighteenth century who liked to make her guests guess how the tea got into the pot. I have never tried to make a cup of tea in one, but I should have thought that getting the tea-leaves out presented a problem. The Chinese original from which it was copied was probably a wine pot rather than a teapot.

Cadogan teapot

Cake Moulds

Those who know the rich variety of quaint and interesting designs which are to be found in Britain on the moulds once used for gingerbread, marzipan and other confectionary, may find it interesting when they are in Amsterdam to bend their steps towards, say, the shops around the Keizersgracht or the Nieuwe Spiegelstraat.

There they will find many examples of the *koekplanken* or *Koekprinten* (literally cake boards and moulds) which come in greater variety and certainly in much greater numbers than in most countries. The housewives seem to have gone on using them after the pastry cooks had given them up–or alternatively more skilful reproductions of such moulds have been made there than anywhere else. They are also to be found in the Scandinavian countries.

Cameo Glass

Vases, bottles and other pieces in carved cameo glass with figures and other designs standing out in relief in opal glass on a darker ground, sometimes appear in the salerooms, and when they do they fetch very good prices. So if you see a good one going cheaply, snap it up.

They derive from a sharp break with the English tradition of cut glass pioneered by John Northwood of Wordsley, in the famous glassmaking district of Stourbridge. Northwood's original work, in which he laboured for years over such tours de force as a replica of the Portland Vase, is rare and priceless, and so also is the handiwork of such disciples of his as the Woodall brothers.

But a later development of this was 'commercial' cameo, which eliminated a great deal of the work of carving the relief figures, and so made it possible to market the ware at reasonable–though by no means low–prices.

The engraving wheel was brought into use to help out with the carving, and the opal glass was 'cased' to the body more thinly, thus leaving less to cut away and reveal the coloured body beneath.

Many of the pieces found nowadays have the classical themes of the times, but personally I prefer the very fine patterns of leaves and flowers, the sort of designs in which the latish Victorians really excelled. But, as I said at the beginning, you will have to be eagle-eyed to get even 'commercial' cameo very cheaply these days.

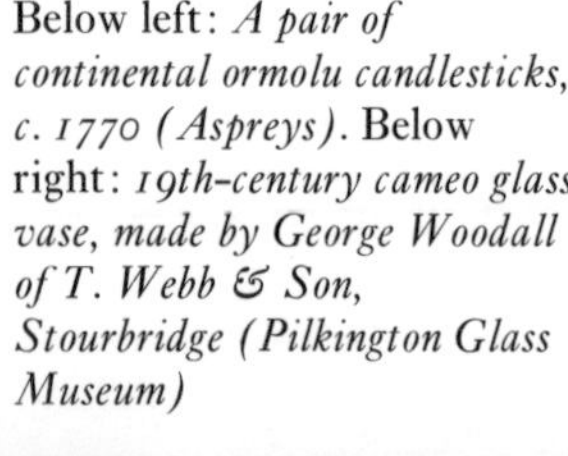

Below left: *A pair of continental ormolu candlesticks, c. 1770 (Aspreys)*. Below right: *19th-century cameo glass vase, made by George Woodall of T. Webb & Son, Stourbridge (Pilkington Glass Museum)*

Candlesticks

The butcher and the baker are still around–just–but their colleague the candlestick-maker has now ended his work: it seems a good moment to see what it has to offer us collectors.

We should pass over rushlight holders, for we are not here concerned so much with bygones as with hasbeens; and we want to think of our candlesticks not merely as holders of candles but as expressions of decorative ideas. Once again, we are junk-shop haunters looking for small ways of showing grand ideas.

In doing this we shall have to pass by gold and silver–unless it be that lovely soft metal from China and Malaysia which the British and American silver fanciers unaccountably pass up. But this still leaves us bronze, brass, pewter, the whole family of ceramics, painted wood (or wood needing painting) and other materials.

Bronze, from Japan and China, may give us a tall pricket candlestick of the kind seen on high altars; while from India we can have something which is a true holder, and

Candlestick shapes 1600–1650; 1650–1700

stands on a writhing snake or an elephant.

late 17th century; 1740–45

Coming nearer home, and homely beauty, where will you find a more entrancing outline than the brass or pewter stick of the late seventeenth and early eighteenth centuries, with long cylindrical socket, into which the candle was deeply thrust–and as it burnt away had to be levered upwards through a vertical slit in the side? The foot is wide and domed or stepped, the drip tray placed well down the stem–which may well be given engine turnings to suggest the beading in contemporary table and chair legs.

It is only a little after this that we come to the typical Queen Anne column, and the square or octagonal foot (although we must remember that in our baser metals we are ever a little rearward of the fashion). Now also comes in the baluster, upright or inverted, with cushions and rings on a domed circular foot; while as the eighteenth century progresses we move, Chippendale-wise, first towards elaborations of the balusters and rings, with gadrooned or scalloped feet, and then away from them, with taller straighter stems, and perhaps a Corinthian capital looking like the columns of a Roman temple–which is exactly what it was trying to do.

1751; 1791; 1905

All this time, of course, we have the friendly chamber candlestick, deeply sunken into its tray, with a place for the extinguisher, and if they are brass, a slot in the stem for the snuffers.

The glassmen and the chinamen of these periods had their candlesticks, so too did the enamel men, although from South Staffordshire rather than Battersea. Once we have turned the corner of the nineteenth century, we can find flower-encrusted Rockingham and Coalport, Victorian cut-glass and perhaps the very rare PONTYPOOL AND USK WARE painted tinplate.

Every one of these shapes, sometimes combined in surprising ways, are to be found in late Victorian days, as my Harrods catalogue for 1900 amply testifies.

Cane Ware

Here is a kind of pottery which I think we might look at more closely. As with many another sort, a single piece may not look very much, but a lot can look very interesting, and in fact show a surprising diversity.

What I am talking about is a buff, or tan-coloured, dry (unglazed) STONEWARE, often enamelled in blue and colours. Outstanding pieces are the well-known piecrust dishes made in the form of a game pie and intended to act as a substitute for the pastry which shortage of flour denied the people of Britain during the Napoleonic wars. Another

Below left: *A cane ware jug, 1870.* Below: *A cane ware plate, mug and jug in basketweave pattern, c. 1810. Both from the Woburn Abbey Collection (Wedgwood)*

A Wedgwood game pie dish, made at Etruria, c. 1850 (Wedgwood)

well-known one is the bamboo-style bulb pot which one often sees. These were quite a happy invention, for each stick of 'bamboo' around the pot had a hole at its end for an individual flower, as well as the central holes for the bulbs.

But these are merely the show-offs of the family: I prefer all those nice little teapots and sugar bowls with reliefs of cherubs and other subjects, and sparingly lined in blue or green. Wedgwood was a pioneer in Cane Ware as in most other fields, but it was also made by Turner of Lane End, Mayer and others.

Cannon

If you like firing salutes when friends come to tea it will not cost you a great deal to buy the cannon, nor take you very long to find it.

'To make the mixture fit for great guns, mortars and other pieces of artillery,' says a gentleman named Malachyn Postlethwayt, writing in the year 1751, 'the best and softest tin of Cornwall is a necessary ingredient skilfully applied. There must be six, seven or eight pounds of it to the 100 weight of red copper.' As Britain was laying the foundations of an empire about that time, this recipe seems to have been a reasonably successful one: perhaps we should have stuck to it.

Most difficult sort of cannon to find, naturally, are those which have survived some historic action and also escaped melting down into souvenirs. But there are plenty of nameless ones which have probably done just as well in their quiet (if that is the word) way. They are usually found in cast iron reinforced with stout metal hoops, or in gun-metal, a kind of low-grade bronze. Brass signal cannon of more recent vintage can still be picked up fairly cheaply, though genuine military cannon are becoming decidedly expensive. The addition of such embellishments as a royal cypher, coat of arms and date tend to enhance the value of these guns. Often, however, the presence of a simple ordnance or foundry mark will enable you to date a piece fairly accurately.

Even if your garden consists only of a window box you can have your artillery. Miniature cannon, either of cast iron or engraved brass, say eight to fifteen inches long, can be found for less than half the price of full-sized cannon.

A selection of card cases in various materials—tortoiseshell, enamels, mother-of-pearl and inlaid lacquer (Christies, South Kensington)

Card Cases

People who called on neighbours and acquaintances to 'leave cards' once carried them in beautiful little cases, made of almost every sort of decorative material. They came in tortoiseshell, inlaid pearl, ivory, papier mâché, mother of pearl, wood, metal, filigree, beadwork, moulded wax and even silver and porcelain.

One sees a good many of these little cases about, and still not at all dearly priced, considering the workmanship which has been put into them–which I suppose we shall never see again lavished on such ordinary workaday little affairs.

One reason they're relatively cheap is that they're usually just too slim to take cigarettes, and there aren't many other practical uses one can make of them. But they can look most attractive when set out on a black velvet tray; so if you like beautiful workmanship, why not gather some together–before we all start leaving cards on each other again and they disappear from the shops?

Carpet Balls

You will occasionally come across a set, or more likely a few specimens, of a sort of china ball with coloured rings. These were used on long TV-less Victorian evenings for the game of Carpet Bowls. For this you needed one plain and six patterned balls, or 'taws', which were in fact usually made of stoneware or earthenware.

You also need a fairly long corridor to play the game in style, so if you become the owner of a set you really ought to buy a baronial mansion as well.

Casolettes

Here again is one of these small objects, which offers itself as a collecting subject costing relatively little and making no great demands on your space.

A pair of Blue John Casolettes

In this case, however, since the period range is fairly narrow, one's interest will perhaps lie in the different materials in which it was made.

As you might suppose, the term is French (although the object must have originated in the East), and it started life in Europe in the seventeenth century as the *brûle parfum* or perfume burner, in copper or some other metal. It was useful in times when ventilation meant, roughly, a draught, and it was more comfortable to sweeten the air in a room by burning aromatic herbs than by opening a door or a window.

Starting fairly simply, in the course of a century the casolette had become a highly elaborate decorative piece, usually in the shape of a vase or an URN, perhaps in marble with ormolu mountings and a perforated bowl.

The great majority of your pieces, I imagine, would show Neo-Classical or Empire styles in their various sub-divisions and derivatives, and in Paris you would be looking for it not only in Louis XVI, but also in Louis Philippe, *Restauration* and Second Empire styles.

Cassone

An adventurous department store on the east side of London was very busy some years ago importing some of the more spectacular modern Italian furniture and furnishings: and among these things, apparently, destined for the many small terrace houses of the district, were some very grand and highly polished examples of that very long-lived and basic article, the *cassone*, together with its compatriot the CREDENZA.

Florentine cassone

Basically, it is a chest; and of course it has its counterpart in every other country; but the Italian *cassone* has always been notable for the variety and richness of its decoration. In it, Renaissance styles enjoyed an enthusiastic revival in the nineteenth century, and it appears today, painted or inlaid, with a characteristically glass-like finish.

Castleford teapot

Castleford

Here is another of those wares which are so characteristic in shape and looks that you can spot specimens from the top of a bus.

To my mind, Castleford is quite unjustly neglected, both by collectors and historians, and I for one would like to know a great deal more about it.

Not all these fine stoneware teapots and other wares, decorated with panels in relief and sparingly lined in colours, were made at Castleford, though David Dunderdale and Company, of that Yorkshire town, seem to have been the principal makers and impressed their name or initials in the ware.

It is held that pieces with convex (bulging) corner panels are indubitably Dunderdale, or at least Castleford-made, whereas those with concave panels and a number impressed were made elsewhere. But, as I say, information is scanty, and there is room for informed collecting. Pieces are no longer cheap, but considering their attractiveness, their charming period flavour and their rank in the stoneware hierarchy, prices are certainly not excessive.

Caudle cup

Caudle Cups

Among the odder drinks favoured by our ancestors was caudle, a sort of custard made of oatmeal or biscuit mixed with hot wine or beer, then spiced or sweetened. It was given to invalids, woman in child-bed and anyone else who needed cossetting, also to those visiting them: at first in a covered cup with a spout (in fact, a posset pot), and later in a two-handled cup with a saucer and cover, the imbiber using a spoon instead of, presumably, sucking the stuff through the spout.

Often mistaken for chocolate cups (which had only one handle), these caudle cups sometimes come in matching sets, and even en suite with a tea and coffee service. Worcester made them, so did Chelsea, Derby, CAUGHLEY and several other English potteries. They could, I suppose, be the ancestors of those covered 'cabinet cups' made for display by the Victorian factories in bone china.

A blue-painted Caughley sauce-boat, c. 1780 (City Museum and Art Gallery, Stoke-on-Trent)

Caughley

People talk about Caughley (or 'Salopian') as one of the lesser lights of early English porcelain. 'Even Caughley,' they say, in a derogatory sort of way. For me, if I were going to collect soft paste porcelain seriously, I think I should go in for Caughley just because of this.

But it's a ware which brings its own rewards as well. The factory (at least the porcelain part of it) was started by that Thomas Turner who evolved the famous Willow Pattern, and as he learned his business of potting at Worcester it is not surprising that the early wares are similar to those of the Severn town.

The Worcester hollow 'C' mark was imitated, also the Worcester imitations of Chinese wares; but 'S' or 'Salopian' was the factory's own mark, and in 1799 it was taken over by John Rose of COALPORT.

S Salopian

Chairs

This is where we have to take a very deep breath. Ever since Western man found he preferred to sit only halfway down to the ground, he has been making and buying these useful and sometimes decorative objects in an astonishing variety of styles and materials. Chairs wear out more quickly than other sorts of furniture, and so have to be replaced more often: it has consequently been easier to express in them the latest notion–original or stolen, felicitous or monstrous–of the furniture designer.

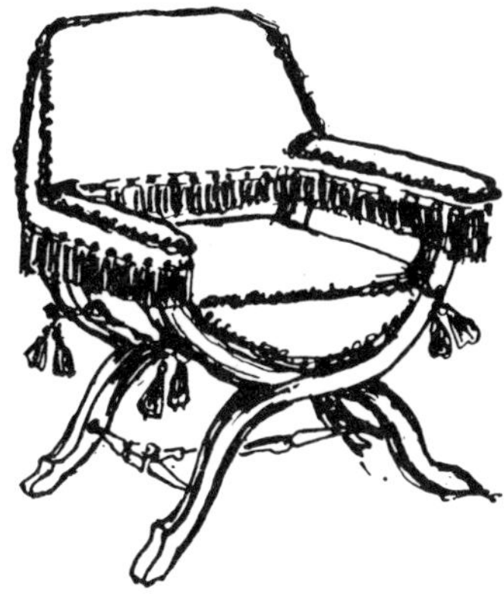
'X', *Dante or Savonarola*

So when we look round even the junkiest of shops we can expect to find hints and echoes of practically every idea these men have ever had. Only the other day I saw a carved wooden X chair which had been chucked on the top of a sideboard and was awaiting a purchaser for a few pounds. In other incarnations, such chairs have occupied proud places in Roman villas, ancient Egyptian temples, Italian palaces of the Renaissance, and stately mansions of the Tudor and Stuart Courts; at various times they have also borne the name of *Dante*, *Savonarola* and *Glastonbury* after their presumed users. They are to be seen in many a Victorian photograph album, and I suspect that most of the ones we see nowadays came out of bankrupt Victorian photographers' studios.

It would be a lengthy and much too tedious job to try to get all these chairs into classifications, but there is one rough division which is worth making. This is a distinction between what one might call 'country kitchen' chairs and the rest. I do this partly because I like the first kind the best, but also because, although you can mix a lot of different furniture, I don't think you would particularly want to mix these two very different sorts of chair.

Right at the heart of the 'country kitchen' school, of course, is the WINDSOR, in all its many flowerings both in Britain and the United States–some say more skilfully in the former than in the latter. An even older distant cousin, enduring down to the present day, is the *ladder-back* or *slat-back*. This usually has a rush seat, but as these wear out you may have to be content, like me, to buy a cheap example with a replacement of shaped plywood. However, there are still craftsmen in England who can give a chair another rush seat when it needs one, though this has become prohibitively expensive of late.

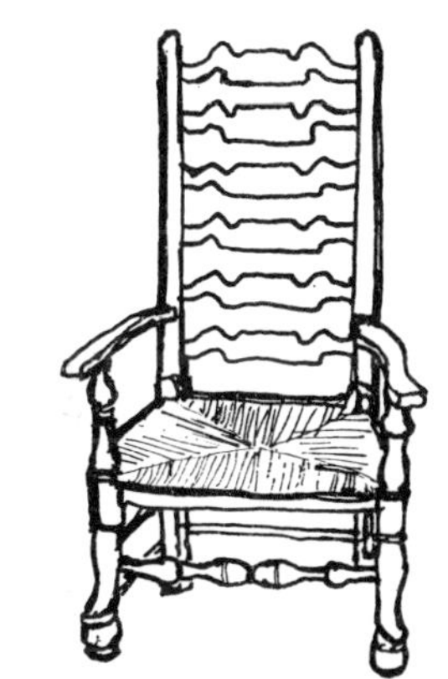
Ladder- or slat-back

These chairs are known also in Normandy, finely carved, from the sixteenth century; perhaps they arrived in the United States via the old French colony of Quebec. As well as the plain slats there are those 'wave' cut, popular in England and also New England; the 'salamander' more often seen in America; and the shape like an oiled and parted Edwardian moustache–which in the older English version is upside down, and was still being made by Ernest Gimson in 1910. It will be noted that the chair in the sketch has a shaped and a turned ball foot which tried to hint at the *cabriole* effect, more often found in the drawing room.

Then we have the *spindle-back* or *bobbin-back*, that most modestly gracious of chairs, used, one feels sure, by the sort of people who like nice things but are themselves much too nice to be able to afford extravagances. This goes back to Stuart times and forward to William Morris, but is suspected of a Scandinavian origin. So far as the English

Spindle–or bobbin-back

Mendlesham

version is concerned they are said to have come up the Severn with the Norse invaders of the north of England where (before sales and auctions scattered them all over the place) they were chiefly to be found. One variety, with the spindles grouped towards the centre rather than across the back, has been called a *Lancashire* chair. Whether spindled or laddered, they also have rush seats, and so enjoy that pleasant 'give' which is as comfortable as any upholstery and a fine tribute to the local craftsmen's skill.

Talking locally again, there are the *Mendlesham*, or *Dan Day* chairs made at the Suffolk village and by the person named: usually of yew and fruitwood, they are a fairly close relative of the WINDSOR but adding nicely placed ball ornaments, a trick which Dan Day's son Richard is supposed to have learned while working for Sheraton. Similar chairs are said to have been made at Scole in Norfolk.

More primitive is the simple *West Country* chair, but it needs no very sharp eye to see its relationship not only with the chairs we have been discussing but also with the American *carvers* and *brewsters.*

West Country

More sophisticated is the whole range of chairs which have been called *Country Chippendale*. These are not really kitchen chairs: they were the middle-class approach to the fine furnishing of the gentry but nowadays they take their place in the kitchen along with all the other honest stuff.

To the wooden family also, but perhaps more often seen in the parlour than the kitchen, belongs a late-comer from Austria, the BENTWOOD chair. Last of our group from the stone-flagged floor, the low ceiling and the casement window comes the *rocker*. This is a chair which the Americans have made more of than the British, having turned it into a national institution, their main types being the *Boston*, the *Sleepy Hollow* and the *Lincoln*. According to Carl Dreppard's *Handbook of Antique Chairs* (1908) there are, first, rockers which have been converted–usually Windsor slat-backs, spindle-backs and the rest, with iron or wooden bends attached to them; and second, the rockers built *as* rockers, with features ordinary chairs don't have.

Country Chippendale

Bentwood rocker

Winged rocker

Regency bamboo-style beechwood

The rocker shown, with wings against the draught was used by John Wesley, and I have seen lots of Windsors with 'carpet cutters'–many were made in the High Wycombe district of Buckinghamshire. Nowadays we have got interested in rockers again, and they are being sold in Britain, not only in traditional styles and materials from Wycombe and Sweden, but also in the latest 'contemporary' manner with nylon-strung back, bent mahogany and ash. Doctors recommend them to ease the strain as the country goes steadily downhill: perhaps this is the era of the English rocker.

Pair of mahogany hall chairs, c. 1770 (Aspreys)

Moving out of the kitchen, through the green baize door and along the hall, the first thing we find is the *Hall* chair, the most universally uncomfortable thing in existence since the eighteenth century, and was so designed, it is thought, (a) because anyone allowed to wait in the hall was expected to leave as soon as possible; and (b) because he was probably wet with rain and mud and so might spoil an upholstered chair. Anyway, there they all are, mostly from Victorian halls, with hard wooden seats, scrolled and carved backs–exquisitely painful to lean against, and surely useable only as decoration.

Cockfighting

Reading or Library

Roundabout or Corner

Abbotsford

Balloon back

Then there is the Regency version of BAMBOO, wherein beechwood was turned to look like the Oriental wood. If we glance into the library or the gunroom we may be able to settle a longstanding controversy about the difference between a *cockfighting* chair and a *library* chair: in both the gentleman sat astride, but the one with the armrest would allow him to lean forward to watch the main more closely, while the one with the book rest would be handy for a book. Why should one sit astride to read in one's library? Possibly because one preferred to keep one's long-skirted coat-tails uncreased.

Prince of Wales

Sewing

Fireside

A much more thoughtful affair is the *roundabout*, which has semi-circular arms, and the seat on the skew so that there is one leg in front. These are sometimes called *corner* chairs, because they fit well in corners, and also *writing* chairs because you can pull them up to a desk or table. These can be found in the 'country kitchen' family as well.

If we are going in for stateliness, there is first the *Dante* or *X* chair already mentioned, and then the *Abbotsford*. As its name suggests, this is a legacy of Sir Walter Scott's historical romances in which Jacobean has got itself gloriously mixed up with Gothic in a pastiche of a chair popular in the reign of Charles II. If you have the right sort of hall, here is your hall chair: you can at least sit upon it. Perhaps the same sort of purpose should be found for the ART NOUVEAU chair, only in this case it will be best if your house was built during, or representative of, that brief flowering of originality in British architecture between 1890 and 1910.

Other chairs in our little group are usual enough. The *balloon-back* chair was popular throughout the Victorian age, and so was the padded armchair. Our specimen shows the *Prince of Wales* style, with its segments of padding representing the Prince's three feathers emblem. The *Victoria* had a looped and waisted back with wooden padded arms; the *Prince Albert* was similar, only with a slightly bowed cresting; the *Princess Adelaide* had no arms, like the *sewing* chair shown.

Finally our drawings show a chair which I have called 'Victorian Fireside'. It is in every junk shop; it is a cross between an armchair and a hall chair, though it was obviously meant for the fireside. It has rows of little bobbins and a carved cresting rail: as it stands it looks horrible and in the days before our currency was decimalized (1971) you could have it for ten bob. Only I just wonder how it would look stripped and painted white, with simple pastel covering.

What other chairs are there? Well, we have said nothing about the *Bergère* chair, comfortably wide with external woodwork or rattan. We owe this originally to the France of Louis XV (although Chippendale insisted on anglicizing the word to 'burjar'). A much wider version if it is known as a *marquise*. The *Prié Dieu* chair, with its low seat and armrests on the back, seems to be as useful for sitting as for kneeling: and reproductions are sometimes found of the *farthingale* chair, with low back and no arms, for my lady to perch her bolsterings upon. There are chairs in WICKER WARE, and a *beehive* chair made of woven rush.

There are also those others which one can only call 'fancy chairs', in all kinds of irrelevant styles, mainly for bedrooms, nurseries and odd rooms, painted or carved in every sort of style from Louis XV to Grecian, from Victorian Sheraton to William IV Edwardian. The only combination I have not yet seen is a Gothic adaptation of Japonaiserie, but there is always hope.

All the same, you can count upon one thing. 'Contemporary' and 'genuine reproduction' have such a hold on us now that unless these amusing and sometimes very charming little chairs become so sought after as to call for reproduction, they will never be made again nor be obtainable so cheaply.

Charms

Anyone who expects his house to fall in or an earthquake to swallow him up might consider making a collection of the various sorts of charms used to ward off these and other evils. We still, if we are female, wear them on our bangles and wristlets, though nowadays they seem to be mostly lovers' tokens, or little vintage motor cars–there are, by the way, 'vintage' versions of these, by which I mean charms in silver which are contemporary with what we now call the 'vintage' car. But the watch-chainless man of today tends also to be going about without adequate protection: so perhaps we can find a few items in the junk shop.

HORSE BRASSES, of course had their origin as amulets or charms, the blinding sunflash on the horse's forehead helping to ward off the 'evil eye' in days when, eerily enough, many people seem to have had this unpleasant attribute. One of these brasses in the porch will keep away such folk, while a horseshoe over the door will help with an outbreak of fire, for if you leave it open end up it is symbolically holding water. Sometimes a dealer will offer you a piece of unicorn horn mounted in Chinese silver; but this is not likely to be unicorn–perhaps rhinoceros horn or the tusk of a narwhal–but either way it will assure you of everlasting happiness.

Pilgrims' tokens and religious medals, of course, have their devotees, but you must make sure that you have not picked up some which having started life as deceptions will presumably have an adverse rather than a beneficial effect. Touchstones and touch-pieces are useful, not only for assessing the genuineness of precious metals, but for warding off scrofula, especially if worn on a white silk ribbon. If you happen to be a farmer, be sure to get one of those stones with holes in them sometimes found in the curio box; hung up in the cowshed or pigsty with your initials scratched on it it will make it no longer necessary to call in your vet to ailing animals.

A good representative collection of Chinese porcelain will be invaluable. Nothing represented in Chinese art ever really contains evil. The dragon, seen on pottery everywhere, symbolizes the renewal of life, the tortoise longevity, the 'cash' or coin with a square hole in it will bring you riches, a leaping carp ensures that you pass your examinations.

Châtelaines

Once upon a time, when every castle had its castellan, it also had a châtelaine. As mistress of the house she carried on her girdle a purse, the keys to her cupboards and other necessary articles for the management of a great establishment.

The name appears again in early Victorian times, when ladies of rank, steeped in the historical novels of Sir Walter Scott, hooked on to their rope-like *cordelières*, or beaded girdles, a large buckle or clasp from which depended all manner of items. The keys to the cupboards and the stillroom were by this time hanging on the leather belt of their housekeepers: so the châtelaine was now free to carry on her silver one such items as smelling bottle or VINAIGRETTE, eye-glass, *étui* or scissors case, writing tablet and pencil, almanac, thimble case, penknife, pin case, even, on occasion, a whistle (to call the police?).

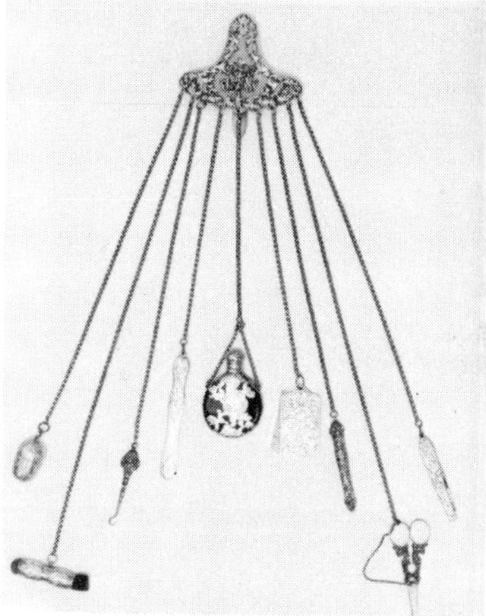

A gold châtelaine with sewing articles, scent bottle, étui, note-pad etc., c. 1840 (The Museum of London)

In the early days the whole affair might be of chased gold or silver, perhaps with enamelling; but after an eclipse in the 1860s there was a revival–some say led by Queen Alexandra when Princess of Wales–in which the châtelaine appeared in the more accessible steel or ELECTRO-PLATE as well as in oxidized silver: C. R. Ashbee (whom we have met in the ARTS AND CRAFTS MOVEMENT) applied his fine workmanship to one in openwork silver in the 1890s.

Chessmen

There are not only collectors of chess sets, but dealers who specialize in them. This is as well, for they have been made in so many parts of the world–even if our form of chess is not necessarily played there–that it takes some specialist expertise to assign them to a country of origin or a period: they did not follow general movements of styles.

There are, of course, the 'traditional' sets, but this is a word which seems to get tacked on to any style after it has been repeated for any length of time. Islam, for example, which forbids the representation of the human figure, makes its own Sunnite chessmen, which look like a lot of pepper pots or cabbage drainers. The Chinese, who have a game of their own, play it with discs placed on the corners of the squares: but all

The Queen from a Wedgwood chess set designed by John Flaxman in 1874 (Wedgwood)

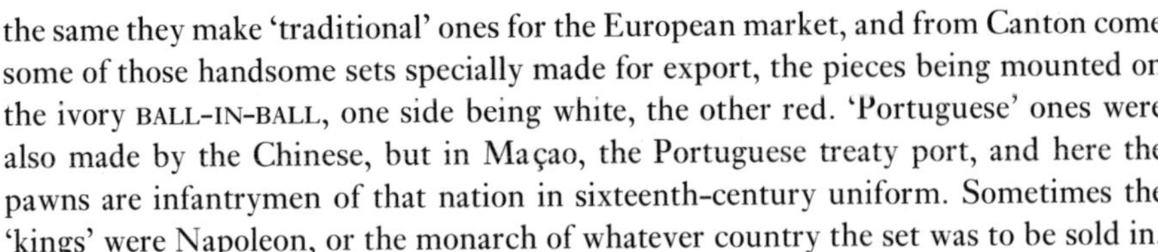

the same they make 'traditional' ones for the European market, and from Canton come some of those handsome sets specially made for export, the pieces being mounted on the ivory BALL-IN-BALL, one side being white, the other red. 'Portuguese' ones were also made by the Chinese, but in Maçao, the Portuguese treaty port, and here the pawns are infantrymen of that nation in sixteenth-century uniform. Sometimes the 'kings' were Napoleon, or the monarch of whatever country the set was to be sold in.

European countries also had their 'traditional' types. There was, for example, the 'St George' type, imported from France; while the 'Staunton' sets, the most popular type in Britain, are named after the first Englishman to win the world championship. Another English type was made by the Hatilow family, their 'signature' being a fluting in the plinths of the pieces.

Not all sets are in ivory: the priceless ones were made in semi-precious stones, but there are others in cast-iron, in wood, either plain or painted. The Black Forest and the Tyrol have sent us carved and painted ones of this sort, the pawns being tradesmen or peasants.

French prisoners of war in England during the Napoleonic period made bone chessmen. There are porcelain sets from Vienna and Meissen: while the English potteries, such as CASTLEFORD and Wedgwood, also made them. The Wedgwood set was designed by the famous sculptor Flaxman in jasperware, with the famous actress Mrs Siddons as the queen. This latter is pretty rare, but I have seen more recent sets modelled in this manner, the one side being in black basaltes, the other in white porcelain.

Enthusiasts tell me that unless you are simply collecting odd pieces for their interest, you should never, never buy incomplete sets in the hope of one day picking up the missing item: as with odd volumes, you almost never do.

Children's Books

A picture by Kate Greenaway, illustrating the inimitable children's fashions she created (Rodney Engen)

Everyone has his or her favourite children's book. I don't want to write a history of them here, but just to call attention to a little race of books I have often picked up from the dusty shelves of unwanted books in junk shops.

They are those engaging little affairs illustrated by Walter Crane, Randolph Caldecott and Kate Greenaway, among others. They were printed, not in the sometimes gaudy late chromolithography of so many illustrated books in colours, but in flat colours from woodblocks, rather after the style of Japanese prints. Walter Crane's work in *Baby's Opera, Baby's Aesop* and other books was totally different from his normal activities as a designer, but they were great favourites with the generation that were children in the 1870s and 1880s.

Randolph Caldecott, in his many picture books like *The House that Jack Built, John Gilpin, Babes in the Wood, Mad Dog, Ride a Cock Horse* and *Three Jovial Huntsmen,* put his children in the eighteenth century. Kate Greenaway's children, in their dateless fancy dress, instead of reflecting a fashion, created one. Her *Kate Greenaway Almanacs* became famous, as did titles like *Under the Window, Birthday Book, Mother Goose, Little Ann* and other poems, all by different authors. Another memorable little book to look out for, one of the first of this type, was William Allingham's *In Fairyland,* with illustration by Dickie Doyle, who drew the famous cover which *Punch* used for so many years. In this little book Doyle's high characteristic note of fantasy in the delicate flat-colour wash of Evans' printing, comes out far better, in my view, than in any of his black and white work.

An illustration by Walter Crane for The Baby's Opera, *first published in 1877, and available again in facsimile (Pan Books Limited)*

Another delightful illustrator for children, one of the great band of wood-engravers of the nineties, was Arthur Hughes. No great shakes as a draughtsman, he nevertheless had a lovely imaginative touch and great skill as a designer. He became famous for his work in George Macdonald's books, such as *At the Back of the North Wind* and *The Princess and the Goblin*: and I see that in a quite modern edition of the former, bought for my own children, the publishers continue to use Hughes' engravings without even giving his name–'illustrated' they ungratefully remark on the title page.

Edwardian swinging cot – the 'Pomona'

Children's Furniture

Nobody can escape giving a little yelp of joy when they see one of those charming little pieces designed for the children of other days.

First there are the cradles, sometimes yielded up unwillingly by a farmhouse or cottage where it has done duty for generations. In this case, probably, it will be tougher and cruder in make, for they had to be shoved around on a stone floor used by the whole family and the neighbours as well. All the same, it might often be beautifully carved, perhaps with the initials of the fond parents, or their first offspring. These are on rockers, like the wicker ones with a hood; but there are others which swing upon supports. From early Victorian days there is a model which has a clockwork rocking mechanism: it keeps going for forty-three minutes even now. And very occasionally one sees a specimen of those upholstered, silk and satin affairs, with canopies and draperies, which the late Victorians and Edwardians loved to use.

Children's high chairs come in the styles of their period, either following country WINDSOR types, or town fashions; but there is also a variety which consists of a little chair mounted on the seat of an adult chair, or on a small table–which can be detached and put in front of the little chair when the occupant is not sitting up at the big table. Most of these look pretty practical, but when the artist designers came on the scene they sometimes let their ideas run away with them. There is an ART NOUVEAU high chair which is so top heavy that it probably explains why children reared at the turn of the century preferred to buy reproduction Sheraton when they grew up.

A walnut child's chair, early 18th century (Aspreys)

Another item of nursery furniture, of course, is the device for ensuring that the little one does not stray too far, or fall in the fire. Baby cages, on casters, helped the little mite to climb up on to its feet, and there is another sort which envelops the child round the waist rather like a wooden crinoline on wheels.

But I prefer the high chairs, especially the little WINDSOR ones. A chair is a chair, but a child's chair is something you want to put your child in.

Children's Plates

Not to be confused with toy china, which were miniatures of adult sets, or with travellers' samples, which were tiny versions or half-pieces of the real thing, carried by peripatetic salesmen. These are plates made directly for use by children, and embellished with decorations designed to amuse, elevate or interest them.

As might be expected, not many have survived. The potters don't seem to have expected them to, for they are generally found in the cheapest sort of earthenware. If they were ever made in STONEWARE (as you'd imagine they would be, in view of the hazardous life they were in for), I haven't seen them.

Surprisingly enough, however, they *can* still be found, and although they have tended to graduate to even the poshest of antique shops these days, the real place to seek them is in the darkest corner of the dingiest junk shop, under piles of old saucers (which, by the way, you should never, never leave unturned over).

Some of these charming items are designed for the very young, with impressed numbers and letters of the alphabet round the rim. Others are seemingly for more advanced infants, as they offer counsel on matters of behaviour up to the age of marriage–though often still keeping up the alphabetical instruction. Pictures and verses recommend virtues like modesty, propriety and industry, but some potters like

Davenport were charitable enough to let the child uncover pictures of animals as he spooned up his food.

A series which has been paid the compliment of a place in the Victoria and Albert Museum, London, is called 'Flowers that never Fade', and really gets down to the 'seen and not heard' business. Two typical verses run:

ATTENTION

'And when I learn my hymns to say
And work and read and spell
I will not think about my play
But try to do it well.'

POLITENESS

'If little boys and girls were wise
They'd always be polite
For sweet behaviour in a child
Is a delightful sight.'

Apart from Davenport, many potters seem to have made these items, notably the Newbottle Pottery in Sunderland. But there is still much to be learned about them, and they could make an engrossing field for collecting.

Has anyone ever thought of poking about in the gardens of old cottage sites in the country? There must be many fragments there which could be pieced together.

China Figures

A shop full of china figures (or figurines, as they're sometimes called) can be a baffling thing to a beginner. Where on earth do you start? How can you possibly find your way through all that undergrowth of Dresden shepherdesses, monkey bandsmen, highwaymen, Jenny Linds and the rest?

I think you start by looking hard at them, and then, very cautiously, buying things you like. You may not like them later on, but as most things are appreciating in value this may not necessarily involve a loss when you sell.

Then you should read up something about them from the experts, and even compare them with other kinds of figures–say sculpture or BRONZES.

You will find, of course, that it occurred to man very early on to want to make likenesses of other people, also of animals and gods. At first there was some motive like giving a dead person an attendant on his journey into the next world. Later, the potter found that people liked to have these things while they were still in this world–to put on their mantelpiece or decorate their tables.

What the earliest potters made are either in the big collections or still under the ground waiting to be uncovered by the archaeologist. In the cabinets of the well-off, too, are those delicious *blanc de Chine* figurines of the Chinese immortals, the breathtakingly fragile and graceful figures from the Italian Comedy modelled at Meissen by Kaendler or at Nymphenburg by Bustelli (which can cost you thousands of pounds a whack at one of the big salerooms); the charmingly anglicized versions of Continental ideas made in English soft paste porcelain factories, such as Bow, Chelsea, Derby and Longton Hall; the delightfully naïve early salt-glazed stoneware figures as exemplified by the famous pew-groups and bandsmen; the earthenware products of potters like Astbury and Whieldon, dripping with glorious coloured glazes apparently thrown on from the other end of the room but all the same arriving at exactly the right spot: there, too, even, are the comparatively late figures of Obadiah Sherratt and Ralph Salt.

So what we are left with nowadays mainly are, *first*, nineteenth-century imitations of the eighteenth-century porcelain figures; *second*, the STAFFORDSHIRE FIGURES of the nineteenth century; *third*, a sprinkling of original figures made by DOULTON, Pilkington and others in the past century or so; *fourth*, PARIAN figures, still relatively undervalued; and *fifth*, a whole selection of items made the other day from the original moulds, still coming out of Europe and Staffordshire wrapped up in their original tissue paper.

Below left: *A Staffordshire saltglaze pew group, 18th century (Christies)*

Printing block for 'Evenlode' chintz by Morris (William Morris Gallery)

Chintz

'Creed, my wife and I to Cornhill,' confided Samuel Pepys to his *Diary* on September 5th 1663, 'and after many tryalls bought my wife a chintz, that is, a painted Indian calico, for to line her new study, which is very pretty.'

That heartfelt sigh 'after many tryalls' gives us a nice picture of the impatient but appreciative Clerk of the Acts attending his choosy French spouse: it also suggests that before even the end of the seventeenth century there were plenty of chintz patterns to be choosy about.

Since then, of course, we have had more than two hundred years of printed chintzes: and anyone looking for something original to collect might well consider this subject, which, like WALLPAPER and PRINTED HANDKERCHIEFS, are just as likely to turn up in an old cupboard or chest-of-drawers as anywhere else.

As Mr Pepys indicates, chintzes originally came from India–hence the French term *Indiennes*–but we adopted for them the Hindi word *Chint*, meaning 'coloured' or 'variegated'. They came to Europe in the same East Indiamen which brought the porcelains of the Far East. A dozen years after Mrs Pepys was buying her imported chintz, Will Sherwin, under a patent from the Crown, was offering them in 'the only true way of East India printing and stayning such kind of goods'–and the industry in England was launched. Through most of the eighteenth century it was bedevilled by restraints and duties designed to help the wool and silk trades, but nothing could keep it down.

Above: *'Avon' chintz by Morris*. Below: *'Brother Rabbit' chintz by Morris (William Morris Gallery)*

None of their work, of course, could quite compare in beauty and subtlety with the hand-painted and dyed Indian product, as shown in the great *palimpores*–bed spreads or hangings, sometimes twelve feet by nine feet, which can be studied in the Victoria and Albert Museum.

Nevertheless the best of the European 'printed calicoes' are fine productions. At first they were printed from blocks, these being laid on the material, and the back of them knocked with a mallet to ensure that the colour was evenly distributed. 'Mordants' of various strengths and types acted upon the dyes into which the material was afterwards dipped and could, miraculously it seems, produce different colours–a process which excited the wonder of Pliny as long ago as AD 70. Later the block work was embellished by 'pinning', similar to PIQUÉ work, whereby small dots were printed by brass pins hammered into the block–a favourite form of ornament until well on into the nineteenth century.

The great revolution occurred, however, with the invention of roller printing from cylinders, said to have been first worked successfully by a Scot named Bell around 1785. Now it was possible to say that 'the peasant's cottage may at this day with good management have as handsome furniture for beds, windows and tables as the house of a substantial tradesman sixty years ago'.

In the middle of the eighteenth century there was a swing away from the 'coloured and variegated' of original chintz to single colour patterns from copper plates–after the manner of engravings, of course, and also printed porcelain from factories like Worcester and Chelsea. Often taken from the same books of ornament their subjects were also very similar–the familiar landscapes, classical ruins, chinoiserie and so on. A method of reserve or 'resist' printing, like that used in LUSTRE WARE, was also developed. Later, however, this particular type seems to have been taken over by Oberkampf with his TOILES DE JOUY.

The English printers tended to favour copies of the Indian painted cottons (which despite all restrictions were still being imported) and especially the 'Persian' types with small brilliantly coloured patterns upon a buff or other ground, sometimes vermiculated. Later, under the neo-classical influence, there were 'architectural' styles, as well as the familiar striped patterns of Regency times.

In the Victorian era–from which we shall expect to find most of our hoards–the most outstanding were the floral patterns in which designers were so successful in other fields: and when, later in the century, William Morris of the ARTS AND CRAFTS MOVEMENT applied to the rather too commercialized patterns his craftsman's taste and skill, you really have something which is worth collecting and preserving.

Apart from these, however, there were many subject designs, commemorating events like royal weddings, coronations, naval victories and political occasions. There were also local views and historic landmarks, but many of these smaller items are more relevantly discussed under PRINTED HANDKERCHIEFS.

Connoisseurs of bird prints may also like to know that in the collection of the Calico Printers' Association there is a roller-printed chintz showing the Song Sparrow and the Red Starling from Audubon's famous book *Birds of America*.

Chip Boxes

One of the most universal of all the small hand-made objects to be found in Europe is the decorated chip box, or *Spanschalten*. Made in much the same way as a Turkish delight or date box, it consists merely of strips of single plywood bent round an oval base and lid, and then decorated by painting.

Sometimes there are quite formal patterns, with flowers or spirals, as in textiles; but there are many with pictorial themes–pairs of lovers, soldiers, nursery rhymes and fables. On the German ones there are often mottoes like those to be found on the beams of ancient inns. Berchtesgaden was one centre of production. In France there is a type which has a copper-plate engraving pasted on the lid.

They varied greatly in size, some of the larger types being designed to take the embroidered caps used on high days and holidays: while the smaller ones might hold the coloured ribbons bought from itinerant pedlars or at fairs.

Chip Carving

Junk shops used to be full of the work of the amateur craftsman, proudly kept in view during the maker's lifetime, then banished to a bedroom or an attic, then finally cleared out at a move or a death. *Ars longa vita brevis.*

One home activity, apparently a precursor of fretwork, is chip carving, which, in its post-medieval form, seems to have broken out in Britain about the year 1888 and remains a fairly popular pastime to this day.

Our wooden tray gives some idea of this work, which consists of so chipping the surface of a piece of wood that a shallow pattern results. It differs from carving proper in that the pattern is not in relief but in a series of V-notches. As in the case of POKER WORK, whitewood goods like boxes, racks, WATCH HOLDERS, wall brackets, key racks, picture frames, etc., were traced for chip carving, and the worker used a knife or chisels to make the simple triangular cuts. But the more ambitious of them worked out their own designs, thus emulating the Scandinavian, Oriental and Maori work, examples of which one sometimes sees. Some very fine and free designs were produced by these methods.

Whitewood tray traced for chip carving

Christmas Cards

Boxes and albums in junk sheds are there to be ransacked and made to yield their unconsidered treasures. Among these can be found letters, postcards, old photographs, VALENTINES–and Christmas cards. The *Art Journal* in 1889 said, 'The fashion of Christmas cards is on the wane.' How wrong can you be?

Why should anyone be interested in Christmas cards? I think the best answer to that is to look at a gathering of them–there are numerous collections in various museums–representative of different periods in the 130 years of their existence. The first fact that comes up and hits you is that here, if anywhere, is an entirely popular art. This was what the public, all sections of it, really liked, otherwise they wouldn't have bought them.

What they bought all through these years has an astounding range. There are, of course, robins, snow, holly, Father Christmases, stage coaches and the rest; but there are also charming little vignettes of early Victorian children, beautiful flower paintings and landscapes, some rather surprising nudes and semi-nudes of adolescents, and fearful warnings about taking the Lord's name in vain: Kate Greenaway's popular little misses and masters in their 'never-never land' costumes; topical cards showing such excitements as the early motor cars; cards from the fighting fronts of various wars, comic humanized animals; cards like cheques so that you can request the Bank of Blessings to pay to the order of the recipient 'Two Thousand Joys'; trick cards with a tab which sets angels bobbing up and down; fold-out tableaux of the Nativity. They come in silk and satin, are trimmed with lace and even dried grasses and seaweed; some even have little dabs of cotton wool or sachets which once bore a drop of some long-vanished perfume.

The history of the Christmas card was first told in a special number of *The Studio* for 1894 by Gleeson White, whose work on the Victorian illustrators is well known. But on this occasion White was rather solemn, objecting to 'unlovely objects' and 'practical jokes of the lowest order'; he didn't even like the robins very much. Not so George Buday whose *History of Christmas Cards* (1965) takes in and hugely enjoys everything the Christmas card has to offer. If you decide to collect them, let him be your guide; if not, read his book for its absorbing little sidelights on the tastes and interests over the past century and a quarter.

Can we trace the first commercially published Christmas card? Oddly enough, it seems we can. It was designed by John C. Horsley–nicknamed 'Clothes' Horsley because of his aversion to the fashion for nude paintings, which became fashionable in mid-Victorian England. Horsley's first card was produced in 1843 and published by Felix Summerly's Home Treasury, an art-publishing house conducted by (Sir) Henry Cole. About a thousand copies were sold at a shilling each, and showed a convivial Dickensian family scene, such as occurred on a memorable Christmas at Dingley Dell. This was severely criticized, says Mr Buday, as being likely to encourage drunkenness.

Since then, as noted, the diversity of cards has been immense. You can find among them the words of such writers as W. S. Gilbert, Christina Rossetti, Robert Louis Stevenson, George Eliot, Lord Tennyson, Lewis Carroll and many shy souls who hide their identity under initials–how interesting to ferret them out and find some 'important' writers among them! As artists you can have Phil May, Kate Greenaway, Lance Thackeray and Singer Sargent among many thousands of others.

And it still goes on: in recent years you have the choice cards by Sir Alfred Munnings, Sir Winston Churchill–and even Picasso. What more could an art collector want?

Clocks

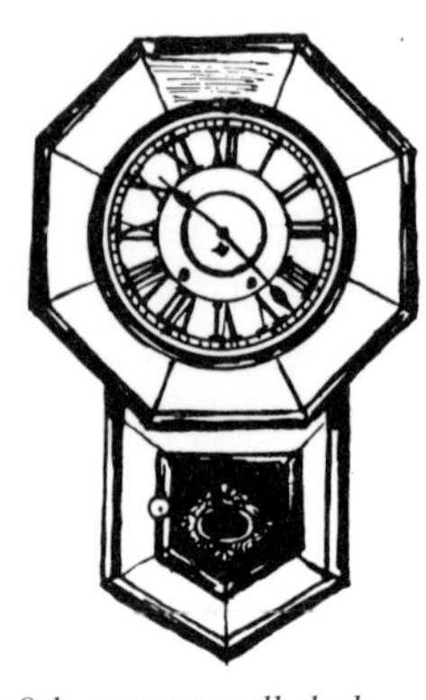

18th-century wall clock

There are men who cannot resist picking up a stopped clock and feeling they want to do something about it.

So I don't think there's much point in saying a great deal about the sort of clocks you see in junk or small general antique shops. If you're interested in clocks at all you'll either know a great deal more about them than I do, or you'll want to rush in anyway.

But I would like to air a few personal enthusiasms. First of all, perhaps, for grandfather clocks–and by the very fact of using that term at all you'll know I'm a tyro in this field like you: an expert would use the old name which was 'longcase' or 'tall' clocks. 'Grandfather', like Christmas and Mr Weller, seems to have come in with Dickens, or even later.

Anyway, there they are, the long and the fat and the tall–hopelessly unsuitable, I suppose, for modern surroundings, although I sometimes wonder if we've *quite* as little room as we pretend to have. For example, I'm at this moment (as it happens) sitting in a modern room with a ceiling high enough to take the tallest grandfather *I've* ever seen.

Of course, like you and everyone else, I'd like one of the early Jacobean ones, with the plain case and the tiny square dial: but these cost money, and so do the later walnut and MARQUETRY ones. But there are still some fine specimens about in the larger and later sorts at a reasonable sum.

Then there are some pretty good specimens of the plainer sorts of wall clocks. You find some splendid movements in this rather austere type, probably intended for butlers' pantries or the offices of the Cheeryble brothers. If you don't happen to like the case there are always nice cases whose movements have long since gone to glory. And don't be too fussy about 30-hour movements (this applies to longcase clocks as well). For some reason people will always pay disproportionately more for an eight-day than a 30-hour movement.

If you want to get really cottagey, there are all those cheap glass-fronted clocks which were sent across the Atlantic from the United States in mid-Victorian times.

With the possible exception of pressed glass this must have been the earliest example of American mass-production methods, for one of the manufacturers, Chauncey Jones of Connecticut, got them over to England so cheaply that the British Customs officials accused him of undervaluing his wares–they cost only a few shillings each. So they bought up the entire shipment at his price–which so delighted Mr Jerome that he promptly sent another load, after which the Customs took his word for it. These clocks have a glass painting on the front as a rule, often with a faded instruction sheet inside at the back. They work on the weight system, strike chimes, and there's many a one in pub and parlour which has been ticking away steadily for a good century or more. Some years ago I bought one of these for a pound, paid thirty shillings (£1.50) to have it put right, and it has since been nearly the best timekeeper I have.

Victorian mantelpiece clock

Talking about getting clocks put right, not everybody realizes that tucked away at the backs of towns, mostly working for the antique trade, there are old clock repairers who will perform miracles for really rather trifling sums. And since clocks, on the whole, are still under-valued today, rather than otherwise, I do invite you to have a closer look at all those Victorian mantelpiece clocks, some of the presentation items, which have survived their proud recipients. There are some good ones about, and if some of them are extravagant, it's surprising what a little careful redecoration can do.

Coalhole Covers

In the fascinating world of DECORATIVE IRONWORK–which we do not look at nearly closely enough–few objects offer more variety of design than the pavement coalhole cover.

This alone would be a good reason for giving them an entry on their own, but in fact they are not only a serious collecting subject already, but there is a posh name for collectors of them: just as stamp collectors call themselves philatelists, so coalhole cover collectors deem themselves to be operculists.

This term (from *operculum*, the Latin word for a cover or lid) was coined by the world's first connoisseur and collector of them, the late Dr Shepherd Taylor. In his peregrinations around London in the 1860s as a medical student he found over 150 different designs; and his booklet illustrating and describing them–*Opercula (London Plates)*–was reprinted in 1965 with an introduction by Raymond Lister. The world's first exhibition of them was held at London's Gallery One in 1962, at which Sir John Betjeman–who has opened our eyes to so many scorned or neglected things–delivered the opening address.

Opercula, otherwise coal-hole covers

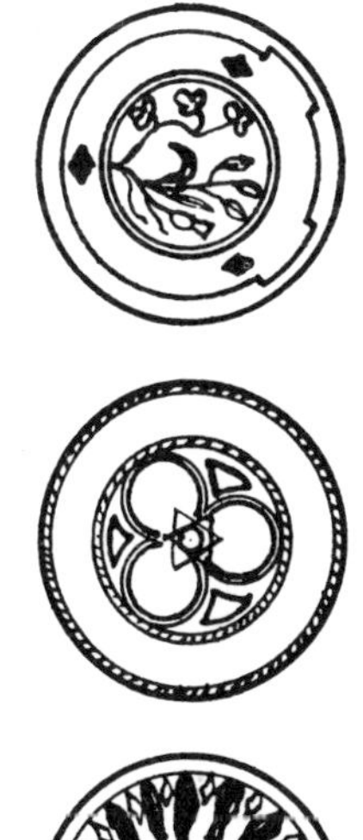

Coalhole covers are usually circular, although there are also squares and oblongs, and, as in the geometrical type of HORSE BRASS, the designers of them found that by dividing a circle with straight lines or arcs, or by multiplying, interlacing and otherwise combining them with other forms like diamonds and squares, they could arrive at an almost infinite number of patterns. Not surprisingly, some of them remind us of Gothic church windows, others of Japanese fans, Chinese trigrams or snow crystals. Occasionally a naturalistic sprig of flowers is to be seen and very often the founder's name is used as part of the design. Some have perforations let into them, to allow air but very little rain to go through; others have little discs or beads of glass, which gives a dim ecclesiastical light to those engaged in filling coal buckets below.

Collectors will realize that, attractive as they may find these covers, they should not steal out at night and leave a gaping hole in pavements. Until the time comes for the house to be replaced by a block of flats (which has no need of coalholes) we should be content to treat them as an outdoor picture gallery. I myself have had to exercize considerable restraint in the matter of what is evidently a privately bespoken *operculum* in the pavement outside a famous (and to me very generous) firm of antique dealers in

King Street, St James's, London, and bearing their name in brass letters. But I suspect that when the time comes for the cover to be taken up, it will have become valuable enough to appear in one of their windows.

Coalport

Coalport

A wonderful example of the way an unlovely name can pick up, by association, a pleasing sound. 'Coalport' now signifies for most of us those fine tea and dinner sevices with green and rose-coloured grounds which were made all through the last century, and in fact, are still being put out by the company's successors in the factory's new (since 1926) home in Staffordshire.

The earlier wares, of course, are the preserves of the affluent collector. The factory was founded in 1796 by John Rose, a porcelain tycoon like Duesbury of Derby, who started as an apprentice of Thomas Turner of CAUGHLEY, and afterwards bought that factory and also the Cambrian Pottery at Swansea–and with it the heart-breakingly lovely porcelains made by the famous and luckless Billingsley. With all this gathering of potting know-how Coalport was in an excellent position to imitate Chelsea, DRESDEN and other styles and to join in the extravagances of Rockingham, in the way of applied flower decoration. Some people blench at some of this: some find it fun. The Victoria and Albert Museum have canonized it by putting it in their cases, so who are we to talk scathingly about 'revived rococo'?

Cockle Plates

It may not be realized that museums often have a huge surplus of items of lesser importance tucked away in cupboards: and that they are usually quite glad to show them to anyone interested.

It was while exploring one of these hoards–acquired by the museum as a legacy on condition that they didn't just pick out the choice bits they wanted, but took the lot–I saw piles of engaging little plates of the shape and size one sees on cockle and whelk stalls. But instead of being plain, as they are today, they were printed with pleasant views, or with mottoes and cheerful pictures of sailors, rather like SOUVENIR CHINA. No doubt many of them did find their way into pockets on boisterous Saturday nights.

Some of them were rather larger than this, with rims impressed with rosettes in the same way as CHILDREN'S PLATES. Still others bore the emblems of Oddfellows and other societies, suggesting that they were used for ceremonial high teas. Rummaging around for little items of this sort–which, after I had seen this collection, I remembered having passed over many times–could take you along a fascinating by-path of social history.

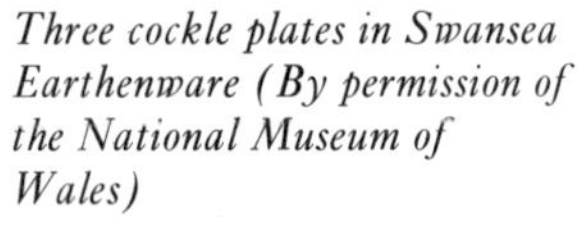

Three cockle plates in Swansea Earthenware (By permission of the National Museum of Wales)

Continental Glasses

When you cross the Channel and leave behind you the typical English drinking vessel shapes, such as *dwarf ales* and *sham drams*, the *opaque twists* and the *air twists*, you will find yourself faced with a whole new family of glass shapes. It may be worthwhile having a look at some of these.

One of the longest lived forms–you meet it still in cafés on the Rhine and the Moselle–is the *Römer* (naturalized in Britain as the RUMMER); still showing in a moulded form the 'spun' thread of the original foot and often still in green glass following the ancient *Waldglas*, or forest glass. There are sometimes 'raspberries' (we call them prunts) on the stem, as on the old beakers called *Krautstrunk* (cabbage stem) or *Warzenbecher* (wart beakers).

Cantarò

Another family derives from the *Stangenglas* (pole glass), tall and cylindrical with a spreading foot, and when this is covered with prunts drawn out into points you have the *Iglglas* (hedgehog glass). But give the plain *Stangenglas* a series of enamelled or engraved threads dividing it into equal parts and you have a *Passglas*, from which you were expected to drink exactly the amount indicated by the divisions before passing it on. Enormous specimens were known as *Willkomm* (greeting) glasses.

Biberon

Still nearly cylindrical, but with a foot more like a beaker or tumbler, is the *Humpen*, the basic beer glass, which in its more splendid forms, showing enamelled double-eagles, becomes the *Reichsadlerhumpen* (Imperial Eagle) and *Kurfürstenhumpen* (Elector glasses). The *Deckelpokal* (covered goblet) was also a favourite object for decoration of all kinds. Given 'wings' you have the *Flügelglas*.

Burette

One oddity, apparently having affinities with the Spanish *porròn*, is the *Angster* (narrow neck?) or *Kuttrolf* (gurgling noise?), with intertwined tubular necks joining a wide mouth, which was apparently used for slow pouring, or perhaps for sprinkling.

The *porròn* will need no introduction to holiday makers in Spain (who have doubtless already found how effective a vessel it is for spraying one's face with wine), but other fascinating forms in that country are the *almorrata* (rose water sprinkler) and the hardly less fantastically Iberian jug called a *cantarò*.

Broc

Italy, having learnt the job from the Syrians and the Egyptians, taught Europe how to make glass. So spread the FAÇON DE VENISE here, there and everywhere: their *tazza* is like our cakestand: and the *biberon* probably started in Venice but took its name from Spain and developed further in Switzerland into the pewter *Brunkessi*. It was the Venetians who started all the great race of goblets, calling them *bicchiere*.

France offers us the *buire* or *burette*, a wide-bottomed type of *biberon*, the narrow-necked BROC À CIDRE and the wider-mouthed *aiguière*.

The traces of all these types may be seen not only in the rarities but among their humbler descendants: and many of them have recently been revived by modern glassmakers, to the great refreshment of our vision.

Aiguière

Copenhagen Porcelain

For collectors of other countries, the most characteristic decoration on Royal Copenhagen porcelain, almost as much a trademark as the three wavy lines which its factory puts on all its wares, is the *Muschel* or 'mussel' pattern, a refined and delicate formal flower design which is sometimes called the 'Danish National' pattern and is still made as the 'blue fluted'. In fact, it seems to have been borrowed from Fürstenberg and ultimately perhaps–like so much else hails from Meissen.

In the Rosenborg Castle in Copenhagen is preserved the factory's masterpiece in the way of table wares, the famous 'Flora Danica' service of 1602 pieces, made originally to the order of Frederick VI for the Empress Catherine II of Russia. The Empress prided herself on her encouragement of intellectual and scientific affairs, and the service offered to her was decorated with highly naturalistic paintings of Danish flora after the great work on the subject by the Danish botanist Oeder. However, Catherine died in 1796, before the service was completed, which is why it remained in the Rosenborg instead of joining, in what was once St Petersburg, Wedgwood's famous 'Frog' service in creamware and also a vast service in Sèvres soft-paste.

After a period of relative stagnation, there was a revival of activity at Copenhagen about the year 1885, when Philip Schou took over the factory and appointed Arnold Frog as his art director. From this date onward the famous and now much collected wares correspond fairly closely to those being made in England at the time, but have a decided originality. They include fine underglaze artist's painting of the kind done so well at Minton's, also crystalline glazes.

There is, in addition, the large family of figure subjects–some of the characters being taken from the fairy tales of Hans Christian Andersen–peasants, animals and birds in soft underglaze colours, predominantly in blue and grey, whose popularity continues right down to the present.

The Royal Copenhagen factory was one of the pioneers of Christmas plates, which made their debut in the 1890s and have since become universally popular. These plates, in their characteristically muted shades of blue, depict seasonal landscapes and subjects with the Danish inscription 'God Jul' (Merry Christmas) and the date. In more recent years this idea has been extended to cover other annual occasions and the commemoration of special events.

Some mention must also be made of Messrs Bing and Grøndahl whose factory in Copenhagen played a not unimportant part in the rise of ART NOUVEAU ceramics in the 1890s. They have likewise been in the forefront of modern commemorative rack-plates, in predominantly blue and white shades.

Copper

There are people who know old copper from new, but not many who know *how* old and *how* new. I can take you to shops which do a roaring trade in copper 'antiques' fresh from their factory tissue paper–all those fascinating little miniature toys, hunting horns for fox hunts and beagles, kettles, pots, scuttles and the rest. They're all coming off a production line which uses much the same sort of tools and processes as in the old days.

And does mere age matter all that much? There's a demand for copper: why not meet it? After all, if a hunt wants to buy a new horn you don't expect them to take the pack all round the Brighton Lanes in search of a new one. (By the way, what happens to the old ones? Do they get dropped down the foxholes?) And if someone wants to buy some pretty miniature kettles or warming pans at the seaside, isn't it nice to think that you're buying some Birmingham workman a Sunday dinner?

But if you *should* want something other than just copper: if you want that authentic glowing red of the old work, if you're attracted by a shape that just couldn't have been made by a modern hand, then that's a different matter. In this case I invite you to look closely at all those oddly shaped and rather crazily finished pieces: those oddities like muff warmers and beer mullers, sets of West Country measures, PLAQUES, Victorian grille work, LAMPS and lanterns. Look especially for signs of hand repairs by the old coppersmiths and travelling tinkers; study their methods of workmanship, good and bad.

Coppers and Cauldrons

Surprisingly enough these appear in junk shops and yards more frequently nowadays than they once did–perhaps because they have only recently been fancied, perhaps because more old houses are being broken up to yield their DECORATIVE IRONWORK.

In later days, of course, the 'copper' was a fixture in an outhouse or a scullery, used mainly by the lady who came on Mondays to boil the wash. But in former times they were used for cooking, it being easier and cheaper to cook food at home by boiling into a stew (roasting could be a matter of taking the joint round to the baker's on Sunday mornings). You plunged your meat into the copper and suspended the vegetables in nets around its rim, to give flavour to the fragrant pottage. This process can still be seen–and deliciously smelt–all over Europe today.

Coppers which were made of copper were hammered up in sheet metal and rivetted; others were cast in bronze or in bell-metal. But the great majority were in cast iron, and sometimes imported from the Netherlands–today a happy hunting ground for them. Those with a lid may have been intended as baking ovens, and could even have been used on military campaigns. One of Marlborough's stratagems for fooling the foe was to set his troops off on a much-advertised journey which the enemy judged would take them about a week, but by baking enough bread in these camp ovens to last a fortnight he could disappear for days and attack at a totally unexpected point miles away.

Corkscrews

To be caught with a fine bottle of burgundy and without a corkscrew is a sad business, and is probably the reason people turn into corkscrew collectors. Corkscrews have been with us since the days of the first Queen Elizabeth, and were originally called bottle-screws, like the devices in ship's rigging named after them. Once upon a time, it appears, after staying with someone who had a particularly good cellar, it was considered polite to send him a handsome corkscrew in silver engraved with his crest or a word of praise.

'Wier's Patent' nickel-plated corkscrew

Corkscrews come in enormous variety, and look astonishingly well when they are mounted on a framed board. There are carved ones in wood and bone, delicate little silver ones for the eighteenth-century gentleman's pocket, perhaps combined with an ear-prick and a firesteel. 'King's' screws have a socket which fits over the neck of the bottle and of course there is the reverse screw for delicate handling of the crusted port. Ladies needed corkscrews for their miniature scent bottles, cellarmen for their stone jars.

In the last century invention ran riot, and it would be an absorbing task in more ways than one to seek out all these clever ideas and try them on your bottles.

Cornucopia

Or 'Horn of Plenty' (from the Latin *cornu*: horn; *copiae*: of plenty). This famous symbol, showing a goat's horn overflowing with fruit, flowers and corn, comes to us from classical times, these bountiful things being showered upon mortals by such friendly personages as Plutus, Tyche, Demeter and others.

Potters and metalworkers all down the variegated years have seized upon it to make a shapely receptacle for the wall or the table and to describe all its forms would be merely to catalogue these wares.

It is mentioned here as a decorative and pretty well inexhaustible possibility for the collector who likes to collect by theme or shape.

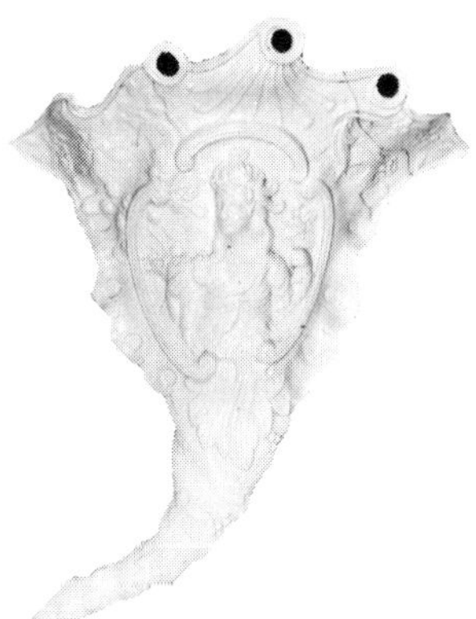

A white saltglaze Staffordshire cornucopia, c. 1760 (City Museum and Art Gallery, Stoke-on-Trent)

Coromandel Screens

You may sometimes come across a piece of furniture in painted lacquer in which the decoration on the various parts seems to have no relationship to that next door to it. It looks, in fact, as though some kind of cannibalizing has been going on.

This, in fact, is what may well have happened. In the late seventeenth century there began to arrive in Europe the first of the long line of lacquered objects which inspired our own JAPANNING. Many of them were large screens, and they came mainly from the Chinese province of Honan; but because they had been shipped either from Bantam, a port in the Dutch East Indies, or from Pondicherry, on the Coromandel coast of India, they were known as 'Bantam' or 'Coromandel' work. The wooden base, after being coated with a chalk composition, was covered with layers of dark lacquer; a design was carved in these layers down to the chalk and the depressions they made were filled with brightly coloured or gilt lacquer. The effect was extremely rich and vivid.

The reason for the cannibalization is that when these very large screens became damaged, as they often did, they were cut up to make smaller pieces. The job has not necessarily been done by modern 'fixers', however, for the author of a treatise on japanning and varnishing, published in 1688, tells us that the practice was already going on in his day. 'In these things,' he complained, 'so torn and hacked to joint a new fancie, you may observe the finest hodgpodg and medley.'

A beautiful – and complete – 18th-century Coromandel lacquer screen (Aspreys)

Costrels

Therewithal a costrel taketh he tho
And seyde, 'Here of a draught or two
Gif hym to drynke.'

What kind of vessel did Chaucer mean? There are some persons (among them that authority on drinking vessels, G. J. Monson-Fitzjohn) who hold that it is a version of the PILGRIM BOTTLE: others that it is one of those attractive pieces of woodwork which look like miniature coopered barrels once taken out into the cornfields filled with ale or cider. Counterparts of them in pottery are known as HARVEST JUGS.

Cottage Prints

Could one use this name for a type of small homely print which was popular as a kind of fairing or souvenir around the end of the eighteenth century or the first third of the nineteenth? I know not what else to call them.

They may be in a curly maple frame, or even one of ordinary painted wood. Many were printed to celebrate some great event–perhaps a Frost Fair on the Thames, actually run off in a temporary printing shop on the ice. There were also biblical scenes, showing saints and martyrs (though not so many in England as on the Continent), naval and sporting subjects. Town and country life contrasted is a subject often found, as well as a cruder version of the Cries of London.

One I bought a long time ago shows a paterfamilias proudly coming out into the garden after a hunting expedition, holding up a rabbit or a hare for the family to admire.

Cottages and Castles

People who do not have to live in them have always loved a cottage, from the days when Georgian ladies and gentlemen built themselves tiny 'Gothick' ones in their parks and played at being milkmaids and shepherds. In Victorian days, as working and middle-class people herded themselves into towns, they too thought wistfully of the charming little nests they had left behind them, set in gardens full of hollyhocks and sweet william.

From these yearnings, pottery and china manufacturers reaped a rich harvest, and because these tiny edifices were generally left in peace on a mantelshelf or in a cabinet, a great many of them have come down to us.

Some are in the form of pastille burners, used to sweeten the air of small, stuffy rooms. Others were designed as night-light holders, a great convenience when you had no electric light switch. But as time went on they were made as ornaments, for MONEY BOXES, DOORSTOPS, TEA CADDIES, TEAPOTS, TOBACCO JARS, inkstands, WATCH HOLDERS–in fact, almost anything which occurred to the fertile minds in the hundreds of little potteries which made them all through the Victorian era.

A Rockingham cottage

Larger versions were made too as ornaments, for the sideboard or the mantelpiece, and coming in such variety and being relatively cheap, they made excellent presents. Apart from the cottages there were castles, churches, tollhouses, garden arbours, summer-houses and so forth. Some of the best of them, considered as pieces of intricate and elaborate potting, came from COALPORT, Minton, Worcester and Spode–all in porcelain, and may also be found in Prattware pottery. It used to be thought that they had also been made by Rockingham because of the flower encrustation typical of that factory, but recent research has now disproved this. The best of these cottages and castles were made between 1820 and 1840 and are now making real money, those with genuine markings of that period now fetching up to £1,500. The more rudimentary examples, however, are still available for much more modest sums.

But beware! The forger is here as elsewhere. In a junkshop in Staffordshire not so long ago I was shown a cottage with all the signs of age on it, which the dealer–a secondhand furniture man really–told me laughingly had been made a few weeks before by a pottery down the road, using the original Victorian moulds. It was a pretty good attempt, both in potting and decoration, but you could see a difference if you knew what to look for. So here, as elsewhere, the serious collector must go to the trouble of studying materials and styles.

Staffordshire pottery castle, late 18th century

Creamware

Here is another of the aristocrats of English pottery and almost the most delightful of them. Nobody who has ever handled, say, one of the early teapots, with its deep buttery glaze, with crabstock handles and spouts, with painting in the vigorous, native Staffordshire tradition, providing the most lovely harmonies and attractive discords, can ever mistake it for anything else.

It arose in Staffordshire, somewhere about 1720–40, made of the same materials

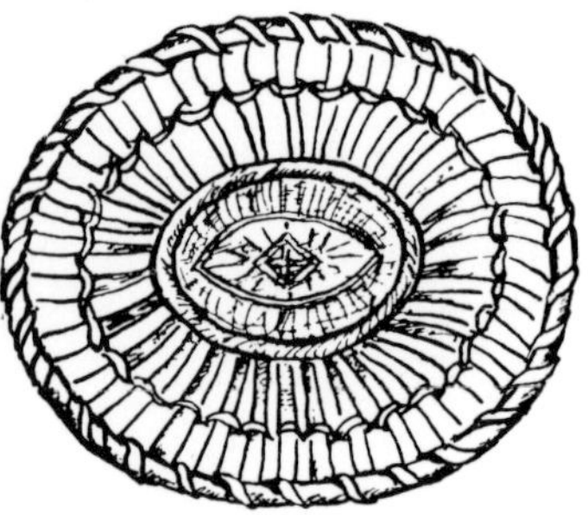

Wedgwood creamware basket

as–but fired at a lower temperature than–the hitherto successful salt-glazed STONEWARE, which it slowly overhauled for all kinds of reasons which one hasn't room to mention here.

The early pieces, of course, have long since gone into the museums or into the big salerooms, and you would have to be very lucky to find them by chance. But, with a little perseverance and especially if you don't mind a crack or a chip here or there, it is still possible to find some modestly priced pieces for a shelf. You certainly won't be sorry, for it grows on you day by day.

There is a wide range to choose from, even among the later wares, when Wedgwood was developing his famous Queen's Ware, with its clean neo-classical lines and restrained, but finely judged, decoration; and when Leeds and other potteries were turning out the pieces in the pierced decoration for which they were noted.

Then there are those much more modest–most of them probably forever unidentifiable–plates, dishes and bowls, impressed with basket weave and other designs, picked out sparingly in blue, brown or green. They are still reasonably plentiful and not over-priced as yet, and they fill a shelf beautifully.

But don't *insist* on a Wedgwood mark, which many of them have. Dealers always ask more when they can show you a mark, and there was just as good creamware made outside Etruria as inside it.

Credenza

Its home is in Italy and perhaps you will come across more examples of this piece of furniture there than anything else except the CASSONE–unless you happened to be a customer of the East London department store mentioned under that head.

It is a long low cupboard rather like an English dresser but without shelves. In the front there are two or three doors and usually drawers in the decorated frieze.

It served the purpose of a sideboard in the same way that the dresser was originally the *dressoir* or sideboard on which you dressed the meat. But in Italy it was used not only in the dining-room but in all rooms in the house and there is a very wide variety of decoration from one part of Italy to another and down through the centuries.

Lozenges and diamonds are the usual form of decoration; and along the frieze you will see the lion or satyr masks which are such a common theme in Italian decoration. Walnut is the wood invariably used although a few others are to be found.

Cuckoo Clocks

If you want a piece of Victorian 'Gothick' in its most romantic mood you can hardly do better than try to get one of the early cuckoo clocks, with their touching landscapes surrounded by carving.

The cuckoo clock is said to have been invented by Franz Anton Ketterer (1676–1750), a native of the Black Forest in Germany; and from there it spread all over the world. The very earliest ones are quite simple and unadorned, after which they picked up the romantically painted scenes. It was much later that they turned themselves into the hunting lodges or chalets, with overhanging gables, that we know today. Some, apart from the cuckoo, have a musical box, and there may be a quail calling the quarters.

Cup Plates

Once upon a time, when we used tea cups without handles, it was actually considered good form to drink from your saucer, which in fact was made deeper for the purpose, sometimes almost like a small basin.

All the same you weren't expected to plonk your cup down on the hostess's snowy linen. So she provided you with a little plate about three or four inches in diameter.

These cup plates, as they are called, come in either glass or earthenware, but they don't come so often as they did, for the Americans have been collecting them for a long time. Some carry the usual patterns of Staffordshire printed earthenware, and the marks of potters like ADAMS, Ridgway, Wood and Clews. The glass ones are sometimes quite plain, and sometimes in colour, with impressed patterns.

Curled Paper Work

Here is one of those crafts, laborious-sounding to us nowadays, which once kept ladies busy in their sitting rooms or boudoirs.

At first sight, curled or rolled paper work seems to be some sort of filigree, but actually it is made by rolling up strips of paper and glueing them 'end-on' in a pattern to the piece being worked, then gilding the edges. Sometimes, in the case of a tea caddy or work-box, this would then be covered with glass.

There was a craze for it about the time of the Napoleonic Wars, and pieces still come up for sale now and again.

Below left: *A fine example of 19th-century gilded scroll paper work (R. J. Phillips)*

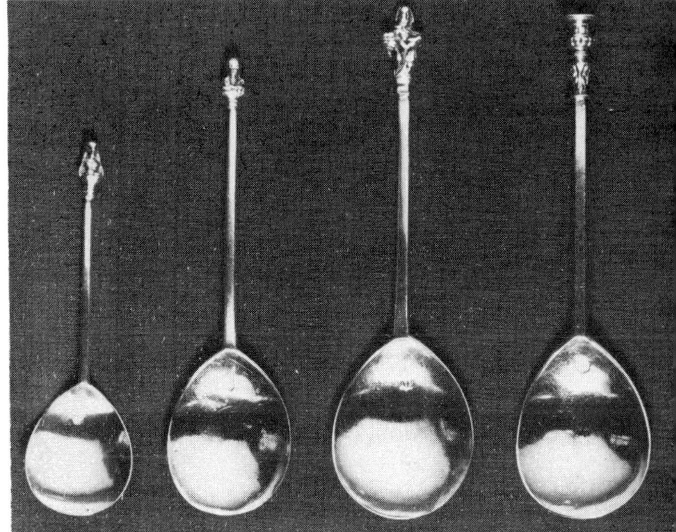

A collection of 17th-century English silver spoons, showing a variety of tops: Maidenhead, acorn, seal, Apostle, etc. (Aspreys)

Cutlery

In most junk shops you will find a box full of knives, forks, spoons, skewers, perhaps liberally mixed up with bradawls, screwdrivers and a baby's dummy or two. These boxes are always worth looking into, for you may very easily come across something interesting in the cutlery line.

Of course, anything the dealers have been able to identify, like sterling silver, will have gone–or not been put there at all. But there are sometimes Victorian fish and fruit knives, beautifully engraved even if they are in ELECTRO-PLATE, some of them with ivory or pearl handles. Bread knives are often quite splendid affairs, many being finely carved in boxwood.

A great deal of this work was done in living-rooms in the back streets of Sheffield by independent workers. Like the buffalo horn and stag handles, they date from before the days of the erinoid and bakelite which one remembers smelling so frightfully when it got burnt on the stove.

Spoons, of course, come in great variety. If you find a wooden one with fine carving on it you have the original spoon itself, for the word comes from the Old English 'spon',

meaning a splinter of wood. But almost every design of fork and spoon has its name–there are over 200 designs being made today–so there is plenty to engage interest.

Don't despise the occasional PEWTER one you may find. Cleaned up and mounted–as they should be–on a spoon rack, which can be made by any handyman, they can look quite splendid. And if you should stumble across one of those with a royal portrait on it, or with acorn, maidenhead or sealtop tops, you will soon have serious collectors breathing over your shoulder.

Davenport

A factory was established by John Davenport at Longport, Staffordshire, in 1793, and continued under his descendants until 1882.

Several kinds of earthenware, stoneware and bone china were made there, and decorations ranged from New Hall and other 'cottage' styles through Japanese Imari to sumptuous affairs in the manner of Derby. Some fine painted landscapes can still be found, though they won't be cheap nowadays, while the charming CHILDREN'S PLATES with zoo animals are also to be seen occasionally.

There are also some delectable little LUSTRE WARE tea-sets. Marks usually include either the name of the firm, or the town and an anchor.

Decorative Ironwork

Penetrate beyond the junk shop and you will find the junk yard, the home of the knackers whose job it is to pull down old buildings when the world no longer wants them.

What the house breakers want are the wonderful fittings which were put into, outside or around these houses–the stair or terrace baluster, the fanlight, the iron

Victorian wrought-iron gates from the demolished old Central Library in Birmingham, which have been refurbished and re-erected in the city centre (Donald Wright)

railings, the fireplace surround. Even a workman's tiny terrace house may yield something–a fanlight or even a FIRE INSURANCE SIGN–while an old shopfront will be carefully taken down to preserve the wooden tracery and glass which has that (seen from the side) shimmering look which proclaims the pre-plate era.

Anyone owning a house and wishing to give it some interesting accent should visit junk yards very frequently, for things of the kind described come in and go out again almost overnight. Alternatively they should leave an order with a specialist dealer asking him to look out for the desired article or articles.

What are these? To see the range or patterns in external ironwork one has only to walk around the terraces and squares of towns like Brighton, Bath and London's Mayfair, where the eighteenth and early nineteenth centuries have left their mark. Cheltenham, Hastings, Cambridge and South Kensington give tastes of the earlier Victorian styles, while seaside towns are full of the neo-baroque frills and furbelows which we now like again. In august South Kensington squares you may find opulence enough to make you feel very rich indeed.

Delftware

Sometimes you will see in a china shop, or perhaps in one of those places by the seaside where they sell SOUVENIR CHINA, a piece of glazed blue and white pottery, probably in the form of a little Dutch boy or girl, and marked 'Delft'.

Delftware apothecary jar

The one thing you can be certain of is that this is not old delftware, for the potters who made this did not use the name. Old delftware, English or Continental, is a coarse earthenware, often pitted, covered with an opaque tin glaze, and usually decorated in a quick, sure style of painting–made necessary by the painter's having to work on an absorbent surface. It gets its name from the Dutch town where a great deal of it came from, but actually it was made in England long before the rise of Delft, the principal centres here being Lambeth, Bristol and Liverpool. It was also produced at Delftfield in Glasgow in the eighteenth century.

Those who like fine porcelain, laboriously painted, may find the free styles of delft difficult to take, and, in fact, it is generally considered a man's pleasure rather than a woman's. But it has its fanatical supporters, all busily pushing the price up–though it's still, I think, a good investment, for nothing like it could ever be made again. To do that we would have to recreate not only the materials of those days but the men who wielded those dashing brushes and mixed those wonderfully vivid colours.

Outstanding among the styles are the blue and white landscapes and seascapes, the Chinoiseries with which the delftmakers tried to stem the tide of imported Chinese porcelain; the early polychrome plates, brightly and vigorously painted with tulips and other flowers; and the very famous blue dash chargers which are now much sought after as major rarities. Apart from the plates (although one ought also to mention those with scalloped or gadrooned edges and with *bianco sopra bianco* decoration) there are those beautifully shaped early wine bottles, predecessors of sealed glass bottles, also the puzzle jugs which form an important part of JOKE POTTERY, and the apothecaries' jars often seen in posh pharmacists' windows. Then there are TILES and PLAQUES.

A Delft armorial tankard, 1753 (Christies)

This ware is so old now that nobody minds a chip or two; and in fact I find them all a part of its charm: you certainly never notice them on a wall as you might with porcelain. But if you do hang old delft on the wall, don't use those gadgets that hook over the rim: they chip the glaze away rather *too* much.

And don't grudge it if you have to pay several pounds for a nice plate. A few years ago, 'Old Elson', as he liked to be called, of Christmas Steps in Bristol, offered me a pair of tulip plates for sixteen pounds, but not having then acquired a taste for delft I was foolish enough to think that I couldn't afford it. Now, of course, so high has polychrome delft gone that I really can't afford it!

It may be well to point out that what we in the English-speaking part of the world call delftware is known in France as *faience* and in Italy as *maiolica*–the latter should not, of course, be confused with MAJOLICA which was a nineteenth-century invention.

Della Robbia Ware

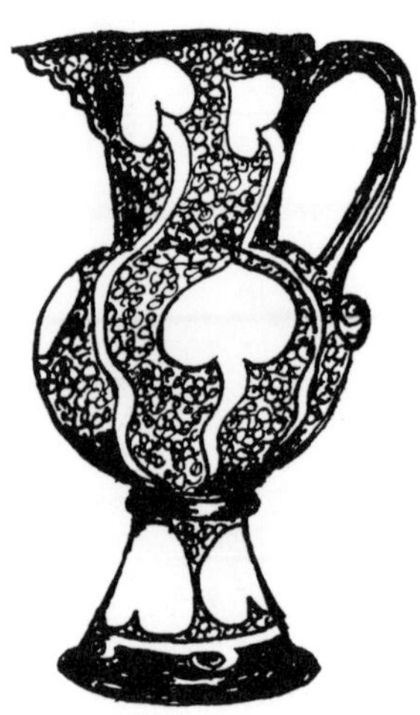

Della Robbia ware jug with painted 'sgraffito *decoration, 1897*

Of the many strange and even startling shapes in pottery made at the end of the last century and the beginning of the present, some of the strangest and most startling were produced by Harold Rathbone at the Della Robbia Pottery in Birkenhead, Cheshire, from 1894 to 1906.

Rathbone carried out the promise of the title of his pottery by making wall panels with figures in high relief which were not at all unlike those made by Luca della Robbia and his family in Renaissance Italy–but, of course, not in tin-glazed earthenware or *faience*, but in the modern coloured lead glazes. The freestanding fountain in the courtyard of the Savoy Hotel in London was modelled by Rathbone himself.

From this, however, he went on to develop vases, bottles, jars, plates and other wares brilliantly coloured, usually in green with a combination of *'sgraffito* work and painting. In this their creators, mostly art-school students, seem to have been allowed their heads completely, although they were made to bear responsibility for them either as painters or incisers, by adding their initials.

A few of them are known and they include, for example, Liza Wilkins, Charles Collis, Ruth Bare, Casandi Ann Walker and Carlo Mazoni–the Italian sculptor who had once run the Granville Pottery in Hanley. The factory mark was a sailing ship and the letters DR.

Directoire

This style-name covers the period immediately after the French Revolution, the time of the Directory and the Consulate, say from 1795 to 1804.

It was a brief and troubled time, when people in France had other preoccupations than cabinet-making; but there *is* a distinctive style, standing somewhere between Louis XVI and Empire. There are straight slender lines, with a single charm and elegance (Hepplewhitish if you like), but, for me, with more warmth and even–not surprisingly enough, perhaps–a hint of the romantic.

Characteristic features are square handles and sunken drawer fronts: classical motifs are still much in evidence, especially the lyre and the fasces, while–as to be expected–there are now Revolutionary symbols like the Phrygian cap, pikes and arrows. There is a provincial *directoire* which is sometimes even more charming than the Parisian.

If you can find a side table in this style–and, as with the English contemporary ones, something very like them appeared again at the end of the nineteenth century and can be found if one looks hard–the most appropriate ornament for it would be a pair of nice large CASOLETTES.

Dish Covers

There was a time when the large SHEFFIELD PLATE or ELECTRO-PLATE–even to some extent the silver–dish cover was loafing about in the shops waiting vainly for a buyer: it seemed so clumsy that there was nothing on earth to be done with it. Well, the silver ones were always worth their value as silver, and this has now rocketed sky-high, but what of the others: has a use been found for them?

Yes, it has. Turn it upside-down and hang it on wires and you have a handsome hanging basket for flowers or plants. Cut it in half and you have *two* handsome wall brackets, also for flowers. Vandalism? Yes, but what else can you do with them and even now they have precious little value in real terms.

One interesting point to look for if you get a Sheffield plate one is the shield. Many owners liked to have their arms or initials inscribed on their tableware, and as Sheffield plate is only a layer of silver fused on to a copper base, any engraving would have gone through to the copper. So they inserted on one side of the cover near the rim a little shield in solid silver which would take the engraving. You can spot this usually by its brightness.

These covers can also be found, by the way, in BRITANNIA METAL, with an electroplated handle.

Dishevelled Birds

Collectors of the fine early porcelains of Bow, Longton Hall and especially Worcester have long been curious about the identity of a peripatetic painter who worked at all these places (or in an outside decorator's studio) painting 'exotic birds' with disarrayed plumage: that it was the same hand on all this work is stylistically incontestable.

My only reason for mentioning the pattern is that for a few shillings in the late 1960s I bought a bowl and two saucers in early Victorian rococo, evidently decorated by an admirer of the eighteenth-century painter.

You could make an interesting collection by finding such latter-day junk-shop versions of expensive original patterns.

Distaffs

We hear a great deal about the distaff side and its doings, but not so much about distaffs.

Yet they can be most interesting and beautiful things, and are still to be found (just), especially on the Continent of Europe. They are, of course, the 'rocks' or short sticks around one end of which your flax, cotton or wool is loosely wound before it is spun off by the spindle.

In Spain, one prolific centre for finely carved distaffs is the province of Alentejo, perhaps because it is a sheep district and shepherds are traditionally great carvers. More elaborate ones are found in the Netherlands, some of them with fine basketwork at the top to take the wool or flax: in others the drawing or carving may be framed in inlaid ivory or gilt nails.

In the Val d'Aosta, as well as geometrical patterns there are carvings of entwined hearts or maybe a figure representing the bride or a couple embracing. Greece is a source of finely carved ones, sometimes showing St George and the Dragon; but perhaps the widest range is shown in those of Finland, some of which have almost naturalistic leaves and flowers.

Finnish carved distaff

An auspicious day to begin your collection might be January 7, the day after Epiphany, which was once St Distaff's Day, when women began to work again after their long, leisurely holiday over Christmas.

Dogs of Fo

I do not know if the owners of Pekinese dogs will feel outraged if I compare their darlings with these little 'dogs', but I am assured that there is a connection.

For these are Dogs of Fo, sometimes called Lions of Fo, sometimes the Lion Dogs of China. Their job was to stand guard on either side of the gates of Buddhist temples. Personally, if I were a Pekinese, I would feel very deeply complimented by being compared with one of these ferocious little animals.

These figures, usually in green enamel porcelain with decoration in other colours, including aubergine, are often to be seen, and are nice to have. They have been made since Ming (1368–1644) times, but the earlier ones will cost you a packet. The female plays with a puppy of the species: the male plays with a ball–but keeps his eye on you.

Don't confuse these–as auctioneers sometimes do–with kylins. These are fabulous animals with a deer's body, scales all over it, and a large bushy head: they are said to embody the Perfect Good. Not surprisingly, therefore, they are rarely found.

Dolls' Houses

There is something rather pathetic in seeing a child gaze wistfully at a lovely old dolls' house across a barrier rope in a museum. Why must it be put out of reach: weren't all those chairs and tables and ornaments and people just made to be played with?

Some of them once were, but to judge by the state in which many have survived, with most of their contemporary fittings intact, it must have been under a very watchful eye–if at all, since the majority of the early dolls' houses were not intended for child's play but for the delectation of grown men and women.

One would have imagined that the building and furnishing of dolls' houses was always a labour of love, the work of amateurs. But it appears that at least as far back as the beginning of the eighteenth century there were trade makers and suppliers of what were then called 'baby-houses'. Dean Swift evidently knew one, for in *Gulliver's Travels* his hero relates how the Queen of Brobdingnag had her cabinet-maker construct for him chairs and tables, silver dishes and the like 'not much bigger than what I have seen in a London toy-shop, for the furniture of a baby-house'.

For those of us who no longer wish to play our make-believe games, there is still much to be learned from them. Collectors of period WALLPAPER and CHINTZ, for example, will often find in them quite rare contemporary patterns, while the tiny

Below left: *A mid-Victorian doll's house.* Below right: *A very elaborate and beautiful wooden doll's house, modelled on an American clapboarded villa (Christies, South Kensington)*

replicas of pottery and furniture will reveal as clearly as anything can, precisely what kind of pieces went into what kind of house, how they hung their pictures, even how the dwellers in them dressed for different times of the day.

In two London museums there are period dolls' houses which are enormously interesting in this way, bringing their story almost down to the present. In the London Museum there is the famous Blackett dolls' house, which dates from about 1740, with original festooned curtains and *chinoiserie* wallpaper. The Lansdowne house, in the same museum, with its handsome red brick façade, brings us forward about a century, for the arms of Queen Victoria are in the pediment; a central spiral staircase gives access to the upper rooms, and there is a nursery in the basement, alongside the kitchen.

Fittings of a generation later are seen in the Princess May of Teck's dolls' house, made in 1879 for the lady who later became Queen Mary (her maiden name is retained to distinguish this house from the celebrated and spectacular Queen Mary's dolls' house in Windsor Castle, designed by Sir Edward Lutyens and made in 1922). By the side of Princess May's, Queen Victoria's house seems a product of the kind of manufacturer described by Dickens in his *Cricket on the Hearth* who made all kinds of houses for the trade.

At Bethnal Green or on loan to the Victoria and Albert Museum (some of which require notice for inspection) is a whole range of houses. Finest of them perhaps is the Tate dolls' house, a fine piece of architecture, made about 1760 with grained paper panelling and bedroom wallpapers of about 1830. Some of the furniture is also original. The giant among them is the Dingley Hall house, five feet high and nearly ten feet wide, and with thirteen fully furnished rooms: it was apparently built by two schoolboys.

In the dolls' house of about 1903, presented to the same museum by Miss Anita Pollock, there is a living room furnished in the ART NOUVEAU style–the house itself, however, offers more than a hint of ART DECO; while of the same date as the great Queen Mary's dolls' house is a miniature of Oakley House, Bedfordshire, the then home of the Honourable Leopold and Phyllis Russell, who made the model.

Perhaps dolls' houses originated in Germany; certainly the well-known 'Nuremberg kitchens' with all their pots and pans and other utensils (as seen in the Victoria and Albert Museum) were being imported into England as far back as 1660. The idea of these kitchens was to teach little girls the rudiments of household crafts, just as the similar butchers' shops, with their serried joints of meat, were intended to teach the housewives of the future the various cuts of mutton, beef and pork. There is a museum of these toy kitchens and shops, I am told, in Schloss Frauenberg, at Bodman on the shore of Lake Constance.

One hopes that dolls' houses are being preserved and also that contemporary ones continue to be made. Has there ever been an exhibition of them?

Door Knockers

Every day one sees more and more houses being pulled down to make way for new buildings. What happens to all their door knockers?

A great many of them eventually find their way into the junk and antique shops, and it is well worth treating yourself to a set for your own house. Once the American tourists get hold of them they will never hang on English doors again.

They range from massive cast-iron ones, with a great ring in the mouth of, perhaps, a gargoyle or a lion, to more delicate efforts in brass (dolphins were a favourite symbol) or bronzed iron, and they can often be dated and traced to a manufacturer by the registry mark.

A sanctuary knocker from Brougham Hall, Cumbria (J. Denton Robinson)

A cast-iron door porter, early 19th century (S. H. Cole)

Ornamental foot-scrapers are worth looking for, also old letter boxes and door knobs. This is a quest which will take you to the local scrapyard–which you should never pass without looking into.

Door Porters

Not, as you might think, men who carry doors on their backs, but articles of cast iron, brass, glass and other materials, used to prop open a door.

These survivals of an age in which, apparently, doors were kept open more than they are now, come in wonderful variety. All through the Victorian age the iron-founders, eager to show off their mastery of new skills in cast iron, turned out by the hundred thousand all those replicas of Punch and Judy, the Duke of Wellington, Ally Sloper, kilted Highlanders, bells, lions and other beasts. Usually there is some part of the figure which can be used to pick up the door stop and drop it elsewhere–like the cocked hat of the Iron Duke, or Mr Punch's curved bonnet.

You could make a fascinating collection of these for the garden, painted against the weather. If you kept them indoors you could always 'blacklead' them and give your visitors a nostalgic glimpse of that unique sheen which long-departed charladies once gave our ironwork.

Other stops come in brass, cast in designs which have been made continuously for a couple of centuries, sometimes weighted with lead, sometimes not. Then there are the green glass ones which at one time were erroneously thought to come from the Nailsea district near Bristol, but which, in fact, emanate from Wakefield in Yorkshire, where the workers at the Kilner glass factory made these 'dumpies' with the metal left over at the end of the day's operation. The more desirable examples have dew-beaded posies and flowerpots fixed inside them–the pattern in chalk dust being turned into tiny bubbles of carbon dioxide when the molten glass was overlaid. A variant of the glass door stop may be found with a circular depression in the base, indicating that it was originally attached to the top of a newel post at the bottom of a flight of banisters.

Doulton stoneware jug

Doulton

This firm has produced an astonishingly varied range of ceramics over a period of over a century, from the art pottery of the late Victorian period to sanitary wares and electric insulators. Their STONEWARE SPIRIT FLASKS are now much sought after, but there are many excellent traditional jugs and bottles decorated in relief which are worth looking for. Also in STONEWARE come the many jugs and vases with applied or incised decoration which, when the colours aren't either too drab or too gaudy, are fine things to have. There is a particularly attractive pale blue which sets off darker colours well.

A Hannah Barlow jug, with charming genre scenes

Very much a personal favourite with me is the work of Hannah Barlow who did some fine, economical drawings of animals in the stoneware while it was still soft, then rubbed pigments into the lines. Each of these is an individual piece of handwork, and they have escalated enormously in value beyond the two or three pounds that was being asked for them in the early 1960s.

But there were many other fine artists at Doulton's and their work is now being carefully re-appraised as a result of renewed activity by the museums. Many of them decorated the china for which Doulton was renowned. Look out for the very fine flower patterns in rich colours by Edward Raby, patterns in raised gold by Robert Allen, orchids by David Dewsbury, landscapes, especially scenes of Venice, by John H. Plant, roses by Percy Curnock, figures with swirling ART NOUVEAU draperies by George White, and animals, birds and fishes by Henry Mitchell and Charles Hart.

Still another production at Burslem were the naturalistic figures by Charles J. Noke (notably the famous 'Old Balloon Woman') which, in view of their excellent

craftsmanship, I wish I could love more than I do: these sentiments also apply to the well-known latter day TOBY JUGS and their more modern character counterparts. Some time ago I saw a beautifully made and coloured figure of a jester (was it Jack Point?) by Noke: but its theatrically 'knowing' look, only just acceptable in a drawing, is difficult to take in modelling.

Returning to Doulton's Lambeth period, I recommend what the firm called their 'Carrara' ware, a stoneware having a white body covered in slightly translucent glaze, gilded and painted with bold flowers. There is much to be said, too, for their so-called 'Faience'–nothing to do with the French earthenware of that name but very similar to MAJOLICA, with thick impasto painting making the bold decoration stand out in relief. You see many FLOWER POTS and pedestals in this ware, but I prefer the smaller bottles and vases.

Above left: *A Lambeth faience flat circular vase on four legs, with seascape, ships and other decoration by Esther Lewis, Ada Dennis and Mary Denley, c. 1900.* Above right: *Two Lambeth faience vases, late 19th century.* Below: *Doulton 'Carrara Ware' vase, by Ada Dennis and Mary Denley, c. 1890 (Doulton & Company Limited)*

Dresden

There have probably been more broken hearts about 'Dresden' than any other kind of porcelain, for no other has been so much imitated, forged, travestied and lied about during the last two centuries.

Let's start by trying to get our terms sorted out. One is often asked the difference between 'Dresden' and 'Meissen'. To explain this we have to make a short excursion into history. Hard paste porcelain, though long in existence in China, was not re-invented in Europe till about 1710, by a young Saxon alchemist named Böttger. He had been locked up in a castle by the Elector Augustus the Strong until he could find the secret of turning base metal into gold, and so help pay for the enormous quantities of Chinese porcelain which Augustus had been buying out of his subjects' pockets. But Böttger discovered the secret of porcelain instead, which, from the Elector's point of view, was just as good.

From this developed the Royal Porcelain Manufactory at Meissen, about twelve miles from Dresden. Here were made all those entrancing figures of characters from the Italian Comedy by the famous modeller Kaendler and others, which can cost you

Dresden (Royal Factory, Meissen)

Paris (Samson imitating Meissen)

several thousand pounds apiece; the famous *chinoiseries*, the beautiful little landscapes and seascapes in reversed panels on the celebrated grounds of yellow, green, lilac and maroon which were to be the inspiration of so much of the work done in the English factories of the mid-eighteenth century.

During the nineteenth century, however, not only did the royal factory go on reproducing its own earlier wares in less refined forms, but other factories, mainly in the Dresden area, as well as in other parts of Europe, joined in the fun too. The result was the export of the huge quantities of 'Dresden' shepherdesses and other figures which filled Victorian mantelpieces and display cabinets.

Not only were the famous crossed swords imitated, sometimes with qualifying initials (like 'S' for Samson of Paris) and sometimes not, but one firm even used one of the very early marks, 'AR' the monogram of Augustus the Strong. A crown over the letter 'D', also the word 'Dresden' itself, may indicate manufacture at, in or around Dresden, but it has nothing whatever to do with the work of the Royal Porcelain Manufactory.

So there we are: 'Dresden', if you like, for all this secondary ware and imitation of the real thing. But if your own piece is to qualify as a rarity, it must be from the royal factory, with the genuine mark; in which case you might as well follow the practice among serious collectors of calling it 'Meissen'.

Dressers

Everyone likes a fine dresser, set out with its china or glass, or sometimes gleaming PEWTER. There are still a good many about if you take the trouble to look for them, and considering the workmanship to be found in them I would not call them dear. I have seen excellent early-nineteenth-century oak and mahogany ones go for less than a hundred pounds, which does not seem a lot for the principal piece of furniture and base for decoration in the living-room of a cottage or a small country house. Stripped pine dressers have been available for more modest sums, but the popularity of this style has encouraged modern 'reproductions' which are, in fact, more expensive than the genuine article!

Before looking at the different sorts of dressers, let us consider its origin. The word comes from the Norman French *dresseur*, which meant that the original dresser was really a sideboard on which one 'dressed' the food before serving it. Later you had that division of purpose whereby the large houses elaborated their sideboards, and perhaps displayed their fine pieces on a Court cupboard; whereas the smaller establishment, such as a farmhouse with a general-purpose living-room, would be more likely to let the dresser acquire shelves for their scoured pewter, blue and white DELFTWARE and perhaps the brown Staffordshire slipware. In some parts of the country, in fact, a dresser is sometimes called a delft-rack, the shelves being built into the walls.

Now for the types. Much has been written about regional types of dressers, but when one gets down to it and looks at those which are still in the houses where they started life perhaps two centuries ago, one has to be pretty wary about laying down rules. The 'Welsh' dresser is well-known, and there is certainly a distinctive type, but I think this word 'Welsh' is often used of any dresser simply because there are probably more surviving in Wales than anywhere else. But the Welsh and West Country (including Cornish) dresser generally seems to be a compact affair with a backboard, often with pierced apron work, or an arched gallery over the upper shelf. They are sometimes covered with red lead and painted black to protect them from damp and pests. Often there are narrow cupboards at the sides of the shelves; in others there may be a clock in the centre flanked by spice drawers.

Quite a different sort of dresser is found on the other side of the country. With an

open back there are rails along the dresser front to keep the plates in, and often the shelves are free-standing. These seem to be common in Yorkshire and Lancashire. There is yet another, which I suspect of having East Anglian affinities because of a certain 'Dutch' feeling; there is a high arched top and the shelves have bobbin railings.

Still another variety does not seem to have local tendencies at all, but has moved out of the kitchen into the sitting-room and acquired cabriole legs, serpentine front and the graceful though simple lines of what is known as 'Country Georgian'. These dressers could hold their own with any sort of furniture, and they are naturally much more expensive than the others.

But–to revert to the 'kitchen' type dresser–if I wanted one badly and could not find one at the right price I would be very much inclined to go back to origins by looking for a good oak side-table with drawers and/or cupboards, and then build my shelving over it. Using old wood, you would have something not at all different from the 'dressers' to be found in many a country kitchen today.

Dumb Waiter

Not what it sounds like, but one of those round, two- or three-tiered contrivances on pedestal feet used as a kind of sideboard, often revolving so that you won't have to walk round it to get the cheese or the decanter of port.

Useful things, these, for one of those cocktail parties where you have to hold a glass in one hand, a sardine on toast in the other, and a cigarette in your mouth.

But wouldn't they look even better at a real party, decked out with flowers, jellies, sweetmeats and other delights? And if the polish were stained by generations of spilt sauces and alcohol, you wouldn't have any sort of bad conscience about painting it up gaily in white, would you?

Two-tiered dumb waiter

Dummy Board Figures

Just occasionally you will see in one of the better-class shops a cut-out figure, sometimes life-size, sometimes only three or four feet high, of a person in seventeenth or more likely eighteenth- or early nineteenth-century costumes. There are shepherds and shepherdesses, housemaids with brooms, soldiers, ladies brushing their hair, boys and girls playing, and domestic animals such as dogs and cats.

Once upon a time these figures were to be found in private houses all over the country, in tea gardens, coffee houses and inns. Why, nobody seems very sure. They certainly stood in front of empty fireplaces in summertime: being of wood, they could not have been used when the fire was alight. They also stood at the ends of corridors in large houses, and in the tea gardens they were generally disposed so that you came on them by surprise, as with a ha-ha. There is also a theory that they were left in windows to hoodwink would-be housebreakers. Probably they were there just for fun, or for companionship.

17th-century dummy board figure

Much more plentiful these days, however, are dummy figures of thin wood or pasteboard used as window display pieces in shops. The majority date from the late nineteenth century when advertising became more sophisticated as branded goods developed. The earlier ones take quite a bit of finding, since they would have been discarded when they became obsolete, but there are plenty of modern examples around so it is a relatively easy matter to begin a collection with current models.

Eggs

Children get chocolate eggs for Easter now, but once upon a time you gave them real ones which were charmingly painted with a picture and sometimes a name. Boiled very hard, they were put away in a cupboard to be kept as mementoes. Later the potters

Silver gilt eggs with novelties by Stuart Devlin, c. 1960 (Christies, South Kensington)

A mounted emu egg of the mid 19th century (Christies, South Kensington)

made them in eathenware and porcelain, and some of these have floral sprays, some pictures of birds, animals and ships. Some years ago I found one which divided in half; it was made of COPENHAGEN porcelain and cost me all of three shillings (15p). Another class bear views of the town in which you bought them as a souvenir of a trip; these were made in Staffordshire, Sunderland and various other places in England, though the late nineteenth- and early twentieth-century examples, with transfer-printed views, mainly hailed from the potteries of Saxony and Thuringia.

Another race of eggs in china and glass, painted with more conventional designs, were used as hand coolers, probably very necessary when you wore lots of clothes in stuffy rooms; and they were made also to use in darning. Darning eggs and hand coolers may also be found in marble, alabaster, malachite and other hardstones, and a cluster of them look most attractive in a wide, shallow bowl on an occasional table.

To put the thing completely in reverse, there were also hand *warmers*. These were hollow, with a silver screw top, filled with hot water, and were carried in the muff or the gentleman's pocket. Quite functional versions of these egg-shaped hand warmers were still being produced up to the Second World War and were regarded as a great boon on the grouse moors, to keep your trigger finger from freezing up. A first cousin to this type is the egg scent bottle, painted in the colours of the actual birds eggs, and therefore a wonderful subject for collecting.

Also worth looking for are examples of ostrich and other large eggs which have been mounted in hardwoods and silver. This charming idea originated in the Middle Ages, when the ostrich egg was regarded as a marvel that lent weight to the fable of Sinbad and the Roc. Silver-mounted ostrich eggs from the days of the Crusaders are, of course, of immense rarity and value, but the idea was revived, as part of the neo-Gothic craze, in the late nineteenth century. There are even some bizarre and grotesque 'curios' from the turn of the century, consisting of ostrich eggs mounted on a pair of birds' feet!

Eight Immortals

This venerable band appear so often in ivory, porcelain and pictures, that it may interest collectors to know something about them. They are (or were) to the Chinese what the saints are to European Catholics, and between them they represent the eight human states of youth, age, wealth, poverty, aristocracy, plebeianism, masculinity and femininity. They stand for the Taoist principles of contempt for material comforts and worldly power, and for the eternal longings of man for a world of faery. All the same, they are a very nice lot of people, with plenty of human traits–sometimes they are shown sitting in a glade having what we would call a glorious binge–and they thoroughly deserve their immortality. They lived at different periods over about a thousand years.

Generally accepted as the leading character is the fat man of the party, *Chung-li Ch'uan*, sometimes represented as a general, but always with a fan. He used this to very good purpose, according to one account, when meeting a young widow who was busily fanning the freshly dug soil on her husband's grave: she had a successor lined up, but could not marry him until her first husband's grave was dry. The general at once dried the grave for her by waving his magic fan.

More often seen, perhaps, is *Lu Tung-pin*, who wears a pleated cap, carries a sword on his back and also a fly whisk. His special interest is sick people, and shrines have been built to him. *Chang Kuo-hao* may be recognized as a bearded man carrying what looks astonishingly like a golfer's bag with two clubs in it: it is a drum made from a bamboo stick. This reverend gentleman had a very handy form of transport in the shape of a white mule (he is sometimes shown sitting on it) which, after being ridden for a thousand miles or so, could be folded up and put in a wallet; he brought the mule into service again merely by pouring water over the wallet.

Ts'ao Kuo-chiu, a bearded man with the cap of a member of the Imperial Court, carries tickets of admission to the Court, but not caring much for parties he gave up the courtly life and became a mountain hermit. *Li T'ieh-kuai* is the beggar of the party, hideous and deformed, with an iron crutch and a calabash or gourd. He acquired his present appearance because at one time he was frequently being recalled to heaven for consultation, leaving his body on earth. After returning from one of these missions he found that someone, thinking him dead, had cremated him without making proper enquiries. However, the Immortal found the body of a lame beggar and used that. Not a difficult man to please.

Han Hsiang-tzu, like Orpheus, could spellbind even animals with his music, though he uses a flute rather than a lute, and is sometimes shown playing it. But he is also seen carrying the broken branch of a peach tree in memory of the occasion when he tried, but failed, to climb to immortality up the tree. He is the patron saint of musicians. *Lan Ts'ai-ho* is sometimes shown as a girl, sometimes as a youth, but either way the figure carries a basket or bouquet of flowers, and is associated with the idea of longevity. But the only veritable lady of the party is *Ho Hsien-ku*, a sort of celestial Cinderella, who had a bullying stepmother and is consequently shown either with a ladle filled with magic fungus, a lotus bloom, or a basket in the mountains.

Sometimes you will see all eight Immortals going to an audience with the Star of Longevity, the venerable *Shou Lao*, who, with an enormous domed bald head, is himself a frequent figure in the antique shops.

Electro-plate

It was around the year 1840 that the still-famous firm of Elkington took out the basic patent for the process whereby a thin coating of silver or gold could be deposited upon a baser metal by electrolysis. It follows, therefore, that since most things in silver also came in electro-plate, pieces made throughout the Victorian era show all those entrancingly interesting mix-ups of motifs which characterize the best–and the worst–of Victorian style.

Electro-plated teapot

Sometimes the base was of copper (as in SHEFFIELD PLATE), sometimes of BRITANNIA METAL, but mostly of what was at first GERMAN SILVER, an alloy of copper, zinc and nickel, later modified into 'nickel silver', thus giving us the initials 'EPNS'–electro-plated nickel silver–which is usually stamped on the base of a piece.

It matters not if your early find is tarnished, or has lost most of its silver deposit; it can be stripped and re-silvered by your local silversmith. As noted under BRITANNIA METAL, the trade is already performing this service for you and offering the result in silver which is, as the advertisement says, whiter than white. They are also doing this to SHEFFIELD PLATE and to copper articles which started life as naked copper.

Embroidery

One doesn't often come across old embroidery surviving in a really satisfactory state–but examples of early Victorian BERLIN WOOLWORK do turn up occasionally in pristine condition and even now are still fairly cheap.

Embroidery, in general, of course, has been with us for many a century, but it took an industrial-minded nineteenth century to make things more or less automatic with mass-produced cross-stitch designs, showing flowers, dogs, cats, birds, horses, deer. On pieces of square-meshed canvas busy fingers young and old occupied themselves all through the long evenings, making firescreens, stool covers, backs of chairs, slippers, even smoking caps and braces for papa.

Later on, and very difficult to find nowadays, is the more original art needlework to which ladies reacted later in the century. Outline patterns were used, but there was room for considerable skill from the needlewoman, and some of these turn-of-the-century designs of flowers and storks and peacocks were very fine. One small item you often find in little piles are the linen 'tidies' with which grandmama kept her furniture clean from sticky fingers, or laid on her sideboards and occasional tables.

Cushion covers are worth looking for, but only if you are prepared to rummage through piles of unusable rubbish to find them. But when you do you won't find them dear. Look out also for patchwork quilts and counterpanes.

One assumes, of course, that Jacobean stumpwork, or even fine needlework of the eighteenth century, won't be found in junk shops. But stranger things have happened. Here the intelligent and knowledgeable needlewoman, who takes the trouble to learn the history of her craft and its materials, might one day get together a small collection which some museum would adore to be given–especially if there is a local interest in the work.

Embroidered Pictures

These are rather a special sort of embroidery–and by the same token rather a special sort of picture. I suppose the sort one sees most are those rather lugubrious mourning pictures, showing a lady leaning on a tomb, or perhaps a biblical scene, with Rebecca at the Well. Many of these were worked in silk which has now faded, or the background crumbled away with time. But there *are* attractive ones: I bought a handsome one some years ago, of a large peacock sitting on a small tree, for, I think, a couple of pounds. It was in reasonably good order, but I believe there are ways of rejuvenating these pictures, either by simply cleaning up or by giving a new background. Here is a chance for the really accomplished needlewoman to see what she can do by drawing in a few threads of bright colour to enliven the old.

More primitive, of course, are all those sailors' pictures in wool, often of their own ships, or showing harbour scenes. Samplers belong to this school: I am not myself an enthusiast, for they so often express sentiments and interests imposed on a child by rather sententious parents and teachers. However, there they are, and many of them give a posthumous fame to some little lady of eight or nine.

These handmade pictures should not, of course, be confused with the charming woven silk pictures pioneered by Thomas Stevens of Coventry in the nineteenth

Below left: *Silkwork picture of Paradise.* Below right: *Woolwork picture of Othello and Desdemona (Christies, South Kensington)*

century and which have continued to be produced sporadically by other companies down to the present day.

Façon de Venise

This is collector's language for a style of glassmaking which derives from Venice, either by fashion (as the name implies), or by emigrating glassmakers.

Unless we become collectors we are unlikely to have much to do with its manifestations in sixteenth- and seventeenth-century Dutch, German and English glass, but we shall come across it in a form which one might more appropriately name 'Anglo-Venetian', or perhaps 'Stourbridge Venetian'.

This appears as ewers and jugs, decanters and drinking glasses blown in a wavy form, often with striped colours and extra decoration, in the shape of little raspberry 'prunts' or lozenges. It was the late nineteenth-century reaction against the rather stereotyped forms of crystal–and the public loved it. To us, now, it looks pretty and engaging, and is well worth the few pounds asked for it.

Another, and posher, type makes use of the Venetian *latticinio* decoration, with opaque white or coloured glass threading, which one sees in a more homely fashion in NAILSEA glass. But there are tall compotiers, candles, and goblets which are Venetian in shape as well.

I note that such forms are being made available in the smart shops again today, presumably from Italy.

Late 17th-century Dutch façon de Venise goblet (Pilkington Glass Museum)

Faiences Populaires

Here is something which you would expect to find only in the country districts of France, but which appears surprisingly often in the shops in Britain.

Alongside the highly decorated *faiences* or tin-glazed earthenwares made in Europe from Renaissance times onwards, there was a much more sparsely decorated, and therefore cheaper, version called, in general, *faience blanche*. They were painted lightly in bright colours–usually blue, orange and yellow–with simple, swiftly-drawn patterns, in some cases not unlike some English DELFTWARE–or at any rate in the same kind of mood.

Faience parlante ('speaking faience') seems to be the term reserved for all those which bear not only decoration but inscriptions of some kind, perhaps a motto; or which commemorate an event, as in some of the STAFFORDSHIRE pottery. In *faience patronomique* we find pictures of saints, with a name or a date, evidently intended as gifts at christening or birthdays.

Faience patriotique *plate from the Nièvre*

Faience patriotique, however, represents a class of wares with national symbols and mottoes deriving from the time of the French Revolution. Nevers was perhaps the most important source of these things, typical of them being a cockerel with the inscription '*La Liberté ou la Mort*'.

These plates and other wares, like PEASANT POTTERY, make no pretension to great art; but some of the *faience populaire*, with its dashing designs of birds and flowers, has a great deal of charm. These faiences have been extensively copied in modern times and, in fact, are still a favourite 'buy' as table-ware decoration in many parts of France.

Famille Rose, Verte, Noire and Jaune

You will not look in shop windows for very long without coming across these styles of decoration in porcelain. Even if you do not see the original work from China, you are bound to find English adaptations of them on china, earthenware and even MASON'S IRONSTONE, which is still being produced.

Famille verte vase

Famille Rose is one of the great 'families' of Chinese porcelain enamelled in various colours–usually three to five. It gets its name from a certain rose pink which appears as one of the colours: and the other 'families' have similar dominant colours–Famille Verte (green), Famille Jaune (yellow), Famille Noire (black). The French names are due to their having first been appreciated and classified by collectors of that nationality.

It is also worth noting, perhaps, that the colour of Famille Rose is something which the Chinese, for a change, owe to Europe: it is produced from a gold chloride called 'Purple of Cassius', after a Dutch chemist.

Many famous patterns derive from Famille Rose originals, notably the Indian Tree of COALPORT, and patterns made today. If you go to museums and get these fixed in your mind, you will have some happy hours spotting them in all sorts of disguises.

Famille Verte is older than Famille Rose, carries much red and powder blue, and appears a lot in figures like the DOGS OF FO. The Famille Jaune and Famille Noire appear often as the ground colour of large jars, baluster vases and 'rouleaux' or four-sided vases. The black ones, with flowers in yellow, green and white, are especially fine, but it should be noted that the original ones are not simply black: a transparent green wash has been floated over the black giving it a unique appearance.

K'ang Hsi famille noire vase

In case you can't find original specimens of these 'families' at your prices, be it noted that the Crown Staffordshire Porcelain Company in the late nineteenth century made excellent reproductions of vases in the colours and styles of the Famille Verte and the Famille Rose, and also, incidentally, wares with powder blue grounds. There was no intention to deceive: the crown and 'Staffs' or 'Staffordshire' appears on every piece–if someone has not removed it.

Pair of Chien Lung famille rose plates (Christies, South Kensington)

Fans

'I have seen a fan so very angry,' wrote Addison, 'that it would have been dangerous for the absent lover who provoked it to have come within the wave of it; and at other times I have seen it so very languishing that I have been glad for the lady's sake that the lover was at a sufficient distance from it.'

In days when tender conversation often had to take place across a room or from one theatre box to another, there was, it seems, a recognized code of signals, rather like semaphore. Collectors, of course, go for the now rare eighteenth-century fans, either those in which you inserted the latest paper song or political rhyme, or *brisé* fans, with

their sticks joined by ribbons. But these are rare now, and we shall have to content ourselves with the painted ones of the Victorian age, with leaves of silk, satin, paper or vellum, or those large black Spanish ones in ebony.

A mid 18th-century fan, painted with a stag-hunt (Christies, South Kensington)

Other kinds of fan which you might still come across include the late eighteenth-century examples lavishly decorated with gold thread and sequins attached to netting, the Italian souvenir fans of the Grand Tour, which had Roman scenery painted on them, and the fans of the Regency period decorated with figures in neo-classical dress. When the use of fans was at its height there were special forms of fan for use in church, at weddings and when in mourning. Other kinds include medallion, Pompadour and puzzle fans, the latter having *brisé* sticks that could be manipulated to produce different pictures.

Quite apart from the various kinds of folding fan, popular in Europe, there is a large family of fixed-leaf fans, mostly of Eastern origin. Early examples are rare, but in the second half of the last century countless thousands of small fixed-leaf fans were imported from China and Japan and triggered off a craze in interior decor, which utilized such fans as decoration for screens and mantelpieces. These rigid or screen fans are still fairly plentiful and are often decorated with charming *chinoiseries*. They were especially popular with the aesthetes of the High Art Movement of the late nineteenth century and were almost as characteristic a motif as the sunflower.

Fashion Plates

There is seemingly no end to the treasure which can be won from Victorian illustrated books–the source of so many attractive engravings of scenery, birds, animals and flowers.

Among these books you will find bound volumes of nineteenth-century fashion magazines, with coloured plates expounding the endless story of changing female forms and fashions. Many of them are fascinating pictures in their own right, for the

The new mode of July 1840 (from The World of Fashion and Continental Feuilletons*)*

Victorian lady liked to see herself, not only *à la mode* but in full action–taking tea in drawing rooms; *soignée* in off-the-shoulder dresses at the opera or at a *soirée musicale*; on walking and boating expeditions; riding to hounds; meeting gentlemen in the park.

Fashion plates were usually hand-coloured lithographs, and the great majority–even in the English and American magazines–came from Paris, then, as always, headquarters of the *haute couture*. One of the most prolific of the artists was Jules David, whose work appeared first in the *Moniteur de la Mode*, and afterwards the *Englishwoman's Domestic Magazine*, published in London by Samuel Beeton, husband of Mrs Beeton–*the* Mrs Beeton.

A nicely-judged succession of these volumes could demonstrate vividly the changing outlines of fashion from about 1780 up to the Second World War–though even individual plates pre-dating the French Revolution are becoming decidedly scarce. There was a lull during the Revolution itself, when Frenchmen–and women–had more serious matters on their minds, but by the time of the Napoleonic Empire in 1804 Paris had recovered as fashion capital of the world. To this period belong those plates, sometimes grotesque, often whimsical, which satirized the *Incroyables* and *Merveilleuses* (the 'unbelievables' and the 'marvellous' ones)–the dandies and ladies whose costume often went to extravagant and ridiculous lengths.

Interest in woman's fashions reached their peak in the second half of the nineteenth century, and this was the hey-day of the fashion magazines. By now such techniques as chromolithography were making the reproduction of colour pictures much cheaper and this inspired a rash of excellent magazines on both sides of the Atlantic–the *Gazette du Bon Ton, The Queen, Vogue, Harper's Bazaar, Godey's Lady's Book, La Belle Assemblée, La Mode Illustré, La Musée des Familles* and *Le Journal des Demoiselles* among others. Some excellent plates were also incorporated in such English magazines as *The Lady's Treasury* and the *Young Englishwoman* (which later became *Sylvia's Home Journal*).

There was a late flowering of this art form at the turn of the century and from then until 1939 artists of the calibre of Paul Poiret and Erté (the acronym of RT–Romain Tirtoff) produced a galaxy of models and mannequins illustrating the latest Paris fashions. Many of these plates were copied in British and American periodicals. Gradually, however, more mechanical techniques of reproduction robbed the fashion plate of its artistry and finally the advent of fashion photography pretty well killed it. There are still numerous examples of early twentieth-century fashion plates to be picked up quite cheaply–and while you are at it, why not consider early dressmakers' patterns, which came into vogue in the 'twenties?

Feather Pictures

A true bird picture is made from actual feathers of the bird which is intended to be shown. The beaks and the feet are painted in watercolour or oils, and very often there is a landscape behind them. Sometimes they are shown hanging on walls with a little trickle of blood coming from them. This really belongs in the department of *trompe l'oeil*.

Another kind of bird picture is seen in the work of Samuel Dixon, a Dublin artist whose best work was done between the years 1748 and 1769. He used copper plates to emboss the design on thickish paper from the back, afterwards painting the relief impressions by hand. Many of the true feather pictures are what you would now term collages, in which feathers are arranged in fancy patterns or arrangements. They look quite tasteful and effective when done skilfully, but too many of the Victorian examples, in which enthusiasm has outpaced ability, look like someone's unfortunate pet hen after a particularly nasty car accident!

A featherwork picture, c. 1800 (Christies, South Kensington)

Finger Plates

Obliging manufacturers are making for us replicas of finger plates which prevent us from making dirty marks where we push open doors. Also indeed of the knobs and the furniture of the lock. It has always been possible, at a price, to pick up some genuine plates or knobs in porcelain or coloured glass; but why not take advantage of the much wider choice that these replicas will give you?

One might also mention in this place that in those mysterious shops which serve 'the trade'–and which can be reached through it–you can buy practically any kind of brass or ormolu fitting for drawers of whatever period you like, and restore your piece to its original style whenever you wish to.

Fire Insurance Signs

You will sometimes see on the walls of old houses, usually at about first-floor level, metal plaques bearing symbols, numbers and names. The 'Sun' is a frequent one; the 'Phoenix' another. They are fire insurance marks, and although collectors do not actually tear the houses down to get at them, they, or the local dealers, generally contrive to be around on demolition day.

These plaques date from the days when fire brigades were run by private enterprise (the insurance companies), which meant that when a fire broke out the firemen elected to save the properties they had insured, and cheerfully left the rest to burn to the ground. Presumably they had a team of salesmen on the spot offering plaques to the improvident.

Originally the plaques bore the actual policy number, and these are the ones which are eagerly snapped up. Tin, iron, copper and zinc were used for most of them, but some are in TERRA COTTA, and porcelain, or were even on a stone built into the house.

In 1833 the various private brigades were combined in the London area to form the Metropolitan Fire Service and gradually the provincial brigades likewise combined. Henceforward even the uninsured could have a reasonable hope of having their fires put out, and so the need for the insurance signs gradually died out. But the plaques continued in use as advertisements until about 1860.

A copper fire mark on God's Providence House (an olde tea shoppe), Newport, Isle of Wight, c. 1790–1800. The policy numbers are not visible and would most probably have been painted in black (Phoenix Assurance Company Limited)

From left: *Fire mark of The London Assurance, dated about 1798; Fire mark of Alliance Assurance Co. Ltd, probably 19th century (both Sun Alliance and London Insurance Group); Lead mark number 53. The earliest Phoenix mark known to have survived, issued in January 1782 (Phoenix Assurance Company Limited)*

Firebacks

Our ancestors knew a thing or two about making the most of an open fire. Here and there you will come across one of the old cast-iron firebacks, taken from an old house which has been pulled down. It stood at the back of an open fireplace, partly to protect the bricks at the back from the heat, and partly to throw that heat out into the room–where it was wanted. In other words, to act as a sort of radiator. Another advantage it had was that once a thick slab of cast iron gets really hot, it keeps hot for a long time; and a fireback would keep a glow in your cheeks long after a fire had died away.

Added to all this, it gave you one more chance to show off your family arms or loyalties. For most of these backs have designs of one sort or another cast into them. A great many are heraldic, often bearing the arms of a specific family. Others feature biblical subjects, such as Adam and Eve, or commemorate some public event, such as a coronation or a victory. The Boscobel Oak, with its three crowns in a tree, symbolizing the escape of the future Charles II, is a favourite device.

Firebacks last as long as a house and in many cases have endured far longer. At least, some of them have. For one of the odd things about these firebacks is that there is apparently an inexhaustible supply of them. I know at least one country antique shop, where one unfailingly sees a dozen or more, always with the same sort of patterns, and I'm sure these have never been inside a house at all.

Making new ones is simplicity itself: you use an old one to make your mould in sand: then cast a new one from it. The more battered and scorched the old one the better, for it will all register faithfully on the new one.

Experts can tell the true from the false by examination of the rust or patina. But non-experts will have to trust the dealer: after all if he's an honest man, he ought to be able to tell you where it came from. If, of course, you mind. A fireback, after all, is a fireback and it's just as effective and decorative if it was cast yesterday or three hundred years ago.

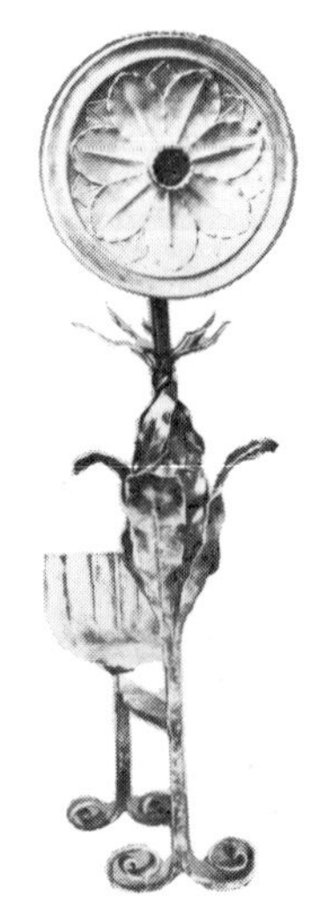

A metal fire dog by The Century Guild (William Morris Gallery)

Fireplace Furniture

A few years ago you could hardly give away old sets of fire-irons. Now you see them displayed on the walls of country cottages like WARMING PANS or old weapons. But fire-irons apart, there are many items which once stood in and around our fireplaces, and which, if unsuitable for collection, have something as decoration.

Having started at the back of the fire–and promising to go to the front of the fire with FIRESCREENS in the next piece–we could plump down halfway on *Firedogs*, which of course were made to support logs so that they would burn freely on the open hearth. Many of these are still about, their uprights often showing cast figures, faces or initials, and are still reasonably priced. A more stately version of this, made for show in the houses of the great, were the *andirons*, sometimes of brass or even silver, beautifully worked, which stood at either end (thus 'end-irons') of the fireplace and supported the fire-irons, especially after the introduction of the coal-burning grate.

A helmet-shaped coal scuttle.

Then there is all that range of smaller things from the hearth itself, like brass *trivets*, to hang from the fire-bars, wrought-iron toasters with sliding forks, and *footmen*, to hold plates or dishes by the fire and keep them warm. There are *smoker's tongs*, with a spring in the handle, for lifting charcoal embers up to your pipe. *Smoke-jacks* and *meat-jacks* of polished brass are occasionally seen.

If you heartily dislike your present grate there are plenty of early ones worth looking at and not outrageously expensive, usually to be found in those junk shops which spread out around themselves in a yard. Don't be afraid of rust or breaks: there are still blacksmiths about. Old *fenders* are worth looking at too if you like workmanship better than that from the local multiple store.

Firescreens

In days when you had to warm a huge room with an equally huge fire there was always the chance of getting scorched by it. Worse, perhaps, it could bring an unattractive glow to the face of your daughter–and that was no way to get her a wealthy and noble husband from among the gentlemen who came up from the dining-room.

So you provided yourself with a range of firescreens. Sometimes they were full-sized ones, placed directly in front of the fire and called–for no very satisfactory reason that I can discover–cheval screens. They were mounted between uprights on swivels so that they could be tilted to the desired angle. When it was desired to shield one particular part of the body, like that rosy cheek I mentioned, there was a pole-screen, a type which, as its name suggests, was mounted upon a pole, sometimes on a tripod support. There was a smaller model for the table and even a handscreen, made to hang by the fireplace, or perhaps at the window, ostensibly to shade the face from the sun, but also useful for peeping out of the window at young cavalry officers without being recognized.

A mid Victorian tripod firescreen (Christies, South Kensington)

These screens came in all sorts of materials, some tough enough to withstand the hottest fire, others obviously designed merely to hide the gaping maw of the fireplace in summertime. Metal, wood, PAPIER MÂCHÉ, EMBROIDERY were used, and one sees some lovely work on many of them. Nobody would ever want to collect them, I suppose, but anyone who did would have the history of interior decoration in miniature.

Fitted Boxes and Cases

By this I mean not the hundreds of little patch and SNUFF BOXES, BONBONNIÈRES and so on, but real containers fitted with contents for some special purpose.

Let me give you two examples. There is the apothecary's box, with lots of fascinating little compartments and drawers containing bottles, phials, pestle and mortar, and various other tricks of the trade. Also there is the barber's box with three swivel compartments having ivory fittings, scissors, pewter soap-box, etc.

Hat-boxes often turn up, sometimes with a top hat, either lay or ecclesiastical, but there is a wealth of ladies' hat-boxes and bandboxes as they are often known. It was fashionable a century ago to decorate the tops and sides of these bandboxes with pictures of contemporary scenes and this adds to their interest.

A fitted medical cabinet, 1850–1900 (S. H. Cole)

There are many ribbon boxes with their mechanical winders. Thread boxes and WORKBOXES, of course, are among the many interesting items associated with needlework.

There are other sorts of boxes which I suppose one should really call cases, such as those used for comfort on long coach journeys. They are elegant affairs in morocco leather, either with a complete tea service or spirit bottles and glasses, with writing materials or toilet requisites: there are also complete 'coach' baskets containing almost everything of this sort.

Flagons and Tankards

What is the difference between them? Without delving into a richly controversial field of enquiry, it might simplify things if we said that a tankard, covered or uncovered, was a pot for drinking, and perhaps, originally a measure; whereas a flagon, usually covered, is a larger, or at any rate a taller, affair intended for holding or carrying liquor to be drunk from some other receptacle. It is usually to be found in churches, municipal and trade halls and the like.

Finest of all the English tankard shapes are the wide but tapering Restoration types, which sit squarely and firmly on a table and demand that their flat covers be opened as soon as possible. We may not linger with them except to look, however, for whether they are in silver or PEWTER or even wood, they command enormous prices.

Somewhere about the second quarter of the eighteenth century saw the beginnings of the familiar 'bell' and 'tulip' shapes, eventually with a foot, the 'belly' becoming more prominent as time went on. Connoisseurs of them in both PEWTER and silver look carefully at the type and styles of the lids–for the flattened 'bun' shape, the 'double-domed'–also the handles and thumb pieces, for these can be of greater assistance in dating than anything else except a hallmark.

These are the progenitors of all the shapes we can still find in the antique shops, sometimes engraved on the bottom with the name of the pub from which they were liberated.

This also applies to flagons, which often flattened their 'bun' into what is aptly called a 'beefeater', after the cap of the Yeomen Warders of the Tower of London. There are variations in the English provinces and also from Scotland and Ireland. Many Scottish examples have a tapering drum, slightly incurved and with a dish cover; others have bands of moulded ornament. The chief distinguishing characteristic of Irish flagons is their very large and fully curved handle. Other variants which may occasionally be met with include acorn flagons, guild flagons, livery pots, and tankards with 'muffin' covers and 'chairback' thumbpieces.

It is, however, on the Continent that we find the richest variety in both departments–even if the distinction between them sometimes gets even less sharply defined than in Britain. The French *cannette* and the German *Kanne* seem to be what we mean by flagons: there are special varieties like the 'Rembrandt' (not unlike the Scottish 'pot-bellied') and the 'Jan Steen' which has a long spout. *Humpen*, as in glass, appears to be the name for the tankard, unless it is in pottery, when it becomes a *Stein*.

Flatirons

To me there is something infinitely romantic about a flatiron. There it sits on a table, old, black and heavy-bottomed, longing to be taken up and held to a cheek dabbed with a wet finger, and then pressed firmly down into soft damp linen.

I had no idea of the great variety of flatiron shapes there were until I saw a collection in a well-known coffee house in Earl's Court, London. Apart from the ordinary 'T'

Three types of flatiron. Top: *An 18th-century, handmade, brass, Dutch charcoal iron.* Left: *A 19th-century, handmade, oxtongue box iron.* Right: *An English 'Hardings Patent Safety Grip' flatiron, c. 1900 ('At the Sign of the Sad Iron' Limited)*

model, which comes in an almost endless variety of types, there is the charcoal iron, with its hollow body, interior furnace and slender chimney. In the box iron, with its elegant leather covered handle, you opened the door at the back and somehow poked in a lump of red hot iron, heated in the fire. There are narrow irons for tailors, some with curved bottoms for pressing the inside of sleeves.

Continental versions, as in so many other things, have profound differences of line and balance.

Flower and Bulb Holders

For a very long time now people have been wanting to bring the delights of the garden into the house. Potters, especially, have been eager to cater for this, and if vases for cut flowers came first, bulb-holders and flower stands pierced with holes have also been with us since the days of the early Chinese potters.

You can find them in pretty well everything from DELFTWARE to DOULTON. Early Derby did exquisite ones in porcelain with painted flowers and views, Wedgwood came up with the CANEWARE box with holes for the bulbs and surrounded by imitation sticks of bamboo, each with a hole for a flower. Here too, BASALTES comes into its own, for Wedgwood's black hedgehog, with flowers sprouting out of holes instead of quills, provided exactly the right foil for your blooms. There were bulb pots in jasper ware as

A Wedgwood hedgehog bulb pot in black basalt, first made in 1800 (Wedgwood)

well as in other kinds of STONEWARE.

Personally I would start to look quite closely now at those in the later Victorian bone china, in TERRA COTTA and in earthenware like the Minton MAJOLICA. But before doing so, spare a glance for those fun-shaped affairs with five or six sockets for fixing on walls. The most delightful of them are in French faience, but the English Prattware ones, with their hectic native colours, are worth having–if you can find them. Other kinds of flower holder include CORNUCOPIAS and POSY HOLDERS.

Flower Pots and Pedestals

It is always rather a mystery to me that when, after being overlooked for many years, something is wanted it suddenly appears as if by magic. Where has it been hidden all this time? The mystery thickens when it comes to those large Victorian plant pots and holders, some of them standing on pedestals, which are now to be seen in serried ranks outside the country antique and junk shops. These must have been very difficult indeed to hide, so one can only suppose that there are a lot more conservatories and unmodernized houses about than one had imagined.

Wrought-iron flower stand for window or fireplace

Anyway, there they are, and people with a fresh eye for Victoriana are buying them to put in their small town backyards or on terraces in their gardens. And when you come to look at them they are really something in the way of potting. This was 'art pottery' in its day, and firms really went to town with pots in their rich MAJOLICA glazes, in STONEWARE with incised decoration or moulded leaf shapes; also in ware in which fabric patterns were impressed upon the wet clay. Copeland produced pedestals in blue and white which are quite five feet high; others are more modest affairs, urn or vase shaped. Burmantofts, makers of TILES, were also in this field, and their name is often found on the bottoms of jardinières.

Coming to the table, one often sees all the little white table decorations in china moulded as leaves or with bowls supported by cherubs or prettily dressed children, rather like those in MARY GREGORY glass. There were also window flower stands in pleasantly convoluted wrought-iron whereby you could suspend your eathenware pots three at a time, either in line or echelon.

These are to be found, all nicely painted for you at rather staggering prices, but my advice to you is to ask friends with old greenhouses or outbuildings to let you poke around and see what you can find. There are also sometimes some interesting things of this sort at the back of old blacksmiths' workshops.

Food Warmers

What a great many different things have been used at various times to keep our food warm by day or night, at the table or by the bedside. I wonder how many of them are still known to a generation, the greater part of which, when at home, eats its food only a yard or two from the place where it was cooked.

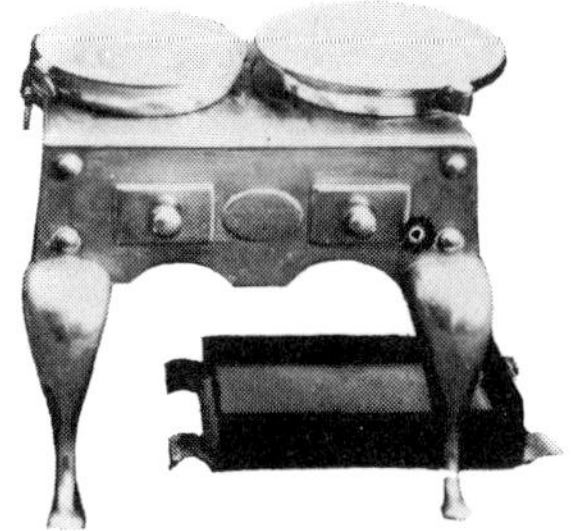

A Victorian charcoal and water food warmer (S. H. Cole)

Aristocrat of the species, I suppose, is the *Veilleuse*, or *rechaud* (in France), *Suppenwärmer* (in Germany), *scaldavivande* (in Italy) and *food warmer* (in Britain). It is a simple enough contrivance, consisting of a bowl and cover suspended in a stand which has an opening for a *godet* or lamp. It therefore provided not only heat for the posset, CAUDLE, or whatever was left by the bedside, but light as well. There are vents under the handles on either side. The earliest of them were in eighteenth-century delftware and porcelain, all elaborately decorated in the styles of the day, but plainer versions may be found in CREAMWARE by Wedgwood and his European imitators. If you try to collect a *veilleuse* in the Marché aux Puces at the weekend, bear in mind the warning of Harold Newman, the authority on these things, that they are quite likely to be brand new.

Next we have the *tea warmer* in which Wedgwood was also implicated, whereby a kettle takes the place of the soup bowl: there is a handsome gilt and painted specimen in porcelain from Clignancourt, Paris, in the Victoria and Albert Museum, which also has a red earthenware Staffordshire and a Leeds creamware kettle which have apparently lost their pedestals.

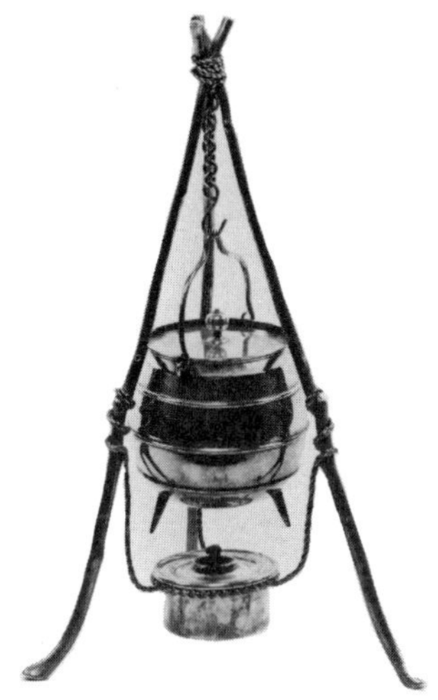

A Victorian egg boiler in the form of a cauldron on a tripod (Christies, South Kensington)

Apart from ARGYLES, there are *warming plates* which are to be found in Staffordshire blue and white. This is a plate of double thickness, having a small aperture just under the rim into which you pour hot water, or, I believe, hot sand. There are Chinese versions of this too, some of them having holes to attach a cover. I am told that there are others with two foot-rings close to each other so that the plate can fit over a bowl of hot water or sand.

From the tea kettle to the *tea-maker*, shaped like an egg which you drop into the pot: how long ago is it that we gave up making tea in this terribly un-English way? They were certainly being sold by Harrods in 1900–perhaps foreigners bought them. Then there are *egg steamers*, in silver or ELECTRO-PLATE, with revolving tops and rustic mounts elegantly engraved: and even a *spoon-warmer* in the shape of a cockleshell. The *chafing-dish*, with ebony mounts, sometimes has its little stand, as does the small *brandy warmer*.

Gallé

You will not find the work of Emile Gallé (1846–1904) cheap nowadays. Time was–and not so very long ago either–when the art glass vases and bowls of Emile Gallé were priced by dealers more by guesswork than sound judgement, in the hope that sooner or later a collector would turn up with the money to match. As for the scent bottles and such ornaments as car mascots and radiator caps–well, they attracted little or no interest at all. But this has changed rather dramatically and any kind of glassware which can be attributed to Gallé now fetches the earth, and even the long-despised and unfashionable car mascots fetch real money indeed when they appear in the saleroom.

Gallé glass vase

Gallé

The glass of Emile Gallé, irrespective of its size or function, testifies to his consummate artistry and skill. He used every trick in the book, and a lot more of his own devising–cracking and crackling, repeated 'flashings' in different colours, cutting and carving in relief, etching and engraving. You can see the influence of Japan in his work, and it epitomizes the very essence of ART NOUVEAU with its emphasis on naturalistic forms and motifs.

The best work was done in Gallé's own lifetime, and these pieces usually bear his scrawled signature, together with the place-name, 'Nancy' or *Deposé* (registered) or perhaps the initials 'E. G.' The work carried on after his death, more or less on factory lines, lacks the touch of the master–although it can still be very acceptable for the likes of you and me–and usually bears the name of 'Gallé' only.

If you get interested in a school of glassmaking in which France made a notable comeback after several undistinguished centuries, look also for the work of Joseph Brocard, Albert Daiguperce, Emile Munier, Julien Roiseux, Gabriele Argy-Rousseau, René LALIQUE, Daum Frères and a firm which marked its wares '*La Verrerie Française*'.

Perfume bottle, 1889, by Gallé, made at Nancy (Pilkington Glass Museum)

Garniture de Cheminée

In spite of all the removals and smashings of the years one regularly sees at sales examples of the *garniture de cheminée*: in other words, the chimney-piece set.

What splendid affairs these looked, if we had an impressive enough mantelpiece! Most often seen, perhaps, is the set of porcelain vases and beakers, sometimes three in number, but more augustly five. Arranged on brackets in steps, or standing like soldiers on parade, the three vases and two beakers not only presented their front view but also their back, by reflection in the mirror behind. As well as the fine Chinese ones, in blue and white, which were enormously popular for two centuries, there were those in the various FAMILLE styles, made by the early English porcelain factories, such as Bow, Chelsea and Worcester.

Garniture de cheminée of Chinese blue and white porcelain

Many of these *garnitures*, it is sad to reflect, may have been split up either by breakage or by dispersal among daughters. Full Chinese porcelain *garnitures* must have come to Europe all through the nineteenth century, to judge by the number left: but the English potters seem to have decided by 1851 to cater for smaller chimney-pieces for the catalogues offer *garnitures* of only three pieces.

It is thought that the *garniture* may have been suggested by the Chinese bronze altar set of incense burner, pair of candlesticks and pair of vases. This does seem closely related to another sort of eighteenth-century *garniture*, which comprises a clock, a pair of candelabra and a pair of CASOLETTES or covered urns.

German Silver

There is silver from Germany, but this is not the same as *German Silver* or *Neusilber*, which is not silver at all, but an alloy of copper, zinc and nickel. In fact it is pretty nearly the same as 'tooth and egg', which is not Tutenag but Paktong. The Italians correctly call it *Pacfong*, the French *Maillechort* (after the first makers in Paris, Messrs Maille and Chort). Others refer to it as *Argentan*. As for the English-speaking world, it knows this useful substance under the name of BRITISH PLATE.

Ginger Jars

There is one kind of ginger jar, with 'cracked ice' blue and white decoration, which has long been recognized and highly priced accordingly; but there is a humbler kind found in a much coarser ware, usually with the neck left unglazed, and decorated under the glaze with scenes in the broad summary brush strokes which hark back to the very earliest days of Chinese pottery.

These jars tell the story of three fisherman brothers, one a hunchback who fished only by the sea-shore with a rod and line. The other two put to sea in their junk, which you see with a great question mark above it, the sign of an approaching typhoon. Apparently they never returned, for on the shore is their shuttered cabin; their hunchback brother stands alone, casting his line and waiting eternally for his lost brothers.

One of the delights of collecting is the way you can find an ordinary commercial grocery container telling a story, like Keats with his Grecian urn.

Glass Pictures

There are two kinds of glass pictures. The more ambitious ones, popular in the eighteenth century, were actually *Mezzotints*, mounted and coloured. The mezzotint was stuck face downwards on a sheet of glass, and the actual paper removed from its back, thus leaving only the ink of the print remaining. Colouring was then applied over this by an intricate technique which often puzzles modern collectors, for the marks so made do not necessarily follow the forms of the picture on the front. Needless to say, all this was extremely skilled work, and some of the earlier specimens are very fine and fetch a high price.

The second type of glass picture is a crude affair, almost a peasant art, but not without some charm, where a landscape has been directly painted on to the back of the glass in lively colours. Most of those I have seen show a castle or large house and a lake, often with a figure on the bank or a vessel sailing. Good specimens of this type with a curly maple frame often turn up in matched pairs.

Glass Toys

Once upon a time these delightful little items in plain, opaque and coloured glass were called 'friggers', for many of them were the spare-time product of a glassblower 'frigging about' to earn himself the price of a drink from visitors to the glasshouse. Even today, if you go over a glassworks, they will often put on a show for you, blowing a long sausage of glass and making it explode with a report, or magically transforming a hot lump of treacly orange glass into a tiny duck, using nothing but a pair of tweezers.

But for many years now these things have been made on a full-time basis, probably in the same sort of small back-street workshops as those in the Potteries where so many STAFFORDSHIRE FIGURES were once made. About 1960, while nosing around the Stourbridge area of Worcestershire looking for coloured glass, I was directed to an outhouse at the back of an ordinary semi-detached cottage, where I found two men, father and son, in something about the size of a toolshed, making little sets of foxhounds, ducks, swans and other kinds of animals and birds. No elaborate equipment was needed. They each had a gas jet flaming out across the table away from them and they made up these tiny things by melting sticks of coloured glass in the flame and manipulating them into shape.

In Victorian times, these toys covered a far wider range than the glass menageries you see in the shop nowadays. There were little trumpets and swords, BELLS, umbrellas, village pumps with buckets, walking sticks, tiny tobacco pipes–in fact, anything which would be a challenge to the blower's skill and delight a customer. They seem to have been particularly fond of hats, for these come in all shapes and sizes, from bowlers to toppers and policemen's helmets. Some are in the form of salt cellars, others are inkwells or medicine bottles.

Goss China

I suppose that, properly speaking, 'Goss' should go under SOUVENIR CHINA. It was usually as a souvenir of a seaside holiday or a stay with distant relatives that there came into Auntie Flo's cabinet those small pieces of 'ivory porcelain', bearing the arms of a town or county and made in a world of different shapes–shoes, houses, bottles, vases, Etruscan lamps and Grecian urns.

But now that 'Goss' is not only being collected again, but has become accepted as a generic term to denote the miniature china made by other firms as well, it deserves a separate entry.

Goss crested china

The Goss family, who went on producing right down to the 1930s, made other items which are being looked at nowadays. One is called 'jewelled china', or 'jewelled porcelain' and consists of a very thin china decorated with little jewels, or imitation emeralds, rubies and other precious stones made from enamels. Some of this was in PARIAN WARE. Goss, who ran the Falcon Pottery at Stoke-on-Trent, also made a series of Parian figures in a vein of late-Victorian sentiment which you have to like to be able to take. I saw a pair of hunchback crossing-sweeper boys as long ago as 1960, with a price tag of seven pounds on them. His miniatures of Anne Hathaway's Cottage, Burns' Cottage at Alloway and similar historic buildings rendered in pottery, have fared rather better in the eyes of collectors and now fetch hundreds of pounds.

The miniature china with civic crests produced by other firms are generally not as well designed or finished, and their colours are flatter or more garish. Nevertheless, with renewed interest in *anything* collectable with pronounced local appeal, even these Goss imitations are beginning to fetch real money now.

Gourd

One of the most frequently seen shapes in pottery and metal is that which looks like a tightly laced Victorian lady without a head. It is called the gourd shape, a term which long puzzled me, for the gourd is a round fruit sometimes with a long neck, with no such tight lacing as is shown in the bottles.

Then I realized that if you hollowed out a gourd or calabash, tied a string round the neck, and dried the shell hard, you had an excellently handy bottle.

The shape given by this simple primitive device attracted the attention of potters and metal workers of ancient Persia, India and China, was copied by the Dutch DELFTWARE makers, and has come right down to Victorian bone china. Doubtless somebody is making the shape today without in the least knowing why.

Gypsy Wagons

If you want to buy one, so that you can live in it at the bottom of the orchard on retirement, the most comfortable sort–but of course the most expensive–is the Reading wagon. It was first built by the Dunton family of that Berkshire town, and it stands between tall wheels, has a high arched roof with a clerestory skylight and a shuttered window, straight outward sloping walls of beaded matchboarding with chamfered ribs and elaborately carved front and rear porch brackets. Inside you will find all home comforts–stove, bunks, settee, cupboards, chest of drawers, usually with fine carving and gilding.

Gypsy wagon

Less lavish living is provided by the more commonly-met-with Showman or Burton wagon, which has a flatter arch, wheels under the body, nearly upright sides and carved oak plaques on panels front and back.

The Ledge or Cottage wagon starts narrow at the bottom but then extends out on ledges over the wheels, supported by brass scrolls, while the side matchboarding projects fore and aft and provided carved porch brackets.

If you want to take to the road and prefer not to see the passing cars, perhaps the most comfortable and durable type is the Bow-topped wagon (also called the Midland, Leeds, Lincolnshire, Yorkshire Bell and Barrel-topped), built with ledges, but having a round canvas top on a bowed wooden frame, the front and back walls being of rib and matchboard, with carved porch boards. A patterned chenille lining under the canvas roof gives you insulation.

Room for pots and pans, a wife and extra sleeping accommodation is afforded if you have another horse and a Four-wheeled Tilted Pot-cart, which is more or less a boat-shaped farm wagon with a hood or tilt of canvas on a bowed wooden farm frame slotted into the sides–perhaps it was the original Covered Wagon or Prairie Schooner.

Halberds and Partisans

Enthusiasts for swords and daggers are seldom to be seduced from their main obsession, which makes it a little easier for the rest of us to buy all those staff weapons or pole-arms with such other-wordly names, and at the same time such realistic properties in the way of cutting, slashing, chopping and poking. And, strangely enough, decorating.

There is the halberd, with its axe blade and lance point, and the partisan–a simple long-handled axe. There are lances, rawcons, spontoons, glaives and bills whose shapes I will leave you the pleasure of discovering for yourself. There is also the battle-axe family: I saw one of those rather unsporting Indian ones having a dagger concealed in the handle, and I believe that there are some which even have a pistol concealed in similar fashion.

The idea may outrage serious collectors, but for me these staff weapons have the same sort of decorative appeal as farm and other OLD IMPLEMENTS, a thought which I have developed under that head. Not all of them are as dear as battle-axes. Unless they have some specially interesting or costly metalwork, such as inlay or damascening, they can still be picked up fairly cheaply–often disposed of in job lots at sales of arms and armour.

Hanging Shelves

This is a piece of furniture which one often sees languishing unregarded in junk shops, high above one's head on a beam.

Perhaps people nowadays don't care to be bothered with the job of dusting things kept on open shelves. And yet, in these days of smokeless zones and the Clean Air Act, there doesn't seem to be so much dust flying about as there once was. Gay boxes, shadow boxes and other variants of hanging shelves seem to be coming back into fashion and they have the merit of occupying so much less actual air space in a room than does a glass china cabinet or bookcase. They vary enormously in price, of course, depending on the amount and quality of craftsmanship involved. At one end of the

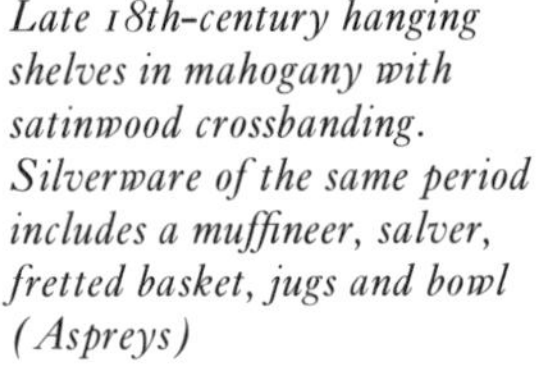

Late 18th-century hanging shelves in mahogany with satinwood crossbanding. Silverware of the same period includes a muffineer, salver, fretted basket, jugs and bowl (Aspreys)

scale, small, relatively simple boxes can be had for a matter of pence; at the other, the more elaborate Oriental and neo-Jacobean ones, replete with ornate carving and turning, now fetch as many pounds.

If you want to spend more, there are much more glamorous ones in, say, satinwood, or with MARQUETRY work on sides and front. You can also find quite handsome examples from the turn of the century, including Oriental-looking ones in BAMBOO, with mirrors and little cabinet.

Harvest Jugs and Bottles

'Harvis is com all bissey
Now in mackin of your
Barley mow when men do
Laber hard and Swet good
Ale is far better than meet.'

Staffordshire harvest jug

With which sentiments, scratched on a slipware harvest jug, everyone who has ever helped to carry in the corn, build a hayrick or feed the thresher, when the dust is apt to tickle one's throat something cruel, will heartily agree. One can even get a little dry when sitting on top of a modern combine harvester.

I am quite sure that there is still time for the dedicated collector to put together a gathering of the stoneware and earthenware harvest jugs and bottles, which, on the old seasonal occasions, the farmer and his men once carried out into the fields or had brought out to them with lunch by the women of the house. It will not be enough simply to haunt junk shops, however: you must delve more deeply.

I once knew a man who sought local pottery simply for its archaeological interest; and the way he went about his business was to study large scale maps in search of such names as Gallipot Street, Potters Heath or Pot Kiln Chace. In olden times potters were often 'gypsies' who, having found a spot where there was wood, or open cast coal for fuel, clay, silica and lead ore for body and glaze, would work there for a few years until the local farmhouses had their full quota of pots, and then move on, leaving behind them only a name on the map.

My friend's trick was to go to places where such names were to be found, carrying with him a plentiful supply of shining coins. He would offer these to the local children asking them to lead him to any spot in the woods where, in their play, they had come across bits of broken pottery. In this way he found many shards which were of enormous interest to him.

An early 19th-century harvest jug (Tunbridge Wells Museum)

On occasion, however, one of these very intelligent children, watching him grubbing around in the dirt for his broken pieces, would in a puzzled way ask wouldn't he prefer to have a complete jug; and the helpful child would thereupon lead him off to some outhouse where a fine harvest jug was being used for carrying water out to the chickens. My friend would then bear off these pots from under the very noses of us pottery collectors proper–quite dangerous behaviour, of course.

Corn harvesting and haymaking being universal operations, every region had its pots, and there was a local style and yet a strong family likeness. This is hardly surprising when one puts them alongside the fine glazed earthenware pots which have come down to us from medieval times: there was obviously an unbroken line of descent. There are many connoisseurs of ceramics (the late W. B. Honey among them) who hold that it is in simple, dignified and even noble wares, made for an everyday purpose by men quite out of touch with art trends or fashions but with an inborn good taste, that some of the finest achievements of the potter are to be found.

The harvest jug family is to be recognized, of course, by the narrow neck, which could be stopped with a cork or a rag while being carried out to the field or lowered into a stream for cool keeping. To take a small trip around the countryside for variations one might start with the fine wares of North Devon, now museum pieces, with '*sgraffito* or 'scratched decoration' and a large coil at the lower end of the handle. Bideford had been making them since the Middle Ages, and the last of them seems to have been produced by Henry Phillips, who died in 1894. Barnstaple has been making fine jugs since the thirteenth century.

Some of these jugs have inscriptions like that given at the head of this piece; others, such as the following, seem to be designed for use after the harvest has been safely gathered in–at least one hopes so:

'Come fill me up and Drinke about
and Never leave till all be out
And if that will not Make you merry
fill me again and sing Down Derry.'

Still others, with mariners' compasses and dolphins, seem to have been designed, not for farming folk but for blue-eyed sailors from Devon and dark-eyed ones from Cornwall to take to sea with them.

Coming to later days, earthenware pots with slip decoration of potters like E. B. Fishley of Fremington in Devon were produced well into the present century. In neighbouring Somerset, at the significantly named Crock Street near Ilminster, the slipware is noted for its glaze stained with patches of green, and therefore one sure descendant of the medieval wares. Of the other known centres one has space only to mention Rye, Brede and Burgess Hill in Sussex, the deep red wares of the Kentish Weald, the famous 'owl jugs' (after their tiny ear handles) of Dorset, the greyish brown stonewares of Essex, and a host of products from Yorkshire and the Midlands.

Harvest jugs are also to be found in finer kinds of earthenware, though still with a strong country flavour: they have a bold PEASANT style painting and were turned out, alongside more sophisticated wares, from the early years of the nineteenth century onwards by potters in Staffordshire, Wales, Bristol, Yorkshire and Scotland.

One would dearly love to ramble on among these pots, but there is space only to warn readers that once having fallen under the spell of harvest jugs and bottles they will be easy prey for all the other kinds of things made in these country wares–the 'milk churn' spirit barrels, money boxes, miniature spice chests and ovens, pilchard pots, butter pans, lamb feeders, cradles and BIRD CALLS, to say nothing of the JOKE mugs and puzzle jugs.

Horn Ware

You will often come across horn drinking cups, but not so often, perhaps, those with engraving on them: this was an art practised in many parts of Europe rather than the British Isles, with the possible exception of Scotland, where horn vessels and cutlery continued in use long after they had become unfashionable south of the Border.

But there are also horn SNUFF BOXES, often inlaid with silver, like the hair ornaments which come under the heading of JEWELLERY. Horn buttons pressed with reliefs are sometimes found; also cane handles of animal heads, the eyes being put in with white opaque glass. Knives and forks are found with horn handles, and spoons with bowls of horn. Of course the oldest 'lanthorns' have horn windows, while horn books, the earliest kind of children's primers, had horn covers. A homely art, but one which brings you close to the daily life of people a long time ago.

There are also the horns you blow: these are treasured relics in many countries, often richly mounted, and capable of making a very loud noise indeed.

Horse Brasses

If the horse age has virtually passed, nobody can say the same for the age of the horse brass. If it had, this would certainly not be the fault of those modern brass-founders who assiduously supply a demand for brasses which is far higher today than when they were used on every farm, in every brewery, in dockyards, railway goods yards, in fact everywhere that heavy horses pulled loads and carters took a pride in their turnouts.

Some say that these brasses originated in the amulets worn in classical times to ward off the devil, just as a piece of moving tinfoil scares off rooks. In eighteenth-century England, the ancestor seems to have been the round sunflash, the simplest form of brass. By the middle of the nineteenth century, however, there were hundreds of different brasses, some of them very beautiful work indeed–horseshoes, acorns, bells, flowers, lions, stags, fox masks, portraits and trade devices like barrels for brewers, railway engines and ships.

Would-be collectors have to remember that these genuine brasses are nothing whatever to do with those sold in seaside shops as souvenirs, stamped out by the thousand. There are also fakes of the genuine old ones. To distinguish them, one must pay some attention to the feel and look of the older brass alloys and look for signs of wear from the constant rubbing of leather. Even these signs of wear are being artificially contrived nowadays.

A champion Shire Horse team from Young's Brewery in London (they stand 18 hands high, weigh a ton each, and twenty of them still deliver 10,000 tons of beer annually to Young's public houses). The horse brasses circle their chests (Young and Company)

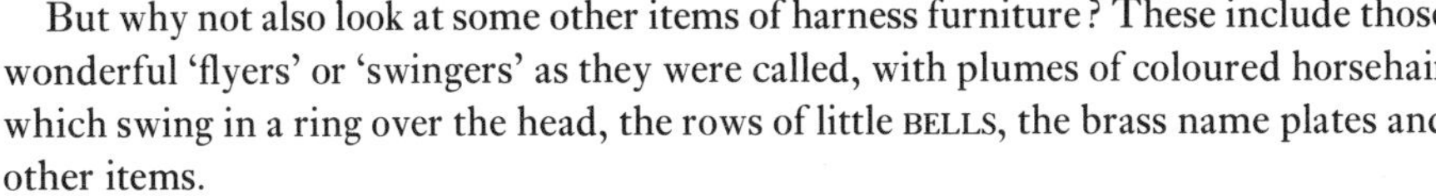

But why not also look at some other items of harness furniture? These include those wonderful 'flyers' or 'swingers' as they were called, with plumes of coloured horsehair which swing in a ring over the head, the rows of little BELLS, the brass name plates and other items.

Hunting Jugs

Hunting jug

These very fine examples of BROWNWARE or saltglazed brown STONEWARE will be recognized by their graceful shapes, their deep reliefs of game and hunting scenes round the sides, and the beautifully modelled handle in the form of a greyhound. At least, it is in one version: there is another in which the hound is a mere rudimentary outline and the jug the typical DOULTON or Brampton shape with a pinched-in spout. These are sometimes called 'dog-handled' jugs. Presumably the first was your fine presentation piece for the kitchen DRESSER, the second for thumping upon an inn table.

Apart from the factories and marks mentioned under BROWNWARE, there are jugs to be found which are impressed on the bottom with 'S & G' and which were once attributed to Shore and Goulding of Isleworth, Middlesex. It is now known, however, that they were made by a firm called Schiller and Gerbing, potters working at Teschen in Bohemia (Tessin in present-day Czechoslovakia). The mark was made in all honesty, so here is a case of collectors deceiving themselves rather than being deceived by others.

Ivory

I have never been enormously attracted to ivory carving, perhaps because much of it is so painstakingly realistic. Being so perfect it's boring, rather like professional billiards. I've seen PLAQUES with Renaissance subjects at no very outrageous price, though I suspect that they were made long after the Renaissance or they would be in the smart antique shops of Bond Street. Religious figures are said to hail largely from Dieppe.

Anyone who picks up a taste for Oriental mythology from Chinese porcelain will find much to interest them in the Chinese and Japanese figures. Chessmen are a quarry for many people, and there is at least one specialist dealer in London who sells nothing else.

But for me ivory is most interesting where it has been used either as a decoration or in making some useful but attractive item for everyday use. The Victorians were very fond of it and used it in all sorts of ways–for such things as CARD CASES, paper knives, bodkin cases, cane handles, 'paper-thin' brooches, boxes and the rest. In JEWELLERY, too, it had its day when highly coloured personal adornment went out in favour of 'plain' things like diamonds, JET and so on: there were many neck chains with huge carved links, not to mention brooches.

Another way of using it, of course, was as an inlay for TEA CADDIES, WORKBOXES, various sorts of furniture including CLOCKS. Not many people realize, too, that the best portrait miniatures were usually painted on ivory.

The modest collector, sorting over the many things made of ivory or making use of it, could get together a charming and interesting collection at very reasonable cost.

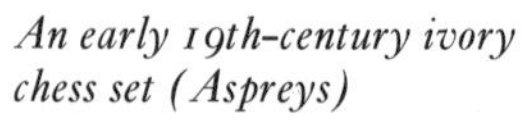
An early 19th-century ivory chess set (Aspreys)

Japanese Sword Fittings

At sales there sometimes turn up collections of small metal objects most superbly worked with chasing, embossing, inlaying, damascening and patination. They are the various fittings belonging to the Japanese sword; and although they vary considerably in price, if you like beautiful workmanship in metal here is one of the cheaper and more convenient ways of putting together a fine collection.

Outstanding is the round or oval flat piece of metal, pierced with a large slit and two smaller holes–the *tsuba* or sword guard, mounted where handle meets blade. Many of the older examples are in hammered iron with silver or even gold inlay, and they show such objects as wild geese flying, dragons, serpents, crayfish, plum trees in copper with silver blossoms, figures of sages and beauties, landscapes like those found in Japanese woodblock prints, and so on. Much use was made for decoration of beautiful soft alloys like *shakudo*, a combination of bronze and gold, and *shibuchi*, bronze and silver, both of which can acquire a beautiful patina.

Japanese sword fitting (much reduced)

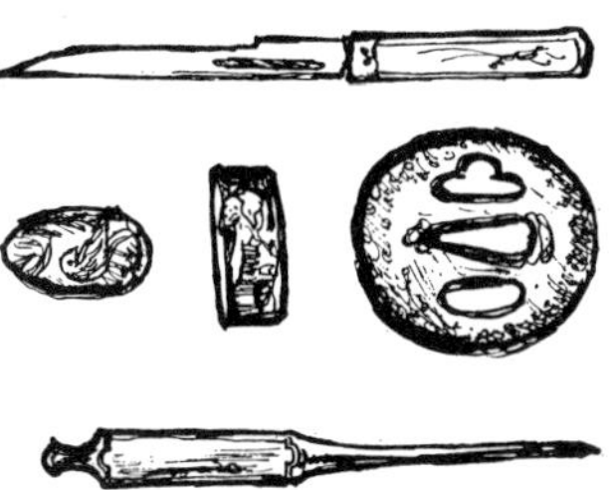

The two holes on either side of the blade hole were for the *kodzuka*, a small dagger which fitted on to one side of the sheath, and the *kogai*, a kind of stiletto or skewer which was housed on the other side. They must have made a very handy set of tools in an emergency, but like the swords themselves, they are not very cheap nowadays. More plentiful are the other small fittings, like the *menuki*, or tiny plates of metal on the grip of the sword-handle; the *kachira*, a metal cap on the top of the hilt, and the *fuchi*, a ring of metal resting on the *tsuba*. Both *kachira* and *fuchi* were often made by the same man, so you get *fuchikachira*. Even in these small things you can discover tigers in bamboo thickets, silver bats, battle scenes and landscapes with golden moons.

Japanning

The English 'joyners' of the late seventeenth century wished to compete in the rich field of LACQUER but could not use the true *lac*, since the British climate was unsuitable, and anyway, the material could not be kept for long periods in the holds of ships without hardening. They therefore arrived at a method whereby the wood carcass was first given successive layers of whitening and size and this ground varnished with gum-lac and other materials dissolved in spirits and wine. The ground colour included various reds, chestnut, olive and blue, but most of all the favourite 'black Japan'. Flat designs were drawn on the ground in gold or some form of size; while raised decoration could be given by means of a paste of whitening, gum arabic and sawdust.

In the early days of European japanning, the craft became a fashionable hobby among the gentry, and some of their work, as one might expect, is not up to the standard of the professionals. There was a revival of interest in the middle of the eighteenth century with the coming of 'Chinese Chippendale'; and japanning came in again, more elegantly, in the Hepplewhite era.

Although the Japanese craze of the eighteen-sixties brought a renewed interest in japanned furniture, for most of the last century the word 'japanning' was almost synonymous with PAPIER MÂCHÉ furniture and also PONTYPOOL AND USK WARE, on both of which it was applied copiously.

Jet

Black isn't to everybody's taste, as we've already noted under BASALTES, and you could hardly have anything blacker than jet. Yet most JEWELLERY boxes have a piece or two of it, and to judge by the way modern manufacturers are imitating it in black glass and ebonite, it may well make a come-back.

True jet–not to be confused with the sharply pointed 'French jet', or black glass–is a form of coal and has been worked in Britain for ornaments since Roman times at least. It comes mainly from the Whitby area on the Yorkshire coast where, in Victorian

Fine japanning on an unusual Queen Anne chest, early 18th century (Aspreys)

Victorian lorgnette or muff chain in Prince of Wales pattern

times, there were over two hundred workshops producing not only jewellery but small household articles as well, such as thimble cases, table vices, egg cups, paper knives and so forth.

Up to about 1850 jet as personal wear was largely associated with mourning, and for a very long time women presented at Court were allowed only jet jewellery. But when Queen Victoria's long period of mourning for the late Prince Albert was over, there was an outbreak of highly coloured jewellery which, by a natural reaction, was followed by a vogue for things with more restraint–diamonds, IVORY and jet. There were enormously long jet chains, with huge beads, also serpents of jet to be worn round the arms. Fair women must have looked magnificent in tiaras made of jet beads.

Jewellery

If we are going to look for jewellery, either in the junk shops or on the market stalls, we should perhaps make up our minds from the beginning that we are not likely to find anything which is *intrinsically* valuable, that is, made up of precious stones or metals. All these places are combed regularly by eagle-eyed dealers and such pieces soon find their level in the more expensive shops where a large overhead for plush carpets and bright lights is immediately added to their price.

But if we have an eye and a taste for workmanship, for the commonly overlooked qualities of the semi-precious gemstones–like the deep purple or lilac amethyst, the yellowish or bottle-green peridot, the deep-red or greenish garnet, the pale blue aquamarine, the reddish carnelian–if we are bored with the jeweller's shop windows which are full of all the standard pieces stuck about with miserable little diamond chips ('We *must* have a diamond ring, mustn't we?'), then here is where a pound or two can still buy you a lot of fun, even if it takes up a lot of your time.

Victorian gold horseshoe bracelet

Our first choice will be among pieces which have either been set in pinchbeck, and other cheap materials such as copper, bronze and even iron and steel: or which make the most sparing use of gold, as with filigree work, gilding, early ELECTRO-PLATE and 'rolled gold'. Some fine artistry went into the stick pins, brooches, rings, bracelets, pendants, lockets and clips made in this way as substitutes for precious metals, and we shall be wise in our generation if we look very hard at things which happen to be out of fashion at the moment; they will certainly come in again, as all things do. Sporting brooches and pins, especially those in nine carat gold with pearl daisies, turquoise hearts and horseshoes, 'merry thoughts' and the rest are plentiful. The double moon, wheat ears and flights of swallows can be found, also little baskets with flowers of jewels.

A Berlin ironware bracelet, c. 1835 (Christies, South Kensington)

There were once many, many chains on dresses for attachments to lorgnettes, muffs or CHÂTELAINES, and some of these are still about for the finding, anything up to one and a half metres long, in 'trace', 'curb', 'alma' or 'Prince of Wales' pattern. There is the occasional châtelaine for holding CHARMS in the shape of pigs, shoes, acorns, lucky stars and horseshoes. The late-Victorian motor car, now classed as a 'veteran', but then the very latest thing in transport, may also be found as a charm. Old-fashioned men's jewellery is about too, not only as cuff-links, tiepins and rings, but as 'Alberts', or short chains worn dangling from the watch-chain, with pendants perhaps in the form of a fancy padlock, a seal, a compass or a locket containing a miniature portrait.

Look also for flies and other insects under crystal (or 'lead glass' as it is more likely to be), also ear-rings in the shape of hammers, tongs or ladders. The Victorians liked 'folk' jewellery when it was shown to them in exhibitions–the Scottish silver brooches of claymore and shields set with cairngorms, the distinctive Luckenbooth brooches and polished pebble mosaic brooches as well as the famous ptarmigan or grouse claw brooches mounted with silver and cairngorms.

A pair of Victorian hair ear-rings, c. 1860 (Christies, South Kensington)

Hair jewellery is sought nowadays by collectors, either actual things made of plaited hair, or as little glass boxes or lockets carrying a pathetic lock of hair which has never aged. There is mourning jewellery in JET which is sometimes very handsome and beautifully worked. There is fine carving in coral as in IVORY, particularly of animals against mountain scenery.

A few other things to look for include marcasite, first popular in Georgian times; it is really iron pyrites, one of the commonest of minerals. It has been made into beautiful things by cutting and faceting, especially as a frame for coloured stones and enamels. These are best when they are *pavé* set, the turned-over edges of the mount adding light to the stone. Cut steel, similar in appearance to marcasite, was another late eighteenth-century craze, as we know from the many Wedgwood cameos mounted on it; but whereas in their early days each steel head was individually set, the invention of die-stamping gave us cut-steel jewellery in ribbons and so brought it down the scale and it was no longer used for the better stones.

The poker-about-in-trays should not overlook AMBER pieces, IVORY and enamelling. Large enamelled jewellery is out of fashion, but it will probably never be made again except by amateurs.

Art Nouveau pendant

Finally, one could recommend a search for pieces made at the turn of the century by craftsmen working under the influence of the ARTS AND CRAFTS MOVEMENT led by William Morris, then in the styles of ART NOUVEAU. French designers headed by LALIQUE of glass fame, broke away completely from the conventional diamond-set

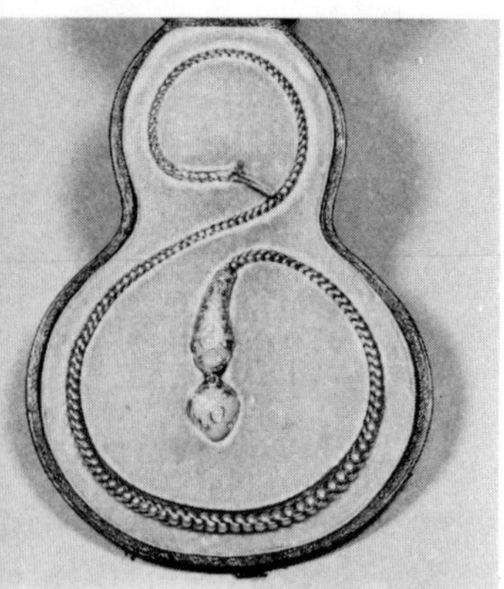

A Victorian gold snake necklet, late 19th century (Christies, South Kensington)

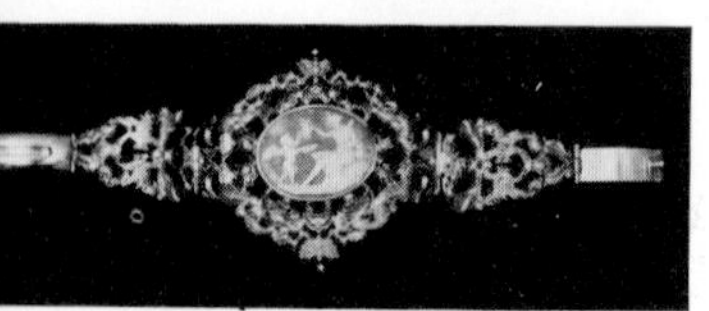

A Victorian enamelled pinchbeck bracelet inset with a classical cameo, c. 1870 (Christies, South Kensington)

A gold and enamel fairy pendant in the Art Nouveau style, c. 1900 (Christies, South Kensington)

jewellery and made lovely things in such materials as horn, black and coloured enamel, ivory and mother of pearl as well as the more precious metals. Instead of using stones for their intrinsic value, they very properly considered only their decorative value, seeking out unusual, though not very precious, minerals like Mexican or fire opals, malachite and azurite, Connemara marble and serpentine, the light green amazonite and the pearl 'blisters' scorned by the seekers after cash values. They also did some fine enamelling. The big names in the movement were Herbert McNair and the Macdonald sisters in Glasgow; C. R. Ashbee, who worked a great deal in silver with a sparing use of gemstones; the Gaskins, husband and wife, who produced some fine work in twisted wire; the French craftsmen Victor Prouve, Eugène Colonna, Georges Fouquet and Emile GALLÉ, better known for his glass; Philippe Wolfers, Victor Horta and Henry Van de Velde in the Low Countries; and Hans Christiansen and Patriz Huber in Germany. But there were many others whose names have not come down to us today, but who made attractive brooches, clasps, pins and pendants, with much finely wrought and beaten work in silver and even aluminium and copper.

As to types of setting, I suppose everyone knows that a *claw* setting is one in which the stone is held by little 'claws' of metal, while with *carved* settings the stone is bedded in solid metal. *Millegrain* leaves the back open and holds the stone with little raised grains of the metal; *pavé* set stones are close together and held by little points of metal; and *cabochon* stones could be set in a box whose edges grasp the stone, the back being cut away to allow the light to show through.

Not many people realize how interesting it can be to put together a collection of gemstones simply *as* stones rather than as decoration in jewellery. They can be bought, either in old and worthless settings or direct from a lapidary–a specialist in stones–at a fairly modest cost.

A gathering of stones will teach you a lot about their qualities. To take semi-precious stones alone, you can get to know the striped agate and onyx, the colour changeling alexandrite, the bloodstone–with its red drops in a sea of chalcedony–the brown and blue zircon, the green and red tourmaline, the sherry-brown, blue and pink topaz, the russet-red sard, the many-coloured spinel, the golden amber, the black JET, the jasper disguising itself as lapis lazuli. By handling and comparing these very cheaply acquired stones, you can get to know a great deal about their *hue*, which means how much actual colour they have; their *tone*, otherwise their lightness and darkness; their *intensity* or vividness. Since there are hundreds of hues and thousands of tones; this should keep you going for some little time. Then, with some stones, one is interested in their *lustre*, or *texture*–whether it is silky, pearly, waxy or glassy. Their *translucency*, as in moonstones, is of interest, also their *transparency*, as in aquamarines. Stones which come in different colours and therefore baffle on that account can be identified by a scale of hardness based on the extent to which one sort of stone will scratch a mark on another.

You measure your stones by the *carat*, which is two-tenths of a grain. Two other points–if you are going to gather these stones don't let them rub together, for the hard ones will scratch the soft ones; and keep them clean and free from dust and atmospheric pollution with a non-greasy detergent. Mount them, for preference, in a silk-lined box with a window.

Nobody can talk about gemstones for long without bringing in birthdays. January's garnet ensures that your lover will be faithful to you; February's stone is the amethyst, which according to a rather scandalous legend about Bacchus and a frightened nymph, keeps you sober. In March you have the choice of aquamarine, which gives you courage and energy, or bloodstone by which you acquire great wisdom. April folk are a lucky lot, for they have the diamond which ensures victory in any enterprise; while May has the emerald, which ensures women wedded bliss and safe child-bearing. June's children have the moonstone which banishes nightmares, and the pearl which makes all brides beautiful. July's ruby frees you from worldly cares; in August the peridot, or evening emerald, makes you merciful to others. September's sapphire stands for truth and sincerity. October has the opal, no longer considered unlucky, and the tourmaline, which since it becomes electrified by a change in atmosphere is said to be as good as a glass of champagne to its rightful wearer. November's topaz cures sleeplessness, and in December the turquoise brings both love and money and lapis lazuli cures melancholy. So everything seems to have been worked out for everybody in the nicest possible way.

Joke Pottery and Glass

Our ancestors had some boisterous habits when they were at their ease in their inns. One of the things they never tired of doing was finding ways of taking the mickey out of their drinking companions by the use of joke mugs and glasses.

A favourite item in the family, which dates back to DELFTWARE times, is the fuddling cup, which consists of three or more cups joined together externally. You are asked to empty one of them, which seems an easy enough task. But the cups are also joined by secret channels, so that in emptying one you have to drain the lot.

A white saltglaze puzzle jug, Staffordshire, c. 1735 (City Museum and Art Gallery, Stoke-on-Trent)

Another is the puzzle jug. This has a whole lot of spouts and other apertures, and it seems impossible to drink out of it without spilling the liquid all over yourself. But there is usually a hole leading back down the handle, and if you stop up some of the spouts, you can get the liquid up through this channel, though sometimes you have to suck hard. One variety is a puzzle even to fill, for it has a hole through the bottom!

Still in the pottery world is the frog mug, which has a frog fixed near the bottom. As you empty the mug, not only does the frog appear and scare you out of your wits, but the air rushing through a small aperture makes a most lifelike gurgling sound.

In glass, of course, there is the 'yard of ale', with a bulb at the foot. It does not seem to be too formidable a job to empty one, but beware! There is a bulb at the end of the glass, and as you tip up the glass to drain the end of the beer, air rushes down into the bulb and squirts the stuff squarely into your face. What a time they must have had cleaning up in those days!

Another little pleasantry, reserved for newly married couples, was the marriage bell. This was a wooden affair, and was filled with wine or beer for the groom to toast the bride. But as the joker handed it over he pressed the handle and caused the wine to disappear into a receptacle at the top, thus leaving nothing for the groom to drink. (Discomfiture of happy couple, as Victorian *Punch* used to say.)

A saltglaze slip-cast Doulton Ware humorous jug 'Before and After Marriage', designed 1924–30 (Doulton and Company Limited)

Knife Cases

You usually find these knife-boxes or cases with their insides pulled out and fitted up as stationery cabinets, with racks for writing paper and envelopes.

For this purpose, they're most practical and they can look very handsome in the centre of a writing table or desk. You can usually pick up a modest Regency one for a few pounds.

You may well wonder why people should have used such elegant containers for their knives, obviously intended as furniture for the dining-room rather than the kitchen. The point was that knives were a costly item in a household, and servants were not very highly paid. It was asking for trouble to let the knives go out to the scullions, so the footmen washed them in the dining-room, under the eagle eye of the butler, and then stuck them into the holes in these cases. You could then see at a glance if any were missing by running your eyes down the rows. They were kept locked–like TEA CADDIES–and the key kept in the pantry or, perhaps, on the CHÂTELAINE carried at the

waist of the lady of the house.

Sometimes these cases are quite plain, sometimes of a wood like mahogany inlaid with other woods, or mounted with silver showing, perhaps, a crest.

And then there's another quite different shape. It's a huge affair like an urn, and you see them standing at either end of those long Georgian buffets, looking very classical and rather funeral. They are sometimes on pedestals which once contained tin-lined boxes for washing up the knives.

A satinwood knife case, c. 1780, showing details of the interior and lid (Aspreys)

Knife Rests

There are some small, relatively unconsidered items which have been made in all sorts of materials from the cheapest to the dearest, and they are the very stuff of junk shop collecting. Among them are the aids to the family carver known as knife rests. Upon these he rested his carving implements while he hastily snatched a few mouthfuls before his sons came back for another helping.

Usually in pairs, they are to be found in porcelain, glass and various sorts of metals: I even seem to remember a pair in Bilston enamel. Sometimes they take the form of short rails with legs at each end, surmounted by some sort of device; others are in the form of flat circle segments with raised sides.

Nobody, I suppose, would ever claim great beauty for them, although Victorian silver ones exist which have been given as much consideration by the designer as anything else on the table. But for those who have to watch the pennies here is a field in which they can line up with the expert, especially in the realm of porcelain. Buyers of more splendid things can fall back upon a factory mark, but as these little things seldom bear such signposts your knife-rest collector will benefit from having to learn his connoisseurship the hard way.

Lace

When a subject is unfamiliar it helps to break things down into divisions. Lace (as I am told, and I hope I have listened carefully) falls into two such divisions, Needlepoint and

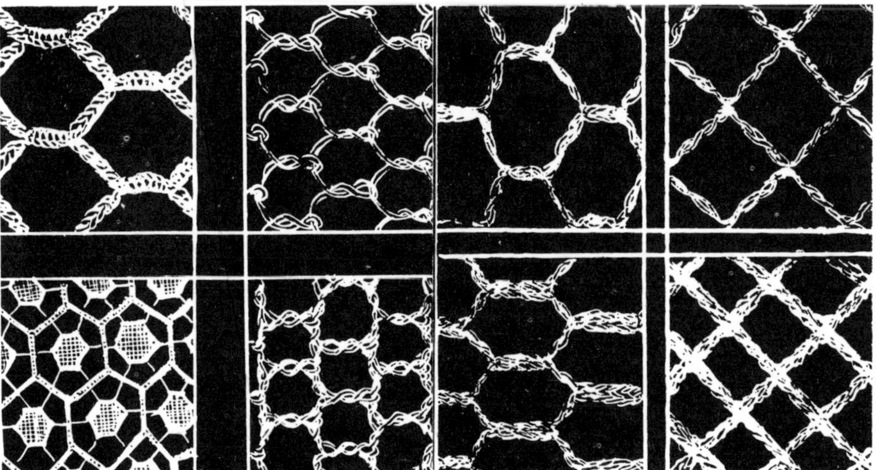

Pillow Réseaux (four squares on left): Top left, *Valenciennes*, top right, *Brussels*, lower left, *Lille*, lower right, *Mechelin*. *Needlepoint Réseaux (four squares on right)*: top left, *Brussels*, top right, *Alençon*, lower left, *Argentan*, lower right, *Argentella*

Pillow: and there is also a mixture of the two. The two charts shown here (taken from an out-of-print book by Mrs Emily Leigh Howes) show the essential differences.

Needlepoint is the earliest of the methods, and it developed in Venice from the early *reticella*. It was done with needle and thread, mainly using the buttonhole stitch. An outline was made on a parchment with a single thread, and then worked over with buttonhole stitches. The *modes* or fillings have a fine network of threads stretched across them, and are afterwards buttonholed into designs. The edges are worked upon with loops or picots.

In *rose point* small stars or roses are worked in; and when the whole surface is sprinkled with these in threes connected by *brides* or bridges which are themselves dotted and purled–it looks like a snowfall–you have *point de neige*. *Gros point de Venise* and *point plat de Venise* are other varieties of Venetian lace which describe themselves: all of them are exquisitely done, were proudly worn by queens and empresses, call for a strong magnifying glass, and are pretty nearly priceless–although you may see some fine specimens in the wonderful collection in the Victoria and Albert Museum, London.

Point laces were also made in Genoa and Milan, but the products of these towns were mostly pillow laces. Here the ground, or *reseau*, is made of plaited threads, and the design is worked with LACE BOBBINS of ivory, bone or wood on a pillow or cushion. In this class there are the early *macramé* lace, *Mechelin* and *Brussels*, *Valenciennes*, *Lille* and *Chantilly*; and the English laces of *Honiton* in Devon, and of *Buckinghamshire* and *Bedfordshire*.

In mixed lace, such as a great deal of the Genoese, the design was woven on the pillow and the ground and fillings were worked in with the needle, either in a network or by *brides* and *picots*.

Point de France had its origin in a migration of Venetian workers to a place near Alençon, and at first was indistinguishable from Venetian. A feature of it is the tiny figures worked in: one specimen shows Madame de Montespan, last wife of Louis XIV, under the French crown. From this developed *point d'Alençon*, whose chief feature is a fine clear ground, the raised *cordonnet* outline to the pattern and the fine patterns in the fillings. *Point d'Argentan* has a larger mesh, but the sides of the mesh are worked with as many as ten buttonhole stitches; while *point d'Argentella* is noted for its fine fillings, outstanding among which are mayflowers, lozenges and dotted patterns.

Of the French pillow laces, Valenciennes (as will be seen from the chart) has a close and thick plait, and was regarded as practically indestructible. At Lille a clearer and

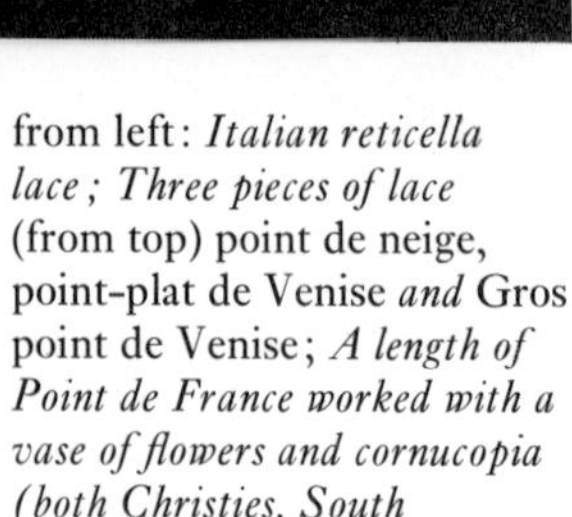

from left: *Italian reticella lace; Three pieces of lace* (from top) point de neige, point-plat de Venise *and* Gros point de Venise; *A length of Point de France worked with a vase of flowers and cornucopia (both Christies, South Kensington)*

larger mesh was used and resembles that of Chantilly. At both of these places black lace was produced–the silk Chantilly fans and shawls are, of course, famous. At this town too were produced the fine silk laces in the natural colours or silvery colours known as *blonde* lace.

The laces of Flanders are renowned, and the arts of the Flemings have been followed in Germany, Sweden, France, Russia and England. Early *Flemish point, Brussels point* and *point d'Angleterre* are virtually indistinguishable from each other, and the fine thread, worked in dark damp rooms, was the finest which could be had.

In later Brussels lace the threads of the pattern follow the curves which also have a distinctive edge. There is no *cordonnet*, but there is a set of looped stitches worked along the edge and whipped over to keep them in place. There are various grounds. The name *point d'Angleterre* (there are also *point d'Aguille* and *point de Gaze*) seems to arise from the fact that when the importation of Brussels lace into England was forbidden in the reign of Charles II the English merchants smuggled it over and sold it as 'English Point' made in Devon. *Mechelin*, the 'Queen of Laces' as it was called, had a a fine silvery thread with a shorter hexagonal mesh than Brussels; being extremely light it was favoured for lawns and muslins.

English laces–as with so many other decorative arts–owed much to Huguenot refugees from France in the reign of Louis XIV. The laces of Valenciennes and Mechelin were copied, although the thread used was coarser. 'Old Buckingham' mesh follows that of Lille. Buckingham made wide lace, but the other southern Midlands counties–Bedfordshire and Northamptonshire–went in for edgings no more than six inches wide.

Lace was made in Devon even before the Huguenot influx; and Honiton, the leading centre, copied Brussels. The most valued pieces are those with hand-made grounds of Flanders flex.

Modern lace, with its machine-made ground, is considered by purists not to be lace at all and in fact a kind of EMBROIDERY or appliqué. It can be distinguished by its regularity and also by the way it remains stiff and wiry when rolled in the fingers.

It forms the foundation of all Brussels lace today, the most common being *point appliqué*, where the sprays, grounds and borders are made separately by hand on the pillow and afterwards applied to the net. *Point de Gaze* with its fine Renaissance patterns is said to be the best of modern laces. Ghent also produces a fine machine-made net and embroiders it in imitation of the earliest Limerick–not the modern type, which is really chain-stitch worked in patterns on machine-made net. Irish crochet, which resembles Venetian Point, is made with a fine thread and a crochet needle.

Honiton lace

Lace Bobbins

Many people like to look for these attractive and highly individual little bobbins used by the lace-makers on their pillows.

What makes them interesting to collect is that they are all different; this in fact was the very point of them, for as the lace-maker worked the design she had to select each bobbin separately. Many of them are dated, and some bear the owner's name or initials.

I suppose most of those one sees nowadays are of bone, ivory or wood, but they are also to be found in brass, pewter and even silver and gold. But it is those in the more humble wood that are the most charming. They evidently, as often as not, originated as tender offerings to a girl with a lace-making pillow from a chap with a handy knife.

'Let me have the wedding day, dear' has been noted, also the rather forward 'Meet me by moonlight alone'. One also sees 'Sweet love, be mine', and 'Kiss me quick, and don't be shy'.

Some bobbins have puzzling inscriptions on them which were evidently some sort of code; or they are about some event like a battle or a Jubilee. Collectors are particularly keen, however, on those that give a hint of the district of origin, whether it be Buckinghamshire, Bedfordshire, Oxfordshire or Northamptonshire, or even in Devon and Wiltshire. You will often come across these things in western Europe, from Sweden to Spain and Italy, and these have many distinctive local styles.

The English types have fancy names which are often highly descriptive. They include the Leopard, Tiger and Butterfly, of turned wood or bone inlaid with pewter, with spots, stripes and wing-shapes respectively; the Yak, a heavy bulbous type, the Baluster or Serrated type with turned wooden or bone bobbins, the Old Maid–a thin straight-sided bobbin with a plain shank; the Wire and Bead, which is self-explanatory; the Trolley or Trailer, a fan bobbin with loose pewter rings, and a variant of this known as Henry VIII's wives, on account of the number of rings. Then there are the composite bobbins, such as Mother-in-Babe, Mother-in-Twins and Mother-in-Triplets which have a hollow shank that unscrews to reveal one or more miniature bobbins inside. Other variants of this type include the Cow-in-Calf, the Bird-cage and the Church Window. These multiple or composite bobbins are naturally the most sought after, and fine and intricate examples fetch quite high prices nowadays.

Lacquer

You should look out for nice lacquer, for it is sometimes overlooked.

The first thing to note is that lacquering is not the same as JAPANNING; true lacquer is the natural juice of the *Rhus vernicifera* or lac tree, and it gives us a remarkable decorative material which does not mind being buried in tombs, providing they are damp enough. Water, in fact, seems to preserve it: some Japanese lacquer was shown at the Vienna Exhibition of 1878, and the ship taking it home was wrecked; but the divers who recovered the cargo eighteen months later found the lacquer objects completely unspoiled.

There are many types of lacquer, but they fall into two main divisions. First there are objects which have been built up from many layers perhaps of different coloured lacquer, each rubbed down finely and then carved in such a way that the various layers are revealed. The Chinese have been producing articles made in this way for many centuries.

Then there is the kind of lacquer where this material has been applied–again in many layers–as a decorative covering, then to be decorated by painting, inlaying or dusting with fine gold or some other material. The Japanese learned this art from the Chinese and, taking it over from them, went on to surpass their masters.

Perhaps the most popular object with collectors in the West is the *inro*, the compartmented cases once carried on the girdle of the Japanese gentleman to hold his medicines, snuff, writing materials and other small items. But there is really no end to the variety of objects which have been decorated in this way, and which offer you a passport to the fascinating artistic themes of the Far East.

Good lacquer sometimes lurks unsuspected in odd corners. Some time ago I bought a small lot at an auction, the main item in which was a large needlework picture; but included in it, totally unvalued, was a beautiful little *inro* in gold *takamakie* with black crows flying over a silver moon.

A Lalique frog car mascot on its original base (Christies, South Kensington)

Lalique

It was back in Edwardian times that we first met the glass of René Lalique (1860–1945). To those of us who lived in Mayfair or South Kensington in London it came chiefly in the form of decorative bowls, figures for the cabinet or mantelpiece, lamp stands, clock mounts and even screens or panels for our furniture. Those of us who lived elsewhere looked for it wistfully in Bond Street windows in the form of SCENT BOTTLES; and in fact Lalique did, as a supplier to Coty, revolutionize the scent bottle industry, so he has to be brought into any collection of them. Did you throw all of yours away?

Lalique started life as a silversmith and jeweller, and when he turned to glassmaking he broke away from the coloured and enamelled glass with which everyone was obsessed, and went in search of what has been described as a 'harmony of whites'. Using a pure colourless glass, he moulded, pressed and engraved getting his best effects with a combination of clear white and matt surfaces. He also produced an interesting range of opaque black glass. He was one of the few artists who managed to produce his work on a factory scale. His son, Marc Lalique, continued the good work.

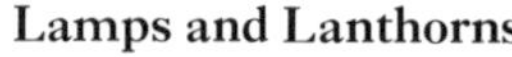

Lamps and Lanthorns

A good-sized part of 'the trade' is involved in what it calls 'lamping', and many a fine and unique vase or figure has, to the fury of serious collectors, been immolated on the 'lamper's' bench.

Of course, there are plenty of things which *can* be 'lamped' without getting people into a bad temper and not necessarily vases either. The lightweight Marly horses in some form of electrotype bronze alloy were once ten a penny, and no one had any compunction about fitting them with a bracket and wiring them for use as lamps. You

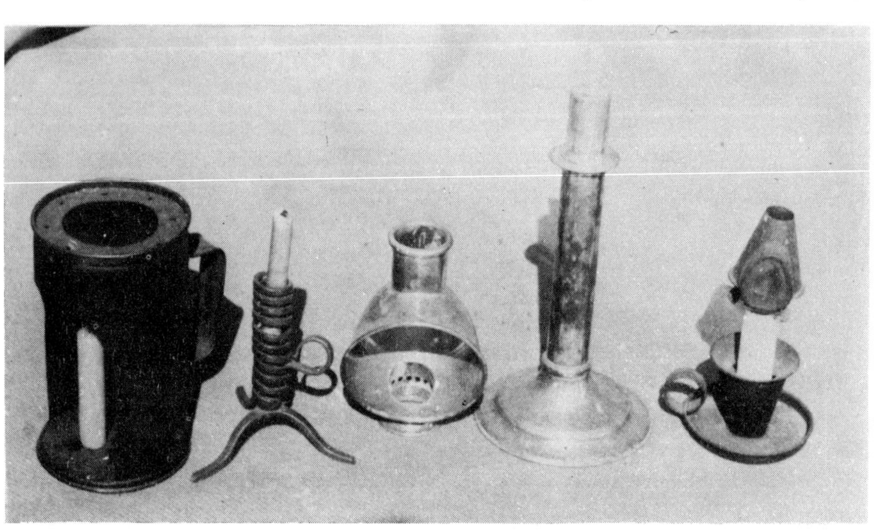

Right: *A selection of 'Lights from the Past', including a child's night light and other candle lamps (S. H. Cole)*

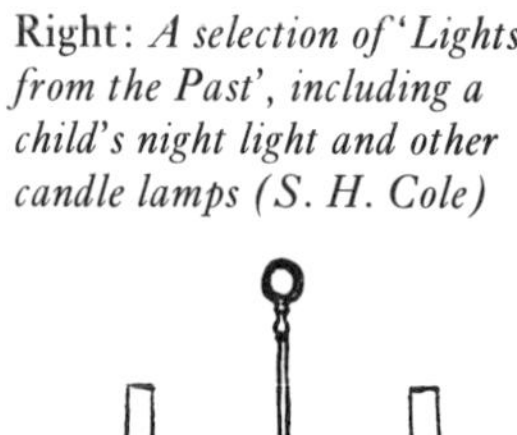

Victorian brass Argand table lamp

Victorian candle lamp

can also have a lot of fun 'lamping' some of these big chemical glass containers, and a great deal of the more commercial STONEWARE that's still around.

As to lamps which started life as lamps, here is a fascinating study for someone. The big old houses of other days, with their many rooms and passages and staircases, must have carried hundreds of lamps of various kinds, from the great candelabra in the drawing-rooms to the small lanterns with one or two candles to fix to walls of passages or to stand on tables at corners. Some seem to have a mirror plate, but no arrangement for a candle: these no doubt carried a glass or porcelain portable CANDLESTICK. The early ones are not easy to find–although this is a deficiency which modern coppersmiths are working hard, it seems, to fill! But there are still to be found the later table lamps, perhaps of BRASS, with globes of blown and frosted glass.

Oddly enough, the Victorian manufacturers put more good taste and good sense into these than most of their wares. No doubt they enjoyed working under the restraint of a practical end. Watch out for the Argand lamp, with a reservoir for colza or other oil which feeds the lamp by gravity; these are now very much sought after. And don't be discouraged if you find lamps that have lost their original shades; if you want a new 'original' glass one, the 'trade' can supply it!

Lancastrian Pottery

One by one the late-Victorian potteries are coming back into favour, and their wares re-appraised by collectors. The best of the Royal Lancastrian LUSTRE WARE has been collected for very many years now; in fact, being real examples of handcraft and artistry these pieces were collected avidly as soon as they were offered for sale. But even quite modest pieces from this factory have now graduated to the level where the dealers recognize the factory mark and realize that, though perhaps not quite fashionable enough to be given away for a pound or two, it will make a great deal more when a serious collector turns up.

The Royal Lancastrian Pottery was founded by William Burton as an offshoot of the Pilkington tile and brick factory at Clifton, near Manchester. Burton was one of those geniuses, like Wedgwood, Spode and Minton, that one often finds in ceramics–part chemist, part artist, part businessman. In the early years he produced some of the best of the wonderful coloured glazes which rivalled those of Chinese porcelain. Some were in monochrome, some had variegated colours, and there were fascinating textures as well.

Next came the famous Pilkington iridescent lustre. This differs from normal lustre in that the effect is of the changing colours on a soap bubble, and the decorators employed under Gordon M. Forsyth, the art director, began to produce with its aid that fine series of painted wares in which classical, Spanish, Persian, Italian and ART NOUVEAU themes were somehow pulled together into what is now beginning to have a very definite character of its own.

The third main class of pottery was what the firm called Lapis Ware, an original kind of STONEWARE in which the painting combined with or reacted against the glaze put on over it in such a way as to produce effects of mottled or speckled flowing colour on tinted grounds.

Lancastrian ware of any kind was never very cheap, and it fell a victim to the industrial depression of the 'thirties; Pilkington stopped making art pottery in 1938.

Except for some of the early glazed pieces made before 1904, Lancastrian is easy to trace not only to the factory, but to the artist, and even sometimes to its year of production. Painters like W. S. Mycock, Gwladys Rogers, Richard Joyce, and designers like Walter Crane and Lewis F. Day, had their special monograms in addition to the firm's 'PL' with two bees (for the brothers Burton). There were also serial numbers beginning at 2001 in 1905.

Some Lancastrian ware I have seen looks rather dulled, as though the glaze has not stood up to heat or washing; but the best of it is really fine stuff and worth looking for.

Latten

Latten is BRASS, but in a particular form. Before brass was founded in Britain (what the Elizabethans called 'brass' was really BRONZE) it was brought across the North Sea from Germany and the Netherlands in flat sheets. From these were made the church monumental brasses from which rubbings are now made. When we applied the word 'brass' to describe what we had once called bronze, the word 'latten' remained to describe brass when it came in flat sheets rather than solid lumps.

Early HORSE BRASSES were made of latten, but this was made in England, the alloy being copper and calamine, instead of copper and zinc as used later on. Such brasses should show the hammer marks on the back. Early brass kettles, skillets, measures and CANDLESTICKS were also hammered out of latten brass.

Linthorpe

We have already met at BRETBY that energetic potting manager Henry Tooth and his enterprising and imaginative designer, Dr Christopher Dresser.

These two men came together when Dresser, on a visit to Middlesbrough during a great depression in the iron and steel industry, suggested to a landowner named John Harrison that on his estate at Linthorpe, on the outskirts of the town, there was a vein of good brick clay which might be worked profitably and so alleviate unemployment in the district. Harrison agreed to start such a venture, and he appointed Dresser as art director and Henry Tooth as manager.

Tooth had never been a potter, but he had been a great many other things, including a theatrical scene painter. He evidently had tremendous drive and also a keen sense of his own contribution to the enterprise. When J. F. Blacker was producing his survey of nineteenth-century pottery about 1900, Tooth was careful to supply him with illustrations of his wares and also the information that 'while it was Dr Dresser who had suggested that this common material be fashioned into beautiful objects, the working out of the idea was due to the energy and skill of Mr Tooth', then added, 'that most efficient manager'.

Between them, at all events, they covered this 'common material' with rich and colourful glazes in the manner of the famous Chinese monochromes, and flambes which were also used at the LANCASTRIAN POTTERY by Bernard Moore and William Moorcroft.

There seems reason to believe, in fact, that it was Linthorpe which actually pioneered this movement. Certainly as early as the year 1882 the London *Graphic* in reviewing an exhibition at the Society of Arts, said that the Linthorpe ware was 'quite a new feature in European pottery; for in depth, richness, variety and glorious beauty of colour it is only matched by the splendid wares of the East'. Here is an interesting problem in ceramic history for some new collector to solve.

Dresser's work for Linthorpe was done in the first three years of its existence; he seems to have left at about the same time that Henry Tooth departed for Bretby. Until Harrison's death in 1889 Linthorpe went on using the glazes on more conventional shapes, with, however, the addition of a great deal of '*sgraffito*, appliqué and painting. Besides Dresser's signature and the factory name one finds also the initials HT during the early period.

Lithophanes

Not very often met with these days–I suppose I have seen one or two over the past few years–are those 'shadow pictures' in china which were so popular in Victorian days.

Lithophanes were made by impressing a design or picture in a thin glassy porcelain in such a way that it could be seen only when held against a light. They were used for lampshades, NIGHTLIGHTS and even as panels in the windows of houses. For subjects the makers generally relied upon the popular pictures of the day. Many were made on the Continent, especially in Berlin, but Minton, Copeland, Wedgwood, Grainger of Worcester and others also turned them out. The average size of lithophane panels is about eight inches square, but some are much larger.

Locks and Keys

When you look at the average modern lock it is scarcely to be wondered at that joiners should have hidden them away in mortices. But old locks, if you can find them, are very different. They were meant not only to be seen but to impress people, and the metalworker really went to town on them. Gilded wrought iron, blue steel, brass sheet, Princes metal (a brass alloy), pinchbeck and copper were all brought into use, and enriched with moulding, engraving and damascening with gold and silver on steel.

Though really fine old locks may be rarities, the old keys made to fit them are much more frequent visitors to the salerooms. These, too, are quite worth collecting merely as fine and very beautiful examples of metalwork. They were important and treasured articles in their day, and each one was given a well-designed 'bow'–the part you hold to turn it in the lock. Crosses, flying cherubs, figures of saints, winged griffins, men and women, coronets and coats of arms were among the motifs used. Not so long ago I saw a group of Roman keys go for very little; and if it surprises you to hear that the Romans *had* keys, let alone locks to put them in, I read recently that even the Ancient Britons had locks–wooden ones which they allegedly bought from the Phoenicians. I did not know they had doors even.

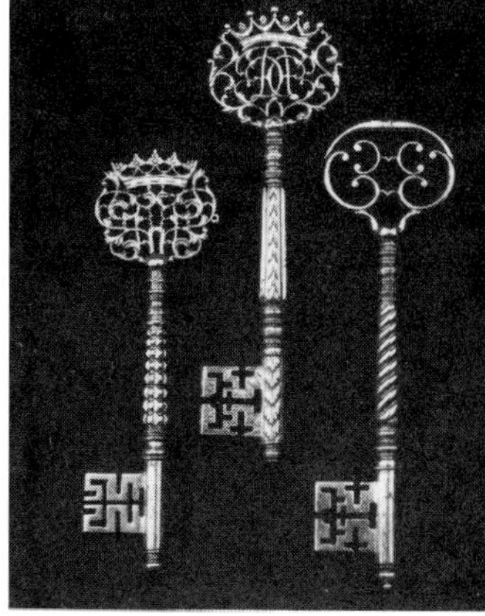

Three 18th-century French keys (Christies, South Kensington)

Love Feast Cups

This heart-warming title describes–in the North of England at all events–a two-handled type of LOVING CUP adorned with texts and/or portraits of John Wesley, Hugh Bourne and other religious leaders.

I owe this definition to J. T. Shaw, Director of the Sunderland Museum and Art Gallery, in whose collection there is a number in the famous local LUSTRE WARE pottery. There are two types, one goblet shaped on a stemmed foot, and the other cylindrical, rather like two-handled mugs, the body tapering from foot to rim.

I have also heard them called Funeral Cups and Communion Cups; but it seems likely, Mr Shaw suggests, that if these were used in Anglican churches where they were not passed from hand to hand, as in the Love Feasts, they would have been simple goblets without handles.

Collectors in different parts of Britain could help us by comparing notes, trying if possible to stimulate local recollections about them before it is too late.

Two-handled 'Love Feast' cup

Loving Cups

Nobody who has attended a public banquet will have escaped the ceremony of the loving cup. This large piece of silver plate, napkin tied to the handle, goes from guest to guest, each of whom remains standing while his neighbour drinks–in case someone has slipped into the Mansion House with a flick-knife and is looking for unwary drinkers.

A more intimate sort of loving cup comes in pottery of the main sorts, and is a small two-handled job for two friends having a quiet drink of toddy together. I have also heard them called 'parting cups', but as journeys end with lovers' meetings, so they must begin with lovers' partings.

Some loving cups had their owner's name or initials printed on them, or perhaps the name of a couple. Others bore mottoes and the arms of Societies such as the Oddfellows. A typical inscription is:

'Cup love and friendship
Peace and good neighbourhood
May we never seen an ould friend
With a new face.'

All these have the value of the wares they are produced in, as well as any historical interest in the inscription, so you are not likely to find good ones at bargain prices. But there are later Victorian ones which are just as collectable. Happily for the future of friendship, the manufacture of loving cups never entirely died out: they were a speciality of the Rye pottery in characteristic striped decoration. In recent years, of course, they have been revived in a big way, and loving cups are now a favourite medium for much commemorative pottery.

Lustre Ware

This is the name usually given to pottery and porcelain which is decorated either partly or wholly with a shiny metallic glaze, sometimes pink or purple, sometimes silver, copper or gold.

In darkish rooms, lit only by candles or oil lamps, it must have gleamed most attractively from the mantelpiece, or on the crowded dresser. It has never lost its popularity and is still being made today, sometimes with new designs–Wedgwood have a very attractive jug–but sometimes in deliberate imitation of the old. It is getting dearer all the time and the better prices make high prices at auction.

Aristocrats of the family are the large silver 'resist' jugs, plain or with canary yellow and other coloured grounds. The 'silver' is really a thin coating of metal, not actually silver but platinum (which was then relatively cheap); and in the same way 'copper' lustre is obtained by using a solution of gold. The name 'resist' arises because of the way the lustre pattern is obtained. You paint it on to the white body of the piece with a substance which will 'resist' or throw off any metal solution. When you dip the piece into this solution the part covered is thus left 'in the white'.

There is another type–which is still being made–which is entirely covered with

Below left: *Wedgwood Lustre ware, c. 1810. The vast range of items produced include the moonlight lustre jug, bell-pull and a steel lustre goblet (Wedgwood).* Below right: *'Flowerpot and Flies' ruby lustre ware plate by De Morgan (William Morris Gallery)*

lustre, but personally I don't find these nearly so attractive, for they seem to me to be just aping silver or gold, as the case may be. I don't see why pottery should try to look like something else–what has it got to be ashamed of?

The most attractive of the older pieces, I think, apart from the resist patterns, are the big jugs with printed views of painted decoration, sometimes combined with relief decoration. These, too, are in the big money class but well worth it. The views of Sunderland Bridge are well-known, and have given the name of this town to the whole class of ware, although it was made in many other places as well, especially Staffordshire.

There is also a whole family of wares with verses, pictures of lovers parting or meeting, to say nothing of those PLAQUES which utter frightful warnings about the next world. These usually feature that special kind of purple lustre which was developed in the Sunderland area, with blotches and bubbles in it; this was done by blowing oil on the glaze with a tube, and it was thought very *chic* in its day.

I notice too that the prices are steadily rising for the ordinary tea-table items, decorated with lustre patterns. Some of this is most charmingly 'cottagey' and it falls into several groups which have not yet been properly sorted out. There is a whole family, for example, which is painted with bold designs of a church or house; another has sprigs of flowers in a New Hall style and limits the lustre to borderings. The quality of the paste varies very widely from a crude earthenware to a very fine sort of china.

Majolica

This word, spelled with a 'j' to distinguish it from *maiolica*–the Italian equivalent of DELFTWARE–was the name given by Minton and other nineteenth-century potters to a distinctive form of earthenware covered with a thick coloured glaze. One still sees a lot of it about, not only on decorative vases and other hollow wares, but also on the outsides of Victorian public houses, in old-fashioned dairies and even public lavatories. This form of pottery was particularly favoured in TILES.

Mangle Boards

Some of the finest wood carving to be found anywhere in Europe is on that humble domestic implement, the mangle board.

Like LACE BOBBINS they were presented to brides as wedding gifts, sometimes–though to judge from their artistry not very often–carved by the groom himself. In Finland they show the braided pattern which has come down from medieval times; in northern Germany CHIP CARVING, the handles often being in the form of fabulous animals.

Mangle boards must have been far better for the figure of the user even than the

A Dutch mangle board dated and initialled 'TBH 1856', with later roller ('At the Sign of the Sad Iron' Limited)

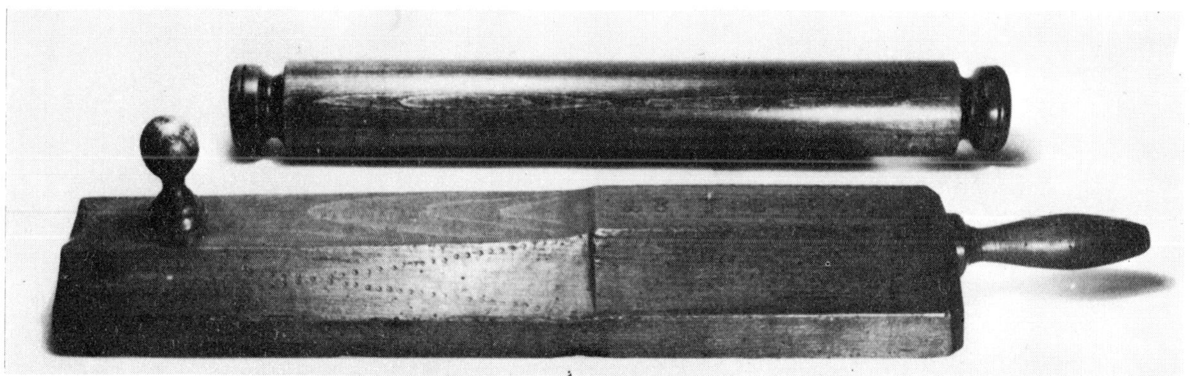

old-style roller mangle. To operate them you took a roller, wrapped the wet clothes round it and laid it on a flat surface such as a stone above a stream. You then took your mangle board by the handle, placed it across the roller and, pressing down on the other end, ran the board backwards and forwards–meantime carrying on a lively discussion with the lady next door.

Even more strenuous exercise–and also fine carving–is provided by the clothes beater: but these seem to be not very different in form from the similarly shaped flax swingle, used for beating out flax–another good form of exercise.

Marquetry

You won't find a great deal of marquetry in the shops unless it wants repairing, which is fairly costly. But it might be useful to point out the difference between marquetry and inlay, so that you can see what is involved in the repairs. Inlaid wood is like any other kind of inlay, being a piece of wood of one kind let into a wood of another kind. But marquetry is a sort of jigsaw veneer. Sheets of different coloured woods are first glued together into a sort of sandwich, and the design is cut through all the layers. Then the sheets are taken apart again, and a jigsaw made up by fitting the 'capes' in one coloured sheet into the 'bays' of another. Then all this is glued on to the 'carcase' of the piece, as with ordinary veneering. And remember, that just as any sort of veneering likes neither damp nor extreme heat, neither does marquetry.

A fine harewood tray with beautiful marquetry in boxwood, stained woods and ivory (Aspreys)

Mary Gregory

Yes, there was a lady called Mary Gregory. But I'm afraid she didn't make much of the decorated glass which goes by her name.

I hope you'll recognize the glass from my description. On a whole range of decanters, jugs, glasses, bottles, boxes, flower holders and vases, you find figures of children painted in white or coloured enamels. Very decorous they are, these young people, in their long frocks or sailor suits, and they're usually picking flowers, blowing bubbles, flying kites or just walking along.

These wares are usually painted in white on coloured glass, in shades of green and red, but clear glass may also be found with the decoration in coloured enamels. For years I have listened to tales of a dear old lady somewhere in the Stourbridge area buying clear-glass decanters and glasses from the local glasshouses and taking them home to her creeper-clad cottage, where she eked out a frugal living painting on them pictures of the dear little children who played outside her door.

Well, something like this may have happened in the case of the crudely tinted ones, no doubt made late in the last century or even after. But the early ones, in good glass and with finely judged white enamel painting, have a very different origin; they were made between 1850 and 1880 at Jablonec in what is now Czechoslovakia, by a firm called Hahn who exported all kinds of decorated glass all over the world. This has been proved beyond any shadow of doubt by an American writer, Carl W. Drepperd, who discovered a catalogue of the firm's products illustrated in colour and with all the pattern numbers.

And Mary Gregory? It seems that she was a lady who worked at the Boston and Sandwich Glass Works doing similar things as the Jablonec glass. And presumably *we* use the name 'Mary Gregory' because American collectors of this glass asked for it under that name, when they toured round the antique and junk shops of Britain. So do legends grow in collecting–and so they are destroyed!

Mason's Ironstone

Everybody will know the famous sets of octagonal jugs with snake handles which are almost the trademark of Mason's and their famous ironstone. It was a tough, practically indestructible earthenware aimed at the middle-class household of the early nineteenth century who liked their crockery to be as showy as the more expensive bone china, but wanted it to last twice as long.

MASON'S PATENT IRONSTONE CHINA

Gathering a full set of the jugs would probably take a lifetime–though it would hardly cost a fortune, even now. These jugs came in sets, ranging from tiny ones a couple of inches high, to giants standing nearly a foot tall. Mugs were also made of course, and immense dinner services come up for auction and are eagerly bought by the trade, presumably for splitting up and selling separately.

Charles James Mason, who patented this famous ware, also turned out some huge pieces, vases five feet high, mantelpieces, baths, bedposts and at least one entire fireplace. The firm of George L. Ashworth and Brothers, who bought Mason's interests in 1851, still make, among their more modern styles, reproductions of the original Mason hollow wares.

Mauchline Ware

Who invented the wooden hinge for the SNUFFBOX? Was it Charles Stiven of Laurencekirk, Lord Gardenstone's rebuilt village in Kincardineshire; was it Jamie Sandy of Alyth in Perthshire; or was it Willie Crawford of Cumnock in Ayrshire? Or did all these Scots pick up the idea from the painted Russian boxes imported for the grand folk of their day?

As every snufftaker knows, a tight hinge and a well-fitted lid are vital in a good snuffbox; and even with the well-seasoned Scots planewood it took real joiner's craft to do this by cutting out tiny wooden rollers from the lid and back of the box, then passing through a brass or wooden pin.

By the early eighteenth century the craft had spread from Laurencekirk to the Ayrshire towns of Mauchline, Cumnock and Auchinleck. The boxes were painted in oils or watercolours or decorated with sporting and other prints. The best of these boxes were produced by the firm of W. and W. Smith of Mauchline, who were also responsible for a series of boxes in the same style as the Russian enamelled wares mentioned above. These were known as 'Scoto-Russian' work, and made great use of tinfoil to give the effect of inlaid silver. They are very handsome boxes indeed, and they deservedly won for their makers a gold medal at the Great Exhibition of 1851.

When the demand for snuffboxes declined the village craftsmen turned their attention to the new craze for tartan decoration, stimulated by George IV's visit to Scotland in 1822. Originally tartan was painted directly on to the boxes, but by the time of Queen Victoria this was applied in the form of tartan paper glued to the surface. Mauchline, however, is chiefly associated with the very distinctive small wooden items in varnished planewood decorated with black transfer-printed pictures of scenery and landmarks. These items became a very popular form of souvenir of tourist resorts in the late nineteenth and early twentieth centuries, doing for wood what GOSS did for china.

The last form of Mauchline ware was known as fernware and consisted of boxes, picture frames and napkin rings decorated with ferns which were specially collected each season from the island of Arran. This work was exceedingly laborious and it was not long before the Smith family devised a simpler method, like their earlier tartan ware, of simulating ferns in specially printed paper which, however, lacks the characteristic raised surface imparted by using actual ferns. Both fernware and the transfer-printed wares continued in production until the 'thirties when a disastrous fire at the Mauchline works put the firm out of business.

Meerschaum

Or as the French have it, *écume de mer*–'sea foam'; but the English-speaking world prefers to use the German term.

Meerschaum gets its name from a fancied resemblance to the creamy spume washed up on the sea-shore. Actually it is silicate of magnesium in its pure state, and its excellent properties for the making of pipes appear to have been discovered about the middle of the eighteenth century.

This property, of course, is the fact that, unlike porcelain, it is porous enough to absorb nicotine (and not simply stew it) and while doing so it can carbonize slowly and evenly.

This means that the more it is smoked the quicker its colour changes from a milky white through various tints of amber to shades of brown; and, of course, just as every rooky bluejacket wants his collar to pale from indigo to light Mediterranean blue as soon as possible, so the owner of a meerschaum wants to smoke until he has all these glorious tints and shades in his pipe.

But this is not all that he desires. The material lends itself admirably to carving, and the skilled carver tries to arrange things so that certain parts of the pipe colour more readily than others, thus producing appropriate effects. For example, a figure will be carved on a bowl in such a way that the face remains a pale cream against clothes of deep egg yolk; or in the case of a negro or a Red Indian, the face goes darker while the clothes remain pale. This process can be helped along, I understand, by some kind of waxing treatment, but it is never wise to press a meerschaum smoker too far for information.

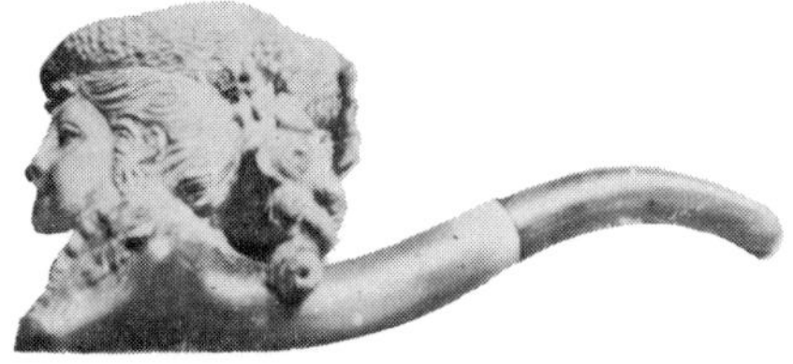

A Meerschaum pipe (S. H. Cole)

There is certainly some fine carving on meerschaums, from naked ladies to battle scenes. The more elaborate sort seems to have begun around 1800 and continued until the briar overtook the meerschaum in the 1860s. One of the leading firms in the business is Sommer of Paris where, I understand, an old craftsman in his nineties was still carving pipes for devotees until fairly recently.

Look out, however, for late and crudely carved specimens made up of pressed meerschaum parings, with a false date in the carving.

Memento Mori

This is a sales cataloguer's term for all those sad things which we once bought to remind ourselves of the dead–and of death.

There are rings, with a ribbon tie of hair in a bezel; there are lockets of all sorts containing hair curls, perhaps tied as a sheaf of corn; there are bracelets, wrist ornaments and pendants. There are also grim little items in which the principal decoration is a skull: the object here seems to be not to lament someone lost as to remind the wearer of his own mortality.

Mineral Water Bottles

Time was when all you had to do was dig around in any old waste ground or dump, but now these bottles have graduated and have become immensely collectable.

They start by following the 'dumpy' shapes of the sealed bottles, but the gases leaked out. In 1814, therefore, a certain William Hamilton patented an egg-shaped bottle which lay on its side and so kept the cork moist, as with vintage wines. This acquired a flat bottom around the year 1870.

The historically minded collector, however, will find it helpful to follow the various forms of closure–which largely determined the shapes. Cylindrical or champagne shaped bottles became possible in fact only after the invention of the internal screw stopper in 1872, the swing stopper (about 1875) and the crown cork (1892). Literally thousands of patents were taken out between 1814 and the end of the century.

My favourite bottle in youth was a late version of the Codd's bottle (though I did not know it as such) with its glass marble pressed against a rubber ring. This was patented by Hiram Codd of Camberwell in 1875; and Mr Codd took out at least fifty further patents all conscientiously designed to stop daft youngsters like me from breaking open the bottle to add to their stock of marbles. I still bear on one finger a small scar earned in this way.

Below left: *A collection of bottles, showing the variety of collectables in this area, not just of minerals: from the leather bottle at the top (c. 1800), through the penny and three-halfpenny glass-stoppered lemonade bottles* (*c. 1890–1912,* middle row, left) *to the late 19th-century soda syphons, heavily caged with wire mesh as protection against bursting in hot weather (S. H. Cole)*. Below right: *Never junk, but so beautiful. An Italian bevelled mirror in a mosaic frame (Christies, South Kensington)*

Mechanics apart, you should try your eye on a range of these bottles. Seen against today's modern standarized product they have a surprisingly fresh variety.

Mirrors

I always think that if you can't afford large elegances, it's worth giving a thought to small ones. A very handy and comparatively inexpensive source of Georgian or Regency elegance is the swinging mirror, or toilet glass, as some people seem to prefer to call it. Put one of these on a bow-fronted chest of drawers and you somehow give the room a distinction which would cost pounds to achieve any other way.

A Georgian mahogany toilet mirror (Christies, South Kensington)

These glasses come in all shapes, sometimes on stands with a drawer, sometimes as simply an oval or shield-shaped framework. Most good antique shops will find you one and they turn up regularly at the sales, sometimes going for as little as ten to fifteen pounds.

Some people are inclined to be put off by seeing the mirror itself in a poor state, but this is the easiest thing to remedy: you can either have them re-silvered, or in bad cases put in a new glass.

Another sort of mirror which is getting very popular again is the small round convex one, which gives you a complete view of the room. In other days the mistress of the house liked to have one of these by the fireplace or wherever she habitually sat, so that she could see what the servants were up to behind her, or who was coming into the room. In combination with other mirrors they certainly opened up vistas all round and made the room seem large.

Talking of that, don't forget the proper purpose of a *pier glass*, which was to help light up a wall between windows. In the eighteenth century most rooms had windows along one side only, so that the 'pier' wall between the windows tended to be in shadow, too dark for a picture. So you put a long narrow mirror there and this not only reflected light from the opposite wall but as the light from outside fell directly upon people in the room, they could admire themselves in it.

And while still on the subject of pictures, don't overlook the possibilities of those old picture frames you see stacked away in the backs of shops, or surrounding some frightful Victorian print or watercolour. You can often pick up very reasonably a curly maple or gilded frame, which can be cut down to fit a mirror. It will give you your small elegance very cheaply indeed.

Money Boxes

Once upon a time, when people saved their pennies more carefully than they do now, every chimney piece had its money box, a little earthenware container so cheap that it was smashed each year for its contents. There is good authority for believing that this was the origin of our term 'Christmas Box', dating from the days when apprentices used them.

But just because so many of them *were* broken in this way, they aren't very easy to find: so I could wish you no better luck than to come across one of the charming little boxes in the shape of fir-cones, pigs, fish, hens, cradles, houses, chests of drawers and so on. They were made in most of the pottery centres, often in brown Rockingham glaze like that used for STONEWARE SPIRIT FLASKS. Serious collectors can sometimes pin them down to a particular factory or centre.

I notice the ones that do survive seem to have a pretty big aperture for the old-fashioned, pre-decimal penny. No doubt in these cases the money was extracted by adroit use of a knife.

A firm favourite with collectors for many years are the cast-iron money boxes and mechanical banks, most of which seem to have originated in the United States in the latter half of the nineteenth century. The best-known–and most plentiful–is the Sambo, in the form of a negro's head, but the more interesting varieties include hunters, redskins and even a fat politician, satirizing a notoriously corrupt Tammany Hall boss of the 1870s. Later tinplate money boxes are now beginning to attract the serious attention of collectors. What they lacked in security they made up in their handsome and colourful appearance–no doubt with the intention of making the idea of saving attractive to young people.

Monteiths

If you like to keep your wine glasses cool, try one of these bowls, which you may find in glass, silver or ELECTRO-PLATE–though not usually in a junk shop, at least not the splendid versions of Gerogian times.

The Monteith is a bowl with notches round the edge, so that you can hook the foot of a wine glass in it and let the bowl hang into the water. It is also a useful way of carrying glasses about after they have been used.

The term is alleged to derive from the name of a 'fantastical' Scottish gentleman who was in the habit of wearing a cloak notched in this way; although it is not clear from the legend–it was set about by the antiquary Anthony Wood in 1683–whether this was due to an eccentricity or to native frugality.

Moradabad Ware

This is a name used by dealers to cover almost anything which does not come under the heading of BENARES or BIDRI. Properly speaking it covers articles of tinned brass made in such centres as Moradabad, Jaipur and Kashmir. In one of the styles, the *sada*, the design is chased in the tinning, showing up the 'gold' of the brass. In the other major style, the *siyah-kalam*, the designs follow the styles of the more precious enamelled wares. They are chased in the brass, and the depressions filled with black or coloured lac. There are plates, dishes, water jars, jugs in all the shapes mentioned under BENARES and BIDRI work, and lots of tumblers and small measures. Some pieces have spiral patterns of tiny rosettes, others arabesque patterns like Arabic writing.

The simpler the design, the older the work, as a rule. Many modern pieces have synthetic colouring instead of the true lac, so it is usually best to go for the black or plain chasing.

Mote Skimmers

The Georgian and Victorian tea table was well provided with accessories and one of them was a longish spoon punched with holes, sometimes plain, but in the later specimens, as the Georges marched on, with cut crosses and crescents, even foliated scrolls, diapers and suchlike.

They were used for removing 'strangers' from your tea, objects which we do not see so often as did our forebears, whose tea had larger leaves. It may also have been used–instead of a TEA CADDY SPOON–for measuring out the dry tea. At the handle end there was usually a barbed spike for clearing the very fat 'gentleman' away from the teapot spout. Larger skimmers were intended for use with tea urns. Large brass skimmers were also indispensable in the kitchen for removing the scum floating on the tops of simmering cauldrons of soups and stews.

Late 18th-century mote-skimmer

Mother of Pearl

No decorative material has been used and loved quite so much as this. It always seems to find its way on to articles which have some personal or even intimate use; and it is no wonder that it has been treasured or that so much of it survives in good order.

A mother of pearl card case (Christies, South Kensington)

It is hard to know where to start talking about it. Perhaps the best place is, as Alice said, at the beginning, i.e. what it consists of. Mother of pearl is nacre, that is to say the iridescent inner layer of shell of various bivalves of the Indian Ocean and the Pacific. Some of the best kinds came from the pearl oyster–the true 'mother of pearl'. Rarely and expensively it appears as whole nautilus shells, in the form of a ceremonial cup, mounted in silver and gold, or perhaps a half shell as the cover of a box.

What we are more concerned with here, however, are all the many things in which the mother of pearl was used cut and split into small pieces as a mosaic, making every use of the iridescent qualities of the material. Jewel boxes, of course, were a favourite subject for this material, but there are also much larger pieces of furniture, now treasured collector's pieces, such as writing tables and cabinets, or complete toilet sets.

But there are many smaller articles about for the eagle-eyed gatherer. Pearl knife handles have sometimes lost their blades and can be given new ones; there are also paper knives and FAN sticks. There are game counters from the eighteenth century, round or square or fish-shaped, perhaps with an owner's monogram. There are also CARD CASES, wafer boxes and boxes for SCENT BOTTLES–the range is infinite.

Moulds and Shapes

Difficult otherwise to describe all those wooden butter and gingerbread moulds, the latter with fantastic figures and other decorations–Punch and Judy, horses, shoes, bells, lovers' knots, pointed questions like 'Do you love me?' and even 'Will you marry me?'

You can also find earthenware jelly moulds of designs you don't see in the shops today. Wedgwood did a fine range of pyramid shapes in creamware and these are now much sought after.

There are fine COPPER ones too. Definitely a quest for those who don't mind ferreting about at country house sales.

Moustache Cups

I know of only one serious collector of these, and since I seem to have used his last letter as a bookmark I shall perhaps never know how far his subject extends across the great field of ceramics. Like the moustaches for which they acted as a lifter, they must have been common to all countries.

An American writer has suggested an ingenious modern use for them in the television age. In drinking consommé he recommends using the shelf as a dry spot for the little croutons of toast, and so leaving one free to watch the screen. This is a refinement of soup-drinking which I must confess had not occurred to me.

In any case, however, moustaches are back, even bushy ones; so perhaps we shall find such cups in production once more.

Muffineers

When you called on friends in Georgian and Victorian times at around tea-time, you might be offered a tray of hot buttered muffins.

Along with it came salt, pepper and cinnamon, and this might be contained in a type of caster later known as a muffineer. It could be vase or pear-shaped, was gilt-lined and had a sprinkler in which there were round perforations–not fret-cut as was usual with pepper casters–or at least not *only* fret-cut.

The muffineer took on a variety of forms in its long life. Around the end of the seventeenth century it looked rather like a small kitchen pepper pot, cylindrical in shape and with a handle on one side and a shallow dome. This style continued popular into the eighteenth century and spread to the American Colonies: I have seen one

Late 18th-century muffineer

example in silver made at Boston in 1725. In England, however, by Queen Anne's reign (1702–14), the muffineer was usually eight-sided, with a bayonet joint in the lid to stop the cinnamon from coming out in a heap.

The next stage, as shown here, was popular in the middle of the century, and was characterized by the classical urn shape on a pedestal. Later still there were tall balusters, standing on three feet, and lavishly ornamented in the 'revived rococo' manner of the 1830s.

Here then is another of those small collecting subjects in silver–like NUTMEG GRATERS–which can give you a history of styles in very little space.

Musical Boxes

A few years ago, when a favourite country pub of mine was overwhelmed by that combination of tasteless wallpaper, hardboard and staring lights which one ought to include under our styles as Brewery Director's Folly–since it is neither period nor contemporary but just damned uncomfortable–I thought to have seen the last of the pub's beloved 'Polyphon Automatic Musical Instument', one of whose brothers appears on this page.

Above: *An upright coin-in-the-slot Polyphon.* Below: *A carved and inlaid musical chair (both Christies, South Kensington)*

For fifty years it had hung on the wall of the saloon bar receiving pennies, in return clunking out music-hall and operatic tunes from its perforated steel discs. Now in its place were three unidentifiable china birds flying diagonally across the wall in line ahead.

But not long ago I saw a Polyphon in a very modern and very comfortable expresso bar, so, like other former habitués of the saloon bar–and for the same sort of reasons–it seems that these old favourites are spending their declining years in more congenial surroundings. The proprietor of the expresso bar told me that, by making a delicate adjustment to the mechanism, the Polyphon now earned 2p instead of one old penny; so that in a very short time it had recovered the thirty pounds laid out by its new master.

The old Polyphon and its cousins–there are many variations–have a very long ancestry. Musical boxes seem to have started life, naturally enough, among the watchmakers, first as mechanism whereby little airs could be played by watches, then as musical movements fitted into bottles, seals, SNUFFBOXES, walking stick handles and even watchkeys and other tiny objects. I have never quite recovered from the shock I had when, dining in the house of a Socialist politician, I raised a fine cut-glass decanter which thereupon played the Eton Boating Song. I hear, too, that there are chairs in which the unmusical ought not to sit.

Ambitious collectors in this field go in for super musical boxes which are really automata. There are singing-bird boxes which spring at you and warble merrily; there are boxes with dancing dolls, monkey bandsmen, marching soldiers on a fort, and all kinds of figures which do many kinds of things for as long as you keep them wound up.

But if you are going in for musical boxes it seems to me that you ought to concentrate on the music. If an old player-piano addict, you can find 'fortepiano' boxes which play loudly and softly at will, having two combs manipulated by a revolving cylinder. There are others which have built-in flutes, to say nothing of drums and bells, whistles and castanets.

Music Covers

In the days before we sold our pianos and bought gramophones (itself a word which now dates one sadly) there was generally a large quantity of sheet music in a house, usually ranging all the way from Spohr to Marie Lloyd and from five-finger exercises through 'Rustle of Spring' to 'K-K-Katy'. Now is the time to see if there is yet a pile of

them in the attic (better still in grandpa's attic)–for they have become collector's pieces.

Like the record 'sleeves' of today the covers of old sheet music announce its contents in some way or another, sometimes in tasteful copperplate, sometimes in vivid illustration.

I find it fascinating to turn over a pile of them in a dealer's shop for they give a wonderful picture of the social life and sentiment of their day. Here you will find the famous stars of music hall, opera and ballet, celebrities of the music hall with their favourite songs ('Champagne Charlie', 'Burlington Bertie', 'Polly Perkins' and the rest), romantic mountain landscapes illustrating some long forgotten song, stirring marches accompanied by battle scenes, historic occasions like the coming of the railways (there was an 'Express Polka' around 1850).

One-colour printing, but unmistakable 'twenties typography for 'Chloe, Song of the Swamp', 1927 (Francis, Day & Hunter Limited)

Some of these covers, especially those associated with romantic ballet of the mid nineteenth century, were also issued as prints for framing–and indeed you may come across actual titles which have been cut down for that purpose (they also appear in scrapbooks).

If you go for illustrated covers, your period starts about 1830, and here you have to look around the European antique shops and printsellers, for illustration on the Continent seems to have been somewhat ahead of English practice. The artists usually signed their work, and among the earliest of the names is the Italian-born Maxim Gauci. One of the pioneers of this medium was T. H. Jones who etched charming little vignettes and also worked with coloured woodblocks.

With the blossoming of colour lithography in the 1830s and 1840s, we began to find the work of prolific illustrators like John Brandard, who specialized in opera and ballet, Alfred Concanen, whose world was the popular music hall, Augustus Butler, who did many military titles, and Alexandre Laby, a Frenchman noted for his romantic backgrounds to ballads and religious music.

Here again is one of those subjects where you can collect on two levels–by haunting the shops which specialize in these things, or by ferreting around in places where *caches* may well still be lying awaiting their knowledgeable discoverer.

Nailsea

This is a term, like 'Battersea' enamels, which is misleading only if you accept it as a guaranteed indication of origin. There are three or four types of glass known in the trade as 'Nailsea', but probably far more of it was made in other centres, like nearby Bristol, Stourbridge, Birmingham, Newcastle and York, than ever came from this Somerset village.

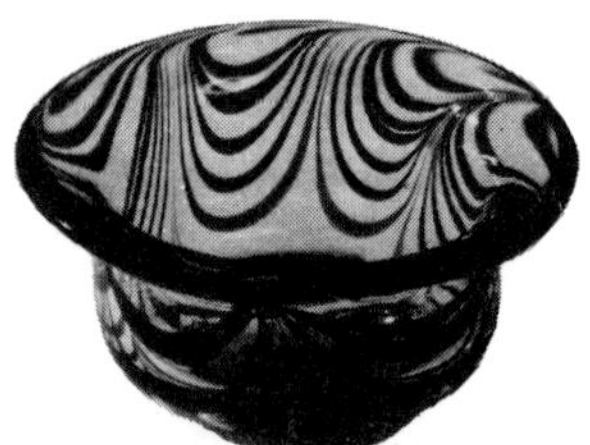

Blue-green Nailsea bowl, c. 1820 (Pilkington Glass Museum)

Glassmaking at Nailsea seems to have started when a Bristol brewer founded a bottle factory there. Clear glass was heavily taxed during the Napoleonic Wars and the factory hit on the bright idea of making decorative items out of the ordinary greeny-brown glass they used for bottles, which was taxed at only a fraction of the rate on clear glass, also the celebrated ROLLING PINS, flasks and other items, no doubt mainly sold as 'fairings' in markets.

Another sort of Nailsea is typified by flasks in clear glass striped with pink or yellow in what is known as a *latticinio* style. People think this style was brought to Nailsea by French glassblowers imported by the owners of the factory. Then there is a whole range of things, some of them described under GLASS TOYS, candlesticks, coaching horns, shepherd's crooks, tobacco pipes and BELLS in various colours.

But remember that glassblowing skill is still about, and there is no doubt that many of the 'Nailsea' items you see have never themselves seen either Nailsea or the nineteenth century.

Needle and Thread

Rummage about in old workboxes and you will find many interesting little items to collect. First there are small thread-winders, predecessors of the reel, used for winding on silk when it came in skeins. There are spindles divided by discs, for the same purpose, sometimes with a hollow shaft for needles. Some attractive work went into cotton barrels of ivory, bone or wood, with a hole where the thread came out. Boxes were made for several reels, each with its own thread-hole.

My favourites are those needlecases, long and slender, with a tiny glass at the top which, when put to the eye, show you a view at the seaside or wherever it was. Some of these come in the form of bellows, rolling pins, parasols and even figures.

As for thimbles, collecting these will take you all round the world and through all the centuries. All kinds of metal ones abound, of course, even in PEWTER, but you also find them in enamels, bone china, MOTHER OF PEARL and leather. Look out too for the presentation boxes they came in, often of tortoiseshell or ivory.

Thread-winders, cotton barrels, ivory silk-winder and needlecase (above *and* below)

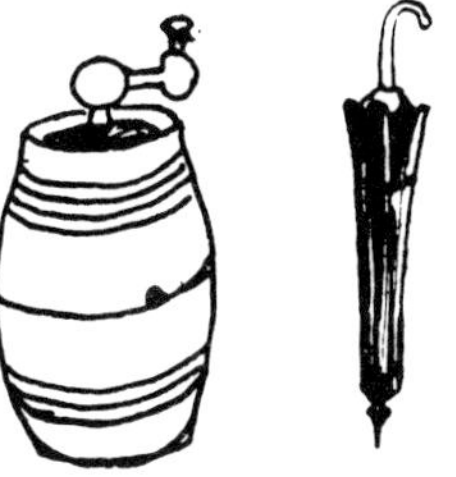

Niello

This is a form of decoration on silver in which the lines cut in the design are filled with an alloy of silver, copper, lead and sulphur, which is fused and then polished. Some wonderful work in this way has been done all down the ages, especially in Italy of the fifteenth century, and later in Russia, especially the work of the well-known Tula factory in the nineteenth century.

Odd pieces of this sometimes turn up at sales; I recently saw a pretty little box in the shape of a pumpkin with stalk, leaves and flowers, all worked with niello, sold for a few pounds. It may interest you to know that the first line engravings were paper proofs taken off early niello work.

Nightlights

Once upon a time, when we were very small and frightened of the dark, it was pleasant to have a light by one's bedside, soft enough to let our eyes droop, bright enough to let us have the comfort of falling asleep with our eyes on the familiar things in the room.

In the junk shops you will find plenty of these survivors of the days before bedside switches. There are those in blue and white Chinese porcelains, their light coming through grilles which throw marvellous patterns on the ceiling, moving and writhing in a draught. There are those in Staffordshire pottery in the shape of COTTAGES AND CASTLES, which are now becoming expensive–and so being reproduced for us. There a·e stands in solid silver, complete with an extinguisher and glass shade; and, by contrast, there is one I have which is in tin and looks like a miniature lighthouse.

Much sought after now are all those small affairs in different sorts of decorative glass. The Price company of Battersea made one they dramatically called 'The Burglar's Horror', but other firms, like Palmer's and Samuel Clarke, used a more tender kind of customer appeal by marketing brands with names like 'Glowworm' and 'Fairylite'. I have a tiny one bearing Clarke's name on the base, and the shade is in NAILSEA stripes which give a delightful effect. I have also seen larger ones, globular in shape, and in clear coloured glass, satin glass, Queen's Burmese glass, Bristol blue, turquoise and green 'vaseline' glass. I have even seen, from the days before luminous dials, nightlight clocks with a little sand for the candle, and a leather case for taking it on a journey.

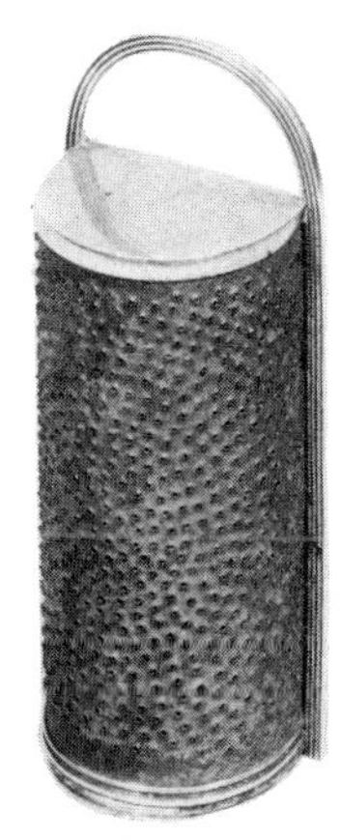

A mid 19th-century silver nutmeg grater (Christies, South Kensington)

Nutmeg Graters

Another small silver collectable–even smaller than the MUFFINEER.

This was not used at muffin time, but later in the evening, when there was hot toddy in the punch bowl or mulled wine by the fireside; or perhaps when you were at a ball or

a rout and your lady wished to spice her glass of custard or some other sweetmeat.

Essentially a nutmeg grater is a box containing a nutmeg and a small grater. It came in a variety of materials–wood, bone, ivory, pewter, brass, silver or Sheffield plate.

From this basic requirement, however, the makers employed much ingenuity in devising shapes for them–they came in the form of eggs, walnuts, urns, acorns and even maces. There is a pun in this last for a mace was not only something carried by a civic dignitary in a procession but also a spice made from the outer rind of the nutmeg.

The earliest of the silver graters date from about 1700, but there are hallmarks from 1760 down to Victorian times.

18th-century iron grille

Old Implements

If you take an old working implement away from its normal setting you will be struck by the interest and strangeness of its shape. When considered in this way a really old three-handled hayfork, a thin-tined muck fork, a long-bladed ditching spade, a wooden grain shovel and a curved wooden milkmaid's yoke all take on an astonishing character not to be found in contemporary tools of the sort. So people are discovering that, in the right context, these things are electing themselves into material for decorating walls. I have seen country tea-serving barns and town expresso bars with walls left rough and crossed and broken up with the fascinating lines and arabesques of iron and wood provided by these old implements. Those who like to shove furniture around frequently will have their chance here; they can ring the changes to suit the mood of new purchases.

It need hardly be said that the place to find these things is the old farm building, the darkest corner of the blacksmith's shop, the derelict farm or cottage garden, the old mills and warehouses of country towns. Look, too, for those rotting wagons which in some parts of Britain still lie where a Home Guard thirty-odd years ago put them in readiness to confound the invader. There are lovely pieces of wood still unrotted, and fine shapes of ironwork.

A penny-farthing bicycle is perhaps not an implement, but it hangs on a wall beautifully among all those straight lines. So do all those HALBERDS AND PARTISANS.

Below, from left: *A yoke still in use quite recently by the 'milkmaid' if we are to judge by the plastic buckets (S. H. Cole); A diunial lantern used to create dissolving views on the screen; Early 19th-century Post Office waywiser (both Christies, South Kensington)*

Old Scientific Instruments

By this I mean those relics of our scientific or mechanical past which have successively been superseded. The fact has been noted in the preceding paragraph that once a thing gets out of date its strangeness interests us, but it is also a fact that many pieces of early equipment, such as engines, carriages, mills and the like have an extraordinary beauty and simplicity of design. It is true that many of them, built in mid-Victorian times, are often embellished with the sort of ornament you might expect to find on temples rather than pieces of machinery. At the Great Exhibition of 1851 there was a cotton machine engine in the Ancient Egyptian style with a front rather like the Carreras building in London: another managed to find room among the wheels and pistons for some very tasty Gothic arches.

In the Science Museum in London you will find a table lathe showing as many rococo curlicues as ever graced the MIRROR frames of the period. On the other hand, some spinning wheels are as tasteful of, say, Hepplewhite, as you will ever expect to find. I find myself fascinated, too, with the lovely workmanship and delicacy of portable sundials and compasses in ivory and brass; of equinoctial ring dials, miniature globes, astrolobes, small orreries showing the movement of the earth, sun, moon and planets, shagreen spyglasses, old telescopes and microscopes, beautifully chased and engraved mathematical and draughtsmen's instruments. There are perpetual pocket calendars in silver and brass, bearing dates from the eighteenth century; hour-glasses in octagonal stands or cylindrical brass cases; quadrants, sextants and octants and many other fine examples of early navigational instruments.

A thaumatrope (Pollock's Toy Museum)

Among the optical instruments one may come across zograscopes for viewing prints, 'Claude Lorraine' mirrors which enable you to see your subject in tones rather than colours if you wish to paint a landscape like an Old Master; magic lanterns and kaleidoscopes; the Camera Lucida for drawing objects in perspective or changing the scale of drawings; and a whole host of optical curiosities of the last century with strange-sounding Greek names–like the Phenakistiscope and the Thaumatrope which operated on the principle of the persistence of vision to create the effect of moving pictures.

There are all sorts of instruments for measuring and weighing, like miniature sets of scales and weights in fishkin cases; pinchbeck pedometers for measuring how far you have walked and dynamometers for showing the strength of your grip; all kinds of dipping, surveying and gauging instruments; and the delightfully named waywiser, perambulator or hodometer, a wheel with a diameter of thirty inches, with a dial attached, which you push along and measure distances in miles, furlongs, poles and yards.

Oriental Department

Seventy or eighty years ago every big department store had one of these and in it, massed for inspection, you would find those exotic things now sitting in lonely splendour among junk of other lands.

Elsewhere in this book will be found the better quality BENARES and BIDRI WORK and the MORADABAD WARE. But here you have the Damascus brass jardinières for the aspidistra in the suburban parlour window, in lacquered *repoussé* work: they came in all sizes, from three inches in diameter to fourteen inches or more. There are also tray-stands from Cairo in carved and stained walnut, bearing large brass trays, and there are those inlaid Syrian stools with ivory, and decorated with little bobbins arranged in patterns; I have a magazine stand and a pot stand of this ware.

Japanese draught screens are, one supposes, a hangover from the craze for *japonaiserie* in the 1870s and 1880s, but there they are with their gold embroidery on black or richly coloured grounds, or painted on light linen with landscape designs. For the dining-room there were those with heavy embossed paper panels. Still in the Japanese corner there are blue and white porcelain teapots with wicker handles, LACQUER glove and handkerchief boxes, TEA CADDIES, trinket boxes and a wealth of small carvings and figures in IVORY. The junk paper sunshades, FANS, handscreens and joss sticks could just as well have come from China, while the carved sandalwood boxes presumably came from India, but very little of the BAMBOO one still sees around has actually come from the Orient.

Ormolu

Before the Second World War a dealer had to work really hard to get a decent price for an ormolu clock, or indeed any sort of furniture so decorated. Nowadays they are looking for it and it doesn't stay in the shops very long. This isn't very surprising, really, for contemporary painters and sculptors have made us appreciate interesting textures–and ormolu certainly has that. It also has the ability to acquire a deep and rich patina. *Real* ormolu, that is, and here we ought, perhaps, to try to get down to brass tacks in more senses than one.

For it should be noted that what we in Britain call 'ormolu' is quite a different affair from the French *or moulu*, that is to say, gold ground down to a fine powder and used in

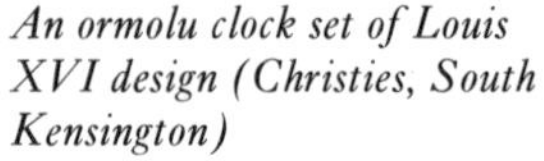
An ormolu clock set of Louis XVI design (Christies, South Kensington)

a mercury amalgam for gilding. In fact the French word describes the gilding on the article; whereas the anglicized version of it refers to the piece itself–usually brass covered with a lacquer gilding. But there *was* good English ormolu, even if it never quite had the finish of the French.

Today you can find odd lamp brackets, waiting for the interior decorator to snap them up, or furniture fittings such as drawer handles, table feet and castors, curtain fittings and bas-reliefs.

If you want real ormolu, of course, you must learn to find your way through the maze of Victorian lacquered and gilded brass alloys. How? The usual way, I'm afraid: either by buying your experience or by taking a first-class dealer into your confidence.

Ornamental Leadwork

In the better class of breaker's yard–which one can commend too often to readers of this book–there may sometimes be found examples of architectural leadwork.

You will not, I hope, expect to find these articles very cheaply priced, for lead itself is nowadays almost as valuable as silver, quite apart from the historic interest and artistry of the articles themselves.

Yet it is difficult to imagine any piece of exterior furnishing which could lend greater distinction to a nice house, large or small, than cisterns, rainwater pipes and pipeheads of sheet lead, moulded with a date or a design. The nineteenth-century French architect, Viollet-le-Duc, reminded us that leadwork (or 'plumbing' as it was then called) borrowed nothing from stone or wood, but was like colossal goldsmith's work.

Leaden pipe head.

The sketch here of one of the more modest types of cistern and pipehead is based on one shown in the little book, *Leadwork: Old and Ornamental and for the most part English*, produced in 1893 by that knowledgeable writer W. R. Lethaby. In a country house the place for your cistern–if the piping system permits it–is beside your front door, as at Poundisford Park near Taunton: in town it goes in a courtyard or down in the front area.

The cast ornament on them includes flowers, fruit, baskets of fruit, stags, dolphins, cherubs' heads, gods like Bacchus and Ceres, and family crests or coats of arms: there are often dates as well.

It is only in Britain apparently that decorated pipeheads are to be found. Some have angles jutting out into salients which, as you may have noticed on going to old stately homes, make excellent nesting places for birds.

Palissy Ware

I have often wondered who buys these strange wall PLAQUES crawling with lizards, crabs, insects, snakes and embellished with moss made from shredded clay. Finer dust-traps it would be difficult to conceive, but they go as regularly as they appear.

Apparently most of them came from Portugal early in this century, but similar wares were made by Frederick Thomas Mitchell at Rye in Sussex in the late nineteenth century.

Such things had a beginning in the work of Bernard Palissy, a French potter of the sixteenth century, so absorbed in his craft that he thought nothing of breaking up his furniture for fuel if he had a really important batch of jobs in a firing.

There is another kind of Palissy ware which has also been imitated in England, especially at Minton's, using their famous MAJOLICA glazes. These are usually large dishes and plaques with classical figures, ornamented rims in relief and in fine glazes of green, blue, yellow and red. If you want colour in pottery here it is: the type was a sensation when it appeared at the Great Exhibition in 1851. (See page 5 for a fine example of this ware.)

Papier Mâché

I remember once as a child being absolutely spellbound by the sight of a large tray in a shop window. I suppose it was an antique shop, but in those days I wouldn't have known. Anyway, there was this tray, which was jet black, and in the centre of it a beautiful painting of an abbey or a church.

For me it was something right out of the middle of a novel by Scott, for the windows glowed with a pinkish light on one side of the tower and a greenish one on the other. Obviously, one window was reflecting the light of the moon, while the other showed the glow of a fireplace. Who could be sitting at that fireplace? What was going on behind that window?

Little did I know it but the tray was made of papier mâché and no doubt it was going begging for a pound or less.

From the eighteenth century up to mid-Victorian times, this highly popular material was used for furniture of all types, not only trays but screens, WORKBOXES, writing cases, vases and even chairs, tables and cabinets. Many of them are beautifully painted in oil colours, sometimes with views, sometimes with flowers or *chinoiseries*. Long after seeing my tray I discovered that my two glowing windows were not actually MOTHER OF PEARL, as my elders then told me, but nautilus shell, pressed into the oil of the painting before it dried.

Trays seem to have survived in greater numbers than anything else, except perhaps for workboxes. Probably this is because of late years they will have been used for ornament rather than carrying things. Most papier mâché items seen in antique or junk shops are in need of repair, but it seems that 'the trade' has resources for putting this right.

Below left: *A Victorian papier mâché painted tray (Christies, South Kensington)*

Above right: *A Parian bust of William Henry Goss, c. 1880, made by Goss (City Museum and Art Gallery, Stoke-on-Trent)*

Parian

Statuesque white ladies, sometimes in flimsy draperies, sometimes with none on at all, but always contriving to cloak themselves with an air of mid-Victorian modesty, are outstanding examples of Parian ware.

It emerged in the 1840s as an attempt to recreate the wonderful unglazed biscuit porcelain of Derby. Both Copeland and Minton were separately engaged in the search for statuary porcelain, as they at first called it, and they eventually named it after the marble from the Greek island of Paros. Wedgwood made a version they called Carrara ware, after the famous Italian marble, while ADAMS, DAVENPORT, Worcester, GOSS and Ridgeway also joined in the fun.

What Parian did was to bring classical or neo-classical style statuary, such as was being made all over Europe at that time, down to a size that would fit into the middle-class drawing-room. Famous pieces like Hiram Powers' 'Greek Slave' were best sellers, as were the various versions of Venus. My own specimen of it is Minton's version of 'Dorothea', the character from *Don Quixote* dressed (only just) as a shepherd, for which I paid seven pounds in the 1950s. A decade later I saw a similar example going for almost half that sum, so either I paid too much or the price had slumped. Needless to say the market value of Parian has since risen quite sharply again.

Types of Parian in the shops today include, first, these statues, sometimes bearing the name of the sculptor, sometimes marked with that of Benjamin Cheverton, which means that the figure was reduced from the full size by means of the machine which he invented; second, there are some quite charming figures and groups of children; third, a whole range of portrait busts, either of classical figures or men and women of the day, all varying greatly in size, from a few inches to several feet. There are also PLAQUES, perhaps the most frequently met with being the famous pair 'Night' and 'Morning' by Thorvaldsen.

Sometimes Parian is tinted–I have seen large figures in a pleasant pale green–while in others the white Parian biscuit porcelain is set off by a glazed background.

There is a good deal of picking over to be done in this field. If a great deal of Parian is apt to be mawkish and sentimental, there is some which is very good; and with the best of it one always has to admire the quality of the material and the excellent craftsmanship of the modellers.

Pearl Ware

Some years ago I found in a pile of plates a large heavy one with a bluish glaze. It had a Chinese pattern under the glaze, and at first I thought it was in fact Chinese porcelain; but on turning it over I saw it was marked 'pearl ware' together with an indecipherable and unidentifiable monogram.

This heavy earthenware, strengthened with flint and white clay, was originally developed by Josiah Wedgwood as an improved sort of CREAMWARE and at first, since the intention was to imitate the pearly colour of nautilus shells, only enough cobalt was used to counteract the cream of the ware, resulting in a greenish tinge. But other Staffordshire potters, and also those in Leeds, used much more cobalt, with the very bluish result shown in my plate.

Pearl ware was used not only for dinner services, but also for jugs, CANDLESTICKS and toilet sets. There were also figures on square bases in the same bluish glaze. Some of them were made by Neale. Spode's mark appears on pearl ware, and so does Davenport's.

Peasant Pottery

As collector's quarry this department of ceramics still offers wide scope–which we sadly need in an age when so many interesting items are soaring out of our reach.

What exactly is 'peasant pottery'? It could be called 'folk', an expression we seem shy of using in Britain but which is used both in Europe and in America.

First, it is certainly not primitive pottery, the art of savages, or of a society which knows nothing better. The kind of pottery we are talking about is made and bought in countries where there are also those sophisticated wares preferred by a cultivated minority. Sometimes the makers of the peasant wares do echo the more polite styles, but usually long after these have gone out of fashion, and often in wild and unconscious parody of them. They may sometimes seem crude, but they have a lively naïve fancy, show a natural love of colour, and have clearly been made for use. They are also as different as they could be from the modern studio imitations of them made by people who are not peasants.

The English pot fancier venturing among the vast range of Continental wares of this kind will at first be struck by the many similarities in the work of widely separated countries, also between them and some of the more provincial English and Scottish wares. If, for example, there is nothing quite so crude there (except on the contemporary Netherlands DELFTWARE) as the portraits which appeared on the English blue-dash chargers of the late seventeenth century, the graceful dashing strokes of the

Peasant pottery plates, from top: *Alsace, Moravia, Kellinghusen*

flowers on Kellinghusen (Holstein) faience look astonishingly akin to the painting on English and Welsh HARVEST JUGS AND BOTTLES and even the roses on Staffordshire saltglaze STONEWARE.

See page 115 for sketches of plates from Moravia in Czechoslovakia, Sarreguimines in Alsace and Kellinghusen in Holstein. But do not delay if you want to find specimens of these wares, for they are rapidly disappearing.

Perambulators and Push Carts

'Small Galloper' push chair

If you want to give your larger infants something which they can satisfyingly feel no other children will have, look carefully around the junk sheds for old perambulators, go-carts and even tradesmen's push carts.

I know an antique shop window where can be seen a perambulator of about the 1840s, with a canopy on top which makes it look so exactly like the surrey 'with the fringe on top' of *Oklahoma* that one wonders if that early American vehicle derived itself from an emigrating version. The dealer, of course, like another mentioned elsewhere, will not sell it because he finds it a wonderful attraction in his window. But neither will he clean it and paint it, which I find a very dog-in-the-manger attitude. Newly gilt, these Victorian baby carriages look enchantingly like the grown-up carriages of that day, just as a little earlier than that the children looked like miniature versions of an adult.

But perambulators are not the only quarry for the person who likes restoring things to their original glory or enamel and gilt. There is a place in London behind the stucco façade of a terrace, where in a stable a man is carefully renovating those little baker's and other tradesmen's handcarts which used to be pushed around the streets. They make splendid toy caravans, which can be fitted up inside for dolls, or can even be turned into little sedan chairs. So don't only peer into junk sheds; look in the outhouses of friendly butchers and bakers and candlestickmakers.

If you want some guidance in your restoration work I would refer you to a little book, published about 1880 and entitled *The Coach Painter's Hand Book and Guide* 'by a Coach Painter of Thirty Years' experience'; and although the book is studded with references to a certain deceased manufacturer's paint and varnish (it seems to have been an early example of a 'sponsored' book), there is no doubt that the author knew his stuff, and won't let you skimp your job. Apart from priming, painting, rubbing, facing, varnishing, flatting and JAPANNING, he discourses on the proper treatment of leather-covered carriages, basket carriages and wickerwork, writing, scrolling and ornamenting–and also gives you hints on how you would paint a locomotive engine if you owned one.

Pewter

A pewter 'tappit hen' (Christies, South Kensington)

This famous and popular alloy of tin and other metals is one of those fields which you can pass by for years–and then suddenly get interested and become a fanatic.

It isn't, I believe, bought so much by the general public as, say, fifty years ago, probably because of the decline in oak, with which it goes magnificently–having, so to speak, grown up with it. But to judge by the prices asked by specialist dealers, there is certainly no lack of collectors to pay high prices for interesting pieces from the eighteenth century and earlier.

So far as our junk shop quest is concerned, except by strokes of real luck, we will have to limit ourselves to early Victorian wares, such as the measures and drinking pots, the inkwells and mustard pots, casters and peppers, spoons, feeding cups and chimney ornaments, small toys, tobacco jars, pipe stoppers, SNUFFBOXES and the rest. Even the 'Tudric' pewterware produced by Liberty's in the early decades of this century has become much sought after, with the recent interest in ART NOUVEAU.

If you are going to look out for measures, you have a whole range of shapes to sort out, from the early balusters to the straight-sided Victorian ones. In collecting these you can learn a good deal about excise matters, for they were constantly being tested and stamped. I have a half-pint pot which bears marks from 1840 right through to 1857–did it go into honourable retirement after that?

A 'Tudric Ware' biscuit tin by Liberty, c. 1900

Some collectors like the tankards bearing the names of inns and public houses. About 1960 I picked up a parcel of pewter items for three pounds and this included one of the capstan-type inkwells, two great quart pots bearing the names of pubs at Sheerness and Deptford, another attractive but unidentifiable mug with a silver-style handle, a pint pot from the 'Bricklayers Arms, Fairfield Road' (where?), also a small pot marked 'James Dixon and Sons, E.P.B.M.'

This last carries a warning. Anything marked 'Dixon' and most items marked 'Sheffield' with a number, are not pewter, but BRITANNIA METAL, a substitute which had no lead in it and tended to follow the styles of silver and SHEFFIELD PLATE rather than of pewter itself. Later in its history this metal was even plated–hence 'E.P.B.M.' which stands for electro-plated Britannia metal.

A word about the appearance of pewter. Some people like it in the dull grey colour it falls into without cleaning, and feel that to put a bright polish on it is to make it ape silver. But in fact the colour and appearance of cleaned pewter is nothing like that of silver: it is a far more mellow and subtle, especially when seen in firelight. So my view is, give your pewter a good clean when you get it, then keep it up by a good washing and rubbing every few months. Some recommend using a very soft abrasive powder (i.e. one that doesn't scratch) and plenty of elbow grease, so as to keep the fine patina which old pewter picks up in the same way as old furniture. Of course, if a piece is badly oxidized, only acid will serve, but if I were sufficiently fond of a piece to want to get it up into good condition I would prefer to hand the work over to an expert.

Pewter made in recent times contains much less lead–it is limited by law to not more than 10 per cent, which gives it a totally different look and feel from some of the older alloys, with anything up to 40 per cent of lead. Put two specimens together and you will have no trouble in distinguishing them.

If you should come across some really old pewter and wish to identify pewterers' touch marks, then I would refer you to the various books written in recent years by Ronald F. Michaelis on the subject.

Photographic Pottery

I don't know if this is the official term to describe china and earthenware decorated with photographic transfers, but the process has certainly been going long enough for such pieces to find their way into junk shops.

One series often found is 'Royal Vistas' ware. There are milk jugs, very tall water jugs, mugs and other items in a white ware covered by a very distinctive yellow-brown glaze, with gilding on the rim. The pictures are in black under this glaze and although the mark claims that they are 'from Paintings by Various Artists' these are undoubtedly photographed rather than engraved. Moreover, the paintings are accompanied by ordinary photographed views. The series bears the mark of Ridgeway's pottery with their crown, but it must surely be after the firm was taken over in 1859 by Brown, Westhead and Moore, a firm which also had a great deal to do with colour printing of POTLIDS.

The reference books aren't much help with this sort of ware, so the interested collector will have to find his own way. As with the early ceramic lithography, it could be a very interesting one–and still relatively cheap to indulge.

Pictures without Paint

If you wanted to you could fill an entire house with pictures which are neither oil paintings nor watercolours nor prints, nor even reproductions.

Some of these fall into definite categories and you will find them scattered about this book under their various titles–FEATHER PICTURES, PIN-PRICKED PICTURES, SAILORS' NEEDLEWORK PICTURES, SAND PICTURES and TINSEL PICTURES. There are also pictures in wood veneers that come under the heading of MARQUETRY. Some kinds of picture in this category, however, such as straw marquetry done by French prisoners of war in the Napoleonic period, could never have been classified as junk and these fragile rarities have long commanded very high prices.

The hair picture is presumably a rather melancholy offshoot of hair jewellery: in this case strands of hair are arranged as though they were lines in a drawing; there are lots of weeping willows and urns and tombstones, all in the manner of 'Charlotte Weeping at the Tomb of Werther' found on jasperware.

The leaf picture had some well-known exponents in the same botanizing age which produced the Victorian flower print–among them Lady Dorothy Nevill, who not only made them but corresponded about them with Sir William Hooker, the famous Director of the Royal Botanical Gardens at Kew.

Full instructions for making them are given in Cassell's *Household Guide* for 1875. What these ladies did, apparently, was to gather leaves in July (Lady Dorothy preferred the *Ficus religiosa*, but poplar and aspen were also in favour, as well as apple, pear and some of the ivies.) They were cleaned with a hard brush and placed in a pan filled with rainwater. The pan was exposed to the sun and air for several weeks, when the soft fleshy part of the leaves decayed, leaving the skeletons, and it was these that made up the picture.

The MOTHER OF PEARL picture appeared in the age of the rococo and nothing could be more rococo of course than shell. There are some pictures in existence which were executed for Frederick the Great of Prussia, which consist principally of an oil painting on copper with the highlights made up in relief with very thin scales of mother of pearl so that they overlap, rather like the scales of a fish. These particular figures look rather like Cockney pearly kings and queen, and are a distant relative of the TINSEL PICTURE.

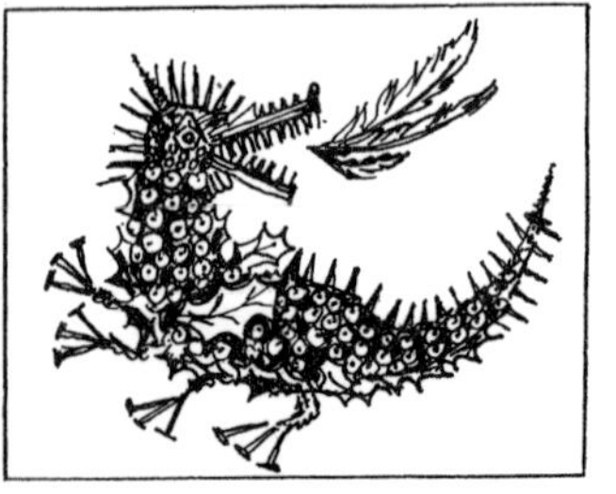
Picture of a dragon in nails and holly

But the craft of the Picture without Paint still flourishes. A few years ago the journal *Farmer's Weekly* ran a competition for making these things, and some remarkable examples turned up. For instance, the picture that won first prize was a mosaic built up out of little scraps, about the size of a postage stamp, of brilliantly coloured fabric. Another was a very lively and beautifully drawn dragon–drawn, I say, but the outline was made up of nails, drawing pins, staples and dead holly leaves. What was particularly interesting was that these spiky sort of materials were so admirably suited to the subject of the picture.

Another pleasant feature of some of these pictures is the way they combine one material with another; for example, I once saw a leaping horse made in straw, but the mane was in white feather and the whole thing was mounted on a moss-green velvet background. In recent years Pictures without Paint have become all the rage–as witness those pictures of vintage cars made up of pieces of old watches, the spiral effects created from weaving silver wire round a pattern of nails on a black board, steel plates cut into fantastic shapes with an oxy-acetylene torch, and the enormous field of collages that combine all manner of materials from old bus tickets and press-cuttings to scraps of cloth and dried flowers and ferns.

Damaged examples of this kind of picture often put one off; and it is true that if the background has worn, as it often does, of course, with the silk pictures, then there is quite a problem. You may almost have to start again. But quite often a little ingenious repair work and cleaning will make the world of difference to a picture: sometimes it is only a matter of cutting them down and reframing them.

Pig Jugs

Once upon a time it was the custom to drink the health of a bride and bridegroom out of a 'hogshead' of ale. This was made possible for ordinary mortals by using a 'hogshead' which was actually the cover of a jug made in the likeness of a pig. The same notion of a cup-cover is to be found in BEAR JUGS.

The only pig jugs–as distinct from piggy banks–I know are the ones once made in Sussex. First, there is the traditional sort made in redware: its distinctive feature is that its ears and nose were long enough so that the cup would stand three-leggedly on the table. These are very rare now, dating probably from the early nineteenth century, so if you should find one in a cottage, do not be mean about it.

The second sort, considerably smaller in size, were made later in the century at Rye in Sussex rustic ware.

Pilgrim Bottle

This is a shape which has interested potters down the ages almost as much as the GOURD.

Worcester pilgrim bottle, c. 1870

No need to question, one supposes, that it stems from the leather bottles carried by Pilgrims to shrines in the East, and that an early necessity was an arrangement whereby the thing could be slung over your shoulder, or suspended from the belt: hence the two holes on either side of the mouth.

The earliest I have seen is one in a brown-glazed STONEWARE in the British Museum: it dates from T'ang days or earlier, i.e. well over a thousand years ago. The latest was made from slag, or what its makers, Sowerby of Newcastle upon Tyne, called 'vitro porcelain', that blue ware made in the late nineteenth century which makes such a good price today. These flasks are usually impressed with a scene from a fairy tale or nursery rhyme.

In between these, the bottle turns up in early Ming blue and white–the Chinese call it the 'precious moon' vase–and the flattened sides were admirably suited to the *Istoriato* painting of Urbino, practised on Italian maiolica from Renaissance times onward. Horace Walpole had a magnificent example decorated in the manner of Raphael which afterwards passed into the Marryat collection.

Enormous ornate versions are found in German *Edelzinn* or 'noble pewter', but it is unlikely that these (or even Horace Walpole's) were ever taken on a pilgrimage–any more than the one in Sussex ware of about 1794, now in the Victoria and Albert Museum, the owner of which had inscribed on it:

> *'Oceans of Brandy*
> *and Rivers of Wine,*
> *Plantacions of Tea and a garle*
> *To my Mind'.*

Anyway it would have been a different kind of pilgrimage.

Coalport, in the course of imitating the wares and even the marks of Sèvres, Chelsea, Meissen and other factories, produced about 1850 some brilliantly coloured pilgrim bottles with imitation Japanese marks. Moore Brothers of Longton made them in MAJOLICA while Worcester used the shape in their *japonaiserie* wares.

All these, of course, merely use the form for its decorative quality, but in the early nineteenth century the Sussex potteries produced them in brown and cream glazed earthenware, not so much to go on pilgrimages to shrines, as to carry spirits home from the pub. Perhaps the most expensive sort of pilgrim flask you can buy is that produced by Minton in the last century in dark blue china, carrying the extraordinary painstaking *pâte-sur-pâte* decoration evolved by Marc Louis Solon, whereby figures and entire groups were built up in relief by brush strokes of a slip paste.

Pinchbeck

How appropriately named is this 'poor man's gold', invented by Christopher Pinchbeck (1670–1732), a London maker of watches and other items.

A warm gold colour, it does not usually tarnish, and is often found on small boxes, on Georgian and early Victorian jewellery, lockets and frames for portrait miniatures. It was an alloy of copper and zinc and it was gradually superseded by low-carat gold. But it has a charm of its own and is well worth hunting for.

An early 19th-century pincusion with the poignant slogan 'Bless the Babe and Spare the Mother' (The Museum of London)

Pincushions

There was a day when we were all held together by pins, and that was also the day of the decorative pincushion. These are still about, often with their tender messages for happy expectant mothers: 'Bless the Babe and spare the Mother'–a grim reminder this, perhaps, of days when motherhood was a major risk. The same thought is expressed in

Welcome little innocent
Welcome to the light of day
Smile upon thy happy mother
Smile and chase her fears away.

They also came in different shapes, sometimes as hearts (from sailor friends and admirers), sometimes diamonds, while much more ambitious were those in the shape of little coaches, spinets, bellows and animals, made up with two solid sides of wood, or MOTHER OF PEARL, IVORY or metal.

A late 18th-century, French, pin-pricked picture of a gentleman with painted face, hair and gloves (Christies, South Kensington)

Pin-pricked Pictures

If you are wandering among the smaller shops in European towns you may come across a picture which seems to be made up of lots of tiny little holes and a wash of watercolour.

This is another of our PICTURES WITHOUT PAINT. The subjects often show a religious theme or figure of a saint with flowers and foliage around him or her; but sometimes also they depict ordinary people going about their work. I believe that a great many of the religious ones were once made in convents, but it seems also that this pin-pricked picture was one of the favourite ladies' occupations all through the eighteenth and nineteenth centuries.

The job seems to have been done first by drawing an outline on a piece of paper which preferably had a groundwork of some opaque colour to throw up the highlights. Then you drew in the faces, the hands and feet, and other coloured features like ribbons in watercolour and mounted the whole sheet on a few sheets of blotting paper of cloth. You now pierced the outline of the figure with a toothed wheel having sharp points; other details could be filled in by pricking with large and small pins. There also seems to have been a kind of embossing and chasing effect, rather as in metal; to achieve this it seems that they turned the picture over and made holes through from the back.

The poet William Cowper seems to have known all about this little craft. In his 'Lines on the receipt of my mother's picture' he implores time to restore the hours:

'When playing with thy vesture's tissued flowers
The violet, the pink, the jessamine
I prick them into paper with a pin.'

Pipe Cases

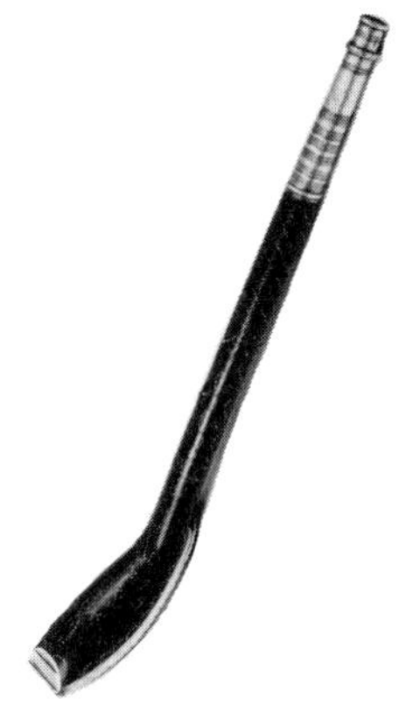

A silver mounted wooden pipe case, c. 1810 (Christies, South Kensington)

When you took your 'clay' along to an evening session with friends or on a coach journey, it was the easiest thing in the world to break it and find yourself without the means of having a smoke. You therefore carried it in a pipe case, which might be a quite plain affair or something very special, with fine wood carving.

The former kind probably because of their plainness, have mostly been thrown away or burnt, but many of the latter have been preserved; and although they take some finding they offer yet another example of the excellent work which once went into the making of articles of everyday use.

Cases of the seventeenth century have tapering, sliding shutters on the underside; but when pipes began to acquire a 'spur' at the bottom of the bowl, for holding or resting on a table, the sliding shutter gave place to an arrangement whereby the case 'bowl' had a hinged lid.

It is difficult to assign these carved cases to a particular country, but the more elaborate of them come mostly from the Netherlands, Austria and France.

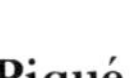

Piqué

Late 18th-century piqué case

Note well the accent over the 'e' in this word, for no sort of pique attaches to this entirely delightful method of decorating what the auctioneers usually call objects of *vertu*–and we think of as pretty things of which we just want to have as many as possible.

Piqué is a method of decorating tortoiseshell, MOTHER OF PEARL and IVORY objects, such as trinket boxes, SNUFFBOXES, BONBONNIÈRES, etuis, trays, POSY HOLDERS and cane handles with gold and silver inlay. *Piqué point* is when the inlay is made up of little points of metal; *piqué clouté* uses larger points or 'nails' arranged in a pattern; while *piqué posé* is where the metal is laid on in flat cut-out shapes.

Either way, the work of the French and English craftsmen of the eighteenth century is quite exquisite and now fetches very high prices. But it is still possible to find Victorian specimens for reasonable sums. It was fashionable in JEWELLERY, such as earrings, studs, clips, pendants, necklaces, brooches and bracelets. CARD CASES may be found with floral motifs in *posé* or *point*, sometimes both together. Other objects include needle cases, writing sets, children's rattles, lorgnettes and spectacle cases.

The early Victorian things tend to be heavier than those of the eighteenth century, though scarcely less skilful in the refinement of the work. By about the 1870s mechanical methods became available and the decorations were stamped out and pressed into the tortoiseshell or mother of pearl between metal plates. All the same, some of these designs, on toilet articles such as brushes, hand-mirrors and trinket trays, are very pleasant and still adorn many a dressing table. It is, of course, *posé* or *clouté* work, the fine *point* decoration being a thing of earlier days. Watch out, however, for imitations in erinoid and mock-tortoiseshell celluloid, with gold 'clous' simply stuck on; luckily these tend to flake off, thus giving the game away.

Although piqué lovers like to restrict the term to work on tortoiseshell, ivory and mother of pearl, similar decoration may be found on other materials such as bone (in LACE BOBBINS), SHAGREEN, HORN, woods of various kinds, and even hardstones.

Plaques

Here is a modest link between the junk shop and the collecting world of the great. Over

Oval plaque of Oliver Cromwell by James Tassie, c. 1790 (Pilkington Glass Museum)

Parian plaque

the years I have come across, without particularly looking for them, small flat pieces of bronze, round, oval or square, with classical figures and scenes in relief. They seldom cost more than a few pounds, are often very beautifully modelled, and when you begin to put a few together you find that you have something like a miniature collection of bronzes. They look magnificent when set out on a bed of silk or velvet.

These small reliefs are not medals, since they do not normally commemorate anything or any person. The smaller plaquettes were often devoted to classical subjects like the Fall of Phaeton, Venus chastening Cupid, Orpheus descending into Hell, Hercules and the Nemean Lion, the Judgment of Paris and so forth. Biblical subjects, such as the Judgment of Solomon, the Entombment, David and Goliath, the Adoration of the Magi, were also very popular. There are fine collections in the British and Victoria and Albert Museums. They were produced all over Europe in a wide variety of materials, though metal, glass and ceramics are those most often encountered.

Plaques and plaquettes seem to have been made from the fourteenth to the sixteenth century and were then revived in the early eighteenth century, enjoying continual popularity ever since. Apart from those designed to hang on a wall, there are many examples which were intended for decorative panels or boxes, cabinets and pieces of furniture. Bronze roundels with scenes in high relief were fashionable in Europe in the sixteenth century and were revived in the mid nineteenth, but numerous examples may be found in porcelain, earthenware and jasperware from the late eighteenth century onwards.

Poker Work

Who has not sat in the saloon bars of pubs and gazed at those wooden plaques on which somebody with a hot poker has drawn archly worded mottoes or whimsical rhymes? I do not know if the industry still exists, but its handiwork does, and is likely to be with us for a long time yet.

But do not imagine that this is the best that can be done with a hot poker. If you look relentlessly in the junk shops you will find such articles as glove boxes, photograph frames, pipe-racks, blotter cases, playing-card boxes and other items decorated in this way with floral and figural patterns. There are even, though not very often, full-scale pictures with work emulating, and very much in the style of, wood engravings.

Dismiss from your mind also that, having knocked up their box or whatever, the characters who made these things simply shoved a poker in the fire, pausing only to mull their lemonade with the orange-bright tip of iron, before drawing their patterns free-hand. On the contrary, they bought their virgin pieces, already traced out with a design from a shop; and so far from using a poker, they bought an outfit consisting of a platinum point heated by 'benzoline gas' from a little bottle. You could even pack the outfit away and take it on your seaside holiday.

Amateurs of old oak will note that small woodware of Stuart times was decorated with a hot poker or needle, sometimes very crudely, sometimes with vigorous peasant designs.

Pontypool and Usk Ware

'Round as a Pontypool waiter' is an old catch phrase, and it refers not to a portly man in an apron but to a small circular tray made of japanned tinware.

Few things keep their period charm like the teapots, tea-trays, coffee pots and urns, kettle braziers and other items in this ware, which would stand up to heat, wear and tear, and yet carry some of the most attractive decoration you could wish for. The grounds of green, sapphire, puce and orange are especially admired.

Pontypool and Usk Ware, a tray and a snuff box (By permission of The National Museum of Wales)

The story of the trade carried on in the Welsh towns of Pontypool and Usk by the Allgood family in the late eighteenth century is a fascinating one. But most of the examples of this sort of ware one sees nowadays must have been made in the mid nineteenth century, when the Welsh industry had died away to a trickle and the business had been taken up by Birmingham and Wolverhampton.

Posy Holders

Has it ever occurred to you, madam, to carry a posy when you go to a party?

It would have been very correct a century ago and you would have equipped yourself with a posy holder either of MOTHER OF PEARL, of gilt-metal pressed and fretted to look like expensive filigree work, or –if you were a real swell–of gold, silver or porcelain.

In the early Victorian days they actually carried these attractive little things in the hand, and some of them have a tiny tripod so that you can stand them down if and when a gentleman asks you to dance.

There is a number of shapes and all sorts of materials but you will have to look a little hard for them nowadays, especially those delightful affairs made of interlaced leaves and flowers.

Posy-holder

Potlids

You will undoubtedly have seen at some time or another small round earthenware lids printed with colour pictures. They are what is known as potlids–a posh name which applies to one category only is pomade tops–and they are the quarry of an increasing number of collectors.

When genuine (and not specimens printed by modern potters using the old plates and a little skill in ageing) they are an early form of selling goods by packaging design. They were lids of pots carrying such necessities as bear grease–a dressing for gentlemen's flowing locks in early Victorian times–as well as fish paste, meat paste and other products, both cosmetic and edible. Today you can sometimes find them in a dark wooden circular frame, which is how many people like to keep them, hanging a group of them on the wall.

Although potlids were rather neglected in Britain for many years they have always had a very strong following in the United States and it was from that country, in the 1960s, that interest in them revived in Britain and Europe, with the result that many examples which were available for a few pounds not so long ago are now priced in the hundreds. This applies especially to the very early ones, often showing bears at work

The Colman Mustard Pot Collection, in pottery and glass, covering the period 1884 to the 1950s (Colman Foods)

A small potlid of bears on a rock, mid 19th century (Christies, South Kensington)

and play in that curiously humanoid aspect so beloved of the Victorians, as well as the sumptuous lids with gilt edges which were prepared in connection with the Philadelphia Centennial Exposition (1876) and the Columbian Exposition in Chicago (1893).

These enchanting lids bring to life most vividly the Victorian scene, its heroes and heroines, its everyday occupations, its sports and pastimes. Most of the early ones were made by F. and R. Pratt & Co. of Fenton, Staffordshire, whose senior partner, Jesse Austin, developed especially for these lids a multicolour printing process similar in many aspects to that used for Baxter prints. For his subjects he copied pictures by famous artists of his own and earlier days–Gainsborough, Landseer, Mulready, Wilkie, Webster and so on; but some of them were originals by Jesse himself.

The rarest and most keenly sought after are the early bear motifs (from bear's grease pomatum or pomade), and the very early versions of English seaside views, particularly Pegwell Bay, whence the first of the potted shrimps and fish paste came. The first of the exhibition potlids were those specially done for the Great Exhibition of 1851 and thereafter lids were produced as a tribute to the great world fairs. Then there are views of London and other large cities, country landscapes, portraits of celebrities and literary characters, sports and games and *genre* scenes of people going about their lawful (and sometimes unlawful) occasions.

As already mentioned, the forger is in the land here as elsewhere, using the original copper plates for his coloured printing transfers, and producing something so much like the original lid that many buyers are taken in. *The Price Guide to Potlids* by A. Ball (1970) lists those lids which are known to have been reproduced in more recent years and includes copious notes on how to distinguish modern reproductions from the genuine article. It used to be thought that a lack of 'crazing' indicated a reproduction, but, in fact, a great many quite genuine lids do not possess this blemish.

Other firms beside Pratt made these potlids and, conversely, the pictures themselves were used on a wide range of dinner plates, jars, jugs, vases and other useful wares, usually referred to by dealers and collector as Prattware. While on the subject of potlids, don't overlook the possibilities of the pots themselves, such as the mustard pots in the Colman collection shown above, which cover the period 1884 to the 1950s.

Pounce Boxes

Among the equipment of the Georgian writing table was the pounce box, so-called because holes were pounced or punched in the top allowing it to serve the office of a caster or dredger.

The substance so cast was not at first sand–as producers of period motion pictures seem to imagine–but powdered gum sandarach; and the purpose was not so much to dry the ink on the writing paper as to re-surface the extremely absorbent early eighteenth-century paper after a scratching out.

Following the great improvements in the sizing and surfacing of paper in the mid eighteenth century, you had a sand caster with rather larger perforations. After shaking it over the wet ink you could pour the unabsorbed sand back into the caster (this is where the film producers *do* get it right).

Pounce boxes may be found in PEWTER, but the more desirable specimens are those in silver.

A Victorian inkstand, fitted with a central pounce box enclosed with a taper candlestick and conical snuffer (Christies, South Kensington)

Powder Flasks

Often called powder horns because so many of them were simply that–a horn mounted with silver or some other metal–these have their interest for the collectors of bygones, especially of firearms. Everyone who toted a blunderbuss, a flintlock fowling piece, a musketoon or a highwayman's pistol, had to have some means of carrying his powder and keeping it dry. So there were flasks–large ones for the charge powder and small ones for the flash powder–which come in leather, wood, brass, copper, silver and gold.

Beautiful work has gone into the making of some of these flasks, with inlay, embossing, engraving, carving and relief moulding. Often they were made en suite with the guns or pistols, but you won't find many of them together nowadays. Earlier specimens are worked by hand, but in the nineteenth century they tended to be stamped from dies, often with shell patterns or elaborate hunting scenes.

Don't expect to find them all actually horn-shaped. There were flat round ones, like a PILGRIM BOTTLE; dumpy affairs like a bag of sweets clutched in a small hand; conical ones with a flat top, and others in special shapes such as a rifle butt. Dixon's of Sheffield, famed for their BRITANNIA WARE and SHEFFIELD PLATE, were prominent makers, and you sometimes find their name stamped on copper or leather flasks.

Printed Boxes and Cans

Here is another subject which has edged its way up from the dustbin or garbage heap and become a quarry for collectors. It is, of course, the industrial descendant of TÔLE PEINTE and PONTYPOOL AND USK WARE, but it can be no less collectable for all that.

We are talking of the tin boxes and cans which were (and still are) used as containers for foodstuffs, biscuits, chocolates, candies, tea and other fancies. But when collectors start to collect they tend to get pretty erudite about it; so the keen folk go right back to Regency times when one Peter Durand was granted a British patent for a cylindrical canister of tinplate for the packing and preserving of perishable foods. Thomas Kensett of New York City was granted a similar American patent in 1825. This shape, of course, has been with us ever since and fills the shelves of our supermarkets–no doubt somebody is collecting them before their paper labels fall off.

When it comes to non-perishable goods, the box and can makers let their fancy run riot, and their boxes and cans appeared in all manner of shapes. There are books, globes, fishing hampers and creels, clocks, roulette wheels, anvils, lanterns, powder flasks, pistols and windmills, to name but a few. Lithographic printing directly on to the tin coating came in towards the end of the nineteenth century and this gave us, in almost as imperishable a form as enamelling, all those pretty pictures of children and

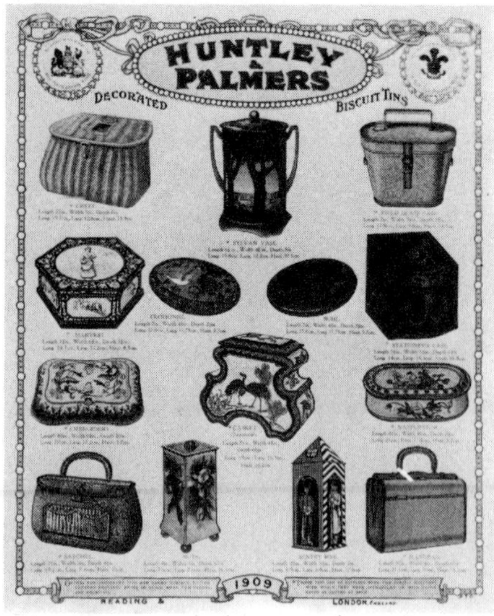

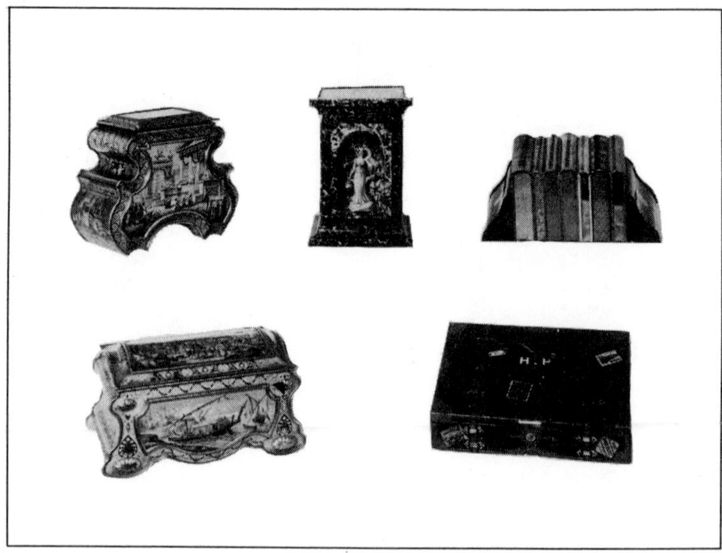

Above right: *A selection of Huntly & Palmers tins: Pompeian, 1893; Statuary, 1910; Books, 1909; Orient, 1899; Suitcase, 1892.* Above left: *A page from a Huntley & Palmers brochure of 1909 (both Associated Biscuits Limited)*

young ladies, comic ones of Scotsmen, or touching ones of kittens and puppies.

Many an early specimen still keeps the place it has held for decade after decade on the cottage sideboard or mantelpiece, as a permanent receptacle for papers and pins, tobacco and tickets, buttons and bills. They stayed there because they pleased the eye, and were thus as genuine an expression of popular art as PEASANT POTTERY, a ship's figurehead or a CHRISTMAS CARD.

Small boys should therefore be taught that kicking cans along the street on the way to school may not only damage the toe caps of their shoes but could also destroy a priceless antique of the future.

A printed silk handkerchief detailing the regulations and fare prices of Hackney coaches and cabriolets (Christies, South Kensington)

Printed Handkerchiefs and Scarves

Imagine yourself looking into the windows of one of those shops where souvenirs are sold, especially printed cotton or silk scarves and handkerchiefs: and then also imagine that you are looking into the same kind of shop a hundred years ago. Would you see there the mid-Victorian counterpart of today's 'Sights of London' or Paris or Rome; the ships and cars, the portraits of celebrities, the cookery recipes and the rest? The answer is that–roughly speaking–you would.

'Squares' were produced by the same textile printer that we met under CHINTZ. Some were made in the late eighteenth century by the early printing processes, but most date after 1831, when heavy taxes on printed calicoes and cottons, designed to help the wool trade, were repealed, the steam-driven roller printing machines came into their own, and the mills poured out squares by the hundreds and thousands.

The subjects have almost as wide a range as those on pottery. There are battle scenes, especially of the Napoleonic and Crimean wars, and the usual sympathetic portraits of Queen Caroline, whom the public thought to have been most shabbily used by her husband, George IV. There were commemorations of all kinds, such as the coronation and jubilees of Queen Victoria, historical and political occasions like the passage of the Reform Bill in 1832, and the stirring events of the Crimean War. There are also many sporting scenes, portraits of famous jockeys and their horses and early railway views. There are maps and calendars, popular ballads, love messages and subjects obviously aimed at children.

There are a few in the Victoria and Albert and other museums, just to give you a taste of them. One of the earliest known shows the famous 'Flitch of Bacon' ceremony at Great Dunmow in Essex, for couples who have been married a year without quarrelling. Another, in a private collection, called 'Woman's Rights, and What Came of It', projects the mid-Victorian reader into the year 1981–presumably the square dates from 1881–and it predicts that if things went on alarmingly as they were then doing, women would be serving in the armed forces, the police and even on the bench; while men would be nursing the babies, washing clothes and scrubbing floors.

It is interesting that Nikolaus Pevsner, whose *Pioneers of Modern Design* (1960) has told us so much about High Victorian taste, expresses surprise at not having found on textiles the same kind of association subjects that are seen so plentifully on Staffordshire pottery, especially in the FIGURES. That he had not come across these things suggests that they have not been sufficiently collected and documented; so if you want to do a little pioneering in a subject which calls for concentration rather than cash, for delving into unsuspected corners rather than into shops, here it is.

Punchbowls

A large bowl is a fine thing to set off a fine sideboard or cabinet. It is even finer when you can take the bowl down on high days and holidays and fill it with hot, steaming punch.

A silver punchbowl in the Art Nouveau style (Christies, South Kensington)

In the old days no family who liked their friends to come and see them failed to have the means of putting up a brew of punch. The name of this cheerful beverage is said to derive from the Hindustani word *panch* or the Persian *punj* meaning five, after the five qualities necessary to a good punch: that it should be hot, cold, bitter, sweet and strong. To provide these qualities the Anglo-Indian nabobs who brought us the drink used sugar, lime juice, water, spices and a villainous concoction called arrack (distilled from coconut juice). In Britain, rum and brandy were preferred.

Punchbowls, according to their period, came in various sorts of pottery–DELFTWARE, STONEWARE, porcelain, CREAMWARE, bone china, IRONSTONE and its variations. I once had one, together with its perforated colander, in ordinary BROWNWARE, which shows that even the humble home liked its bowl of grog. Decoration was a great feature of these bowls, of course, and they range from heraldic and Chinese designs to ships, political messages and portraits of contemporary celebrities, all in the familiar processes of transfer printing, painting, lustre and so on. There are very competent reproductions of these about, and also some fine modern versions issued as commemorative bowls.

You can find lordly ones in silver and SHEFFIELD PLATE, with spreading feet; but surprisingly few glass ones.

Purses

Purses and little money bags are sometimes seen, especially those made of beads or net. Most of these were made at home by the busy fingers of wives and daughters. Some were in silk, some a network of gold and silver thread, and there were many in JET.

The 'miser' purse is a curiosity of Victorian times. They are long purses with an open fold in the middle for the coins, which were kept in place by sliding along rings of metal.

Rings

Every jewel box had its quota of rings, and so does every secondhand jewellery shop. And every ring has its own little story–who bought it, how long ago, where and why.

Some of the rings you see are so large or 'old-fashioned' looking that it seems unlikely they will ever get worn again. But why not mount them in a case, as the jewellers do, and as they do with the magnificent collection in the Victoria and Albert?

What sort of rings are there–apart, I mean, from the materials of which they are

17th-century gold puzzle ring with three hoops and Gimmal betrothal or wedding ring

made? Signet rings have a great affinity with SEALS, but there are all the engagement and betrothal rings: at one time there was no distinction between the two. There are token rings too, such as the 'Gimmal', with its partable parts which come together to show clasped hands; there is the 'Regard' ring with seven hoops and a stone on each which spells out the word with the initial letters of the stone; there are the lovers' knots, the Mizpah ('I will watch over thee') ring; there are rings with guards, snake rings and wishbone rings.

Chinese rings often bear characters conveying a message if you can find somebody to read it–maybe wishing you 'riches and public honours' or 'long life and riches'. There are very precious rings with tiny watches in them; there are smokers' rings with a tobacco tamper mounted on them; there are swivel rings with two sides to show. 'Surprise' rings open up and show some magic sign; memorial rings are among the items discussed under MEMENTO MORI and are characterized by locks of hair, the death's head or similar references to death. Then there are puzzle rings with all their baffling hoops and interlocking pieces. Fraternity and sorority rings bear the symbols of these secret societies.

Rolling Pins

Glass rolling pins fall into several categories. First, there are the solid dark ones, made of bottle glass and flecked with coloured enamel glass, associated with NAILSEA though they are just as likely to have been made in Stourbridge, Wrockwardine or any other glassmaking centre.

Then there are the hollow ones, with a stopper hole at one end. Some of these are in the Nailsea-type bottle glass, but others are in clear glass, often bearing a picture of a ship, or a motto, or a loving message from a sailor to one or other of his sweethearts.

It has been variously suggested that these items were designed (a) to hold, and keep free from damp, the household salt and sugar–very costly items in the eighteenth and nineteenth centuries; (b) as love tokens; (c) as chimney ornaments and charms against spooks; and (d) just as rolling pins. My theory is that they were probably used at one time or another for all these things. The hollow ones with messages could have been bought by our ever-constant sailor, filled with tea or sugar or sweets, and when empty used as a container for more mundane articles. If they were used for salt the best place to hang them was over the chimney, for this would not only keep the salt dry but, according to the wise ones, infallibly discourage any evil spirits that lurked in the house.

Or they could have been used quite simply as rolling pins, filled with cold water. Every good pastrycook knows that both cool hands and a cool roller produce the best results; and as a matter of fact you can today buy highly efficient rollers in your hardware shop.

You can also, I'm afraid, buy highly efficient reproductions of the ones discussed above, with just sufficient age and signs of wear on them now to look antique.

Green glass Dutch roemer, c. 1655 (Pilkington Glass Museum)

Rummer

Shall we try to settle the old argument about the rummer? Most people assume that this means what it implies; that it is a glass for the drinker of rum. If you point out that although the stem is much shorter than that of a goblet, the bowl is quite as big, and would hold enough rum to make even a three-badge A.B. blink sharply, then they reply that it wasn't intended for neat rum but for grog, i.e. rum, hot water and spice.

The scholars, on the other hand, claim that the word derives from the Dutch *roemer,* signifying 'Roman style', or alternatively from a lady named Anna Roemers Visscher (1583–1651), who decorated a lot of such glasses with flowers and fruit. These *roemers,*

by the way, are very like the hock glasses you found still in use when last you worked your way through the winegardens of the Rhineland.

But another, and more thoughtful, school has noted that the Lower Rhenish word *roemer* means 'to boast'; also that when these glasses arrived in England they did so at the same time as Rhenish wine. So the most tenable view, I think, is that they came over to Britain as *roemers*, or 'boasters', got shorter in the stem and were found to be handy for grog; and then became anglicized as rummers. The boasting, no doubt, was anglicized as well.

Sailor's Needlework Pictures

One particular type of the silk and wool PICTURE WITHOUT PAINT is that which has unmistakably been made by a sailor.

By this I mean that it is made up of the kind of materials which a sailor is likely to have: for example, the base or support may be a piece of light sailcloth, or that kind of duck of which the sailor's bell-bottom trousers are made. They might use coloured wools, with perhaps cottonwool to give the effect of a cloud or a wave, and the rigging could be worked in silk. But the real index of authenticity here is the detail of the ships themselves. Some of them are extraordinarily good.

Collectors of these pictures can identify the older types–or rather pin them down to a particular age–by looking at the wool, the silk or the canvas used. Some of them may even have been made by those industrious French prisoners held at Dartmoor and Normancross during the Napoleonic Wars. Not all of these pictures are old, however, and examples may be found right down to the era of the motor vessel.

This is one of the items which may really still be lurking in a cottage; some of the small ports around the European coast still have a lively maritime tradition and keep such pictures in the family. Whether you can ever get inside one of these seamen's cottages, of course, is another matter, but certainly if I were moving around any of the coastal towns and villages of France and Spain I'd keep a very keen lookout for this type of craft.

Sand Pictures

Another of our PICTURES WITHOUT PAINT, and a great favourite in seaside resorts along the south coast of England at one time. Different coloured sands in Alum Bay in the Isle of Wight were first used for this purpose. The picture was outlined in pencil on a card, covered with glue, and the coloured sands sprinkled on appropriately. Landscapes were a favourite subject, but you will often find animal groups and even copies of famous paintings. The pictures were quite often set in one of those nice deep birds-eye maple frames.

One of the masters of the earlier sand pictures was Benjamin Zobel, a native of Swabia in Southern Germany. He came from a family of confectioners and in those days–that is to say, the late eighteenth century–sand pictures were an important part of the enormous panels that were made for table decorations. Zobel had been trained in oil and miniature painting and later came to London to work for a firm of WALLPAPER and CHINTZ manufacurers in Chelsea. He became official table decker, as it was called, at Windsor Castle, and called himself on his trade card 'Sand picture painter to George III'.

Zobel married an Englishwoman and they and their seven children turned themselves into a firm making these pictures–so there must have been a good many of them around at one time. Very few of them are signed, so it is a matter of identifying them by means of their styles and techniques.

Sand pictures remained in vogue until the First World War, and you may even find examples of picture postcards from Hampshire and the Isle of Wight decorated in this fashion.

Scent Bottles

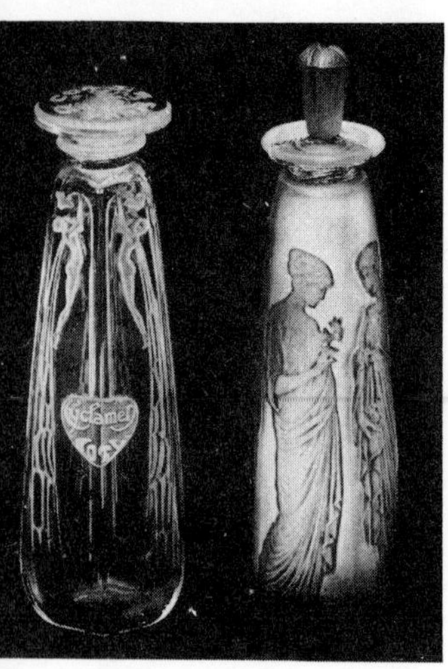

Two original scent bottles designed by Lalique for Coty (Coty)

There is a lifetime of collecting here, and your way will take you through every department of ceramics, metals and glass and a lot more materials as well.

I would say that you have two main fields in front of you: the rare things of the eighteenth century in hardstones, gold, rich enamels, silver and precious stones; or you go for the more modest nineteenth-century affairs, sometimes sold at country fairs as lovers' keepsakes.

NAILSEA made them, and there are double-ended ones, with one compartment for perfume and the other for some aromatic vinegar used by Victorian ladies when confronted with emotional crises. Odd cut-glass ones from toilet sets are worth looking for, especially if you can date them from the hallmarks on silver mounts.

Coming nearer the present day, there are those magnificent little scent bottles made by the great French manufacturers, such as GALLÉ and LALIQUE, and there are plenty of modern bottles around which are worth preserving as antiques of the future. Some of them are most beautifully designed and made, even if they *are* factory products. So if you want to be remembered by your great-grandchildren as a very wise old bird (or girl, as the case may be) fill a box with them and stow it away in the attic.

Screens

Screens are back with us again, not necessarily only FIRESCREENS, but any pleasant screen which will stand on its own–as a piece of furniture in a not too crowded room. What sort of screens we have will depend upon what sort of people we are. If we are rich, then we will not mind spending a few thousand pounds on a LACQUER Coromandel six-fold screen with a continuous design of figures and landscape. If this strikes you as a lot of money for very little, why not try one of those black lacquer ones inset with a variety of *chinoiseries* in MOTHER OF PEARL, IVORY and hardstones such as jade and lapis lazuli, all arranged to show pastoral and other scenes; it should scarcely run to more than three thousand pounds.

However, to come down to reality, there are many screens with needlework behind glass which could surely be adapted to carry some more exciting weaves or perhaps some less faded ones. There are screens in BERLIN WOOLWORK which also are not as bright as they were; and I have seen old English leather screens with oil-painted motifs go for quite modest sums.

One kind which vanishes from the shop almost as soon as it appears is the scrapwork screen, once the pride and joy of the Victorian nursery for which it was often made. Some of these are fairly sedate affairs with a few large cut-out pictures of children or adults in coloured borders; but others are a perfect riot of colour and odd bits and pieces–animals, children, birds, flowers, domestic scenes, fairies, landscapes and seascapes. All this material was culled from popular coloured prints of the day, often given away as magazine inserts or trade cards, and also from the scraps which children still stick in albums.

These screens are sometimes in bad condition through years of neglect in an attic or outhouse. If they are gone too far to patch up, why not recreate them in terms of today? There are just as many, if not more, coloured illustrations about today and they are immeasurably better in quality than the Victorian chromolithograph.

If you want to make a good job of it, though, remember that a good scrapwork screen isn't *quite* an uncalculated hotchpotch: you need some feature to 'pull it together'. One way is to paint the screen with a good strong background colour which can form a ground seen at the edges of your scraps. For your materials, pastes and varnishes, go to the picture dealer.

Seals

There was a time when all of us who had any business with documents, or wrote letters to any extent, carried a seal–or had one on our writing tables and desks.

Many of these seals are still about, for some of them are really pieces of JEWELLERY and not to be lightly thrown away, even if their function has passed away. So today in the shops you can find them set into RINGS–when, of course, they become signet rings, made of gemstones like carnelian, onyx, emerald and garnet, carved at first with crests, but later with any sort of device that would please the buyer.

More collectable than these, because of the fine work that went into their handles, are the desk seals. Wedgwood moved in on this fashion by making them with handles of lilac or blue jasperware; they also appeared in the delightful Chelsea porcelain 'toys' and Battersea and Bilston enamels. Jade, rock crystal, IVORY, smoked quartz, coloured glass, JET, onyx, every kind of metal and even hardwoods were all pressed into service, beautifully worked and sometimes modelled into animals' heads, legs and other shapes.

Those who like using seals for their letters may be interested in some tips given by the late Dr George Williamson, who insisted that everyone, especially ladies who had important and perhaps confidential letters to write, ought to re-learn the art of sealing. What he recommends is, don't just shove the wax into the flame and blob a shapeless mass on the paper: it looks horrible. Your graceful sealer revolves the wax carefully above the flame until it is soft, then rubs it gently on the envelope in an ever-decreasing circle until there is a nice round shape. She then gets some Chinese vermilion of the very finest quality, rubs a tiny portion over the head of the seal with a camel's hair brush, warms the seal by breathing on it so as to prevent adhesion to the wax, then applies it very, very gently and firmly. She blows off the loose vermilion from the border, and has her impression in rich vermilion beautifully framed in sealing wax red. And off it goes, by hand messenger, to some lucky man.

Services

I have sometimes wondered to see people paying largish sums for odd Coalport or Copeland plates, cups and saucers because they liked them, and then buying one of the less attractive sort of new tea or dinner services because, presumably, they think they couldn't possibly afford a whole new service of things they like.

Nankin ware dinner service

They ought some day to go along to one of the larger sales in the big towns, and see what modest prices are sometimes fetched by the old services. Some years ago, for example, I saw a Davenport tea and coffee service painted in puce *en camaieu* with springs of flowers and fluted rims, forty-four pieces in all, sold for only ten pounds. Even now such nineteenth-century services are still quite cheap–and often compare favourably with the cost of current productions.

If you want something smaller, but more exciting, how about a Rockingham claret ground ten-piece dessert set, each piece painted with a different botanical sketch of a flower? Or an attractive Chelsea Derby tea-set with an apple-green ground and painted in the Chinese taste with flowering plants and roots, scattered sprigs and insects? I can even recall a Flight Worcester tea-set which sold for as little as ten shillings a piece–but that wasn't yesterday, I admit. But even today one can still see fine examples of MASON'S IRONSTONE in red, blue and yellow Japanese patterns, Coalport services with floral bouquet motifs and plenty of Copeland and Garrett tea and coffee services with panels and flowers on green and gilded grounds, all in the price range from £30 to £100 for the complete works.

All these services, of course, include their teapots, jugs, basins or tureens and dishes as the case may be, so you can see how comparatively cheaply it works out. It is also worth comparing these prices with what it would cost you to buy new sets.

Serviette Rings

Nowadays both collectors and dealers prefer the term napkin rings–largely, I suspect, as a result of Nancy Mitford's definition of what was 'U' and 'non-U' in the 1950s. But at the time these things were current, 'serviette' was the proper word and 'napkin' was applied only to a towel or a baby's diapers.

Whatever you call them these rings are worth the consideration of the collector with limited resources both in space and money. They come in silver, carved IVORY, bone, glass, wood, all manner of things engraved, embossed and sometimes mounted with jasperware or glass paste cameos and gemstones. How far back in history they go, I know not: it might be an interesting quest to discover that too.

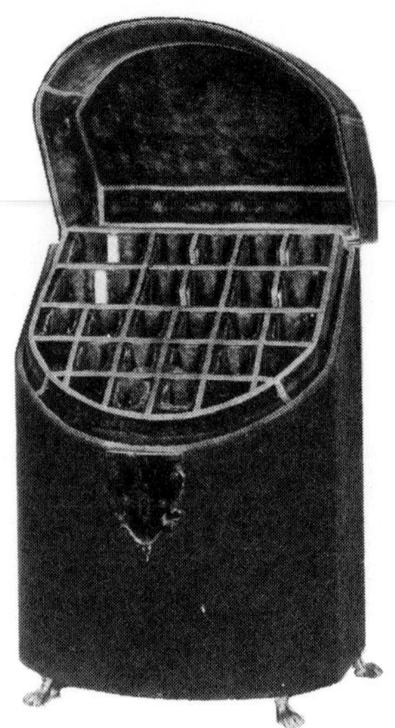

A mid 18th-century shagreen cutlery box (Christies, South Kensington)

Shagreen

The word has a nice old-fashioned ring, and the articles decorated with it an equally nice old-fashioned look. There are small portable writing sets of the eighteenth century, etuis for the lady's purse, penholders, knife and fork cases (for taking on your travels abroad by coach), sword-hilts, spectacle cases: in fact, all objects likely to have a lot of wear, but at the same time needing to be pleasant to look at and handle.

Although most shagreen is dyed green, it comes in other colours as well, even white and grey. The word, in fact, derives from the French *peau de chagrin*, or ass's skin, which itself also gives rise to the other meaning of chagrin–i.e. mortification–presumably from one's having to ride on the rough skin of an ass. But this was only one source. It is also prepared from the skin of sharks, rays and spotted dogfish. Nowadays, of course, you find imitations of it in hides patterned by copper plates and embossed paper.

Shaving Stand

Not many pieces of furniture in the past few centuries have been designed especially for men, so one welcomes the odd shaving stand one sometimes sees.

I bought one for myself about 1960 in a back street junk-shed for 'twopunten'; and I became very fond of it. The mirror was small and octagonal, but adjustable to the unshaven chin, and you could bare your teeth into it comfortably. The top of the stand was prettily galleried with bobbin turning, there was a cupboard big enough to carry all necessary gear and tackle, and the rails at the side carried huckaback towels. Somebody had obligingly removed the old French polish, and in its naked mahogany it looked well with the ladder-back and cane chairs in my bedroom.

Perhaps the most desirable feature of these items is that they are hopelessly inadequate as dressing tables for women; consequently one can not only buy them cheaply but keep them for one's own use.

A shaving stand, probably late 19th century (Mrs D. Dey)

Sheffield Plate

The first time I took any real note of Sheffield plate was when I saw on the top shelf of a junk shop a pile of candle snuffer trays. Blowing off the dust I found they all had a coppery colour showing through the silver. I asked the man about them and he said 'Old Sheffield plate, guv. They're waiting to go for re-plating.' After they'd got their new coating of electro-plating, it seemed, they'd eventually find their way into some more attractive shop. They might even be helped along by having a little of the electro-plating scraped off to let the customer see by the copper that they really were old

A Sheffield plate snuffer tray

Sheffield plate. For, of course, the worn plate, displaying its genuineness to the world, is much preferable to one which has been re-plated.

But Sheffield plating isn't the same as ELECTRO-PLATE and, in fact, it owes its demise about 1850 to the invention of that process. It has been called the poor man's silver (a title one would question on seeing the prices fetched nowadays for good pieces!) and appeared somewhere about 1750 when, the story goes, a man named Boulsover happened to be heating a piece of copper in a vice. On stuffing a sixpence in to keep it firm he found afterwards that he had fused these two metals.

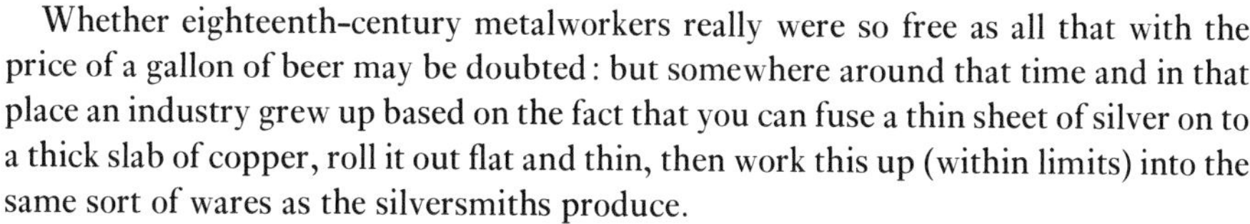

Whether eighteenth-century metalworkers really were so free as all that with the price of a gallon of beer may be doubted: but somewhere around that time and in that place an industry grew up based on the fact that you can fuse a thin sheet of silver on to a thick slab of copper, roll it out flat and thin, then work this up (within limits) into the same sort of wares as the silversmiths produce.

And, in fact, nowadays you really are better off buying your Sheffield plate from the silversmith, or at any rate the metal specialist, than the general dealer–until you learn to find your way about such things as re-plating and the various substitutes. For example, soon after seeing the above-mentioned snuffer tray I happened to inherit one, together with a pair of snuffers, among some family treasures. The tray was Sheffield plate all right, with just enough silver left on to make it attractive when polished up. But the pair of snuffers puzzled me. Where *they* had worn, it showed not copper as you would have expected, but iron or more probably steel. How on earth could this be Sheffield plate?

The answer was that it wasn't: it was close-plating–something which seems to be more valuable. I found this out because on the knife blade there was a maker's mark and name, and the firm was a maker of close-plated ware. This was quite different from Sheffield plating. Instead of fusing the silver on to copper before working up the sheet, you made the desired piece in some base metal, then applied a thin layer of silver afterwards, using tin as a solder. This process pre-dated Sheffield plating but it was revived in the early nineteenth century, and specimens are much sought after.

Then there is the trap of BRITANNIA METAL. I fell right into this one, and didn't come out quite so well as with the snuffers. I thought that anything silvery looking with 'Sheffield' and no silver hallmark might reasonably be considered Sheffield plate. So I paid a pound for a handsome teapot so marked. Mistakenly, however, for this word–often with a maker's name as well–can indicate Britannia metal, a cheap alloy similar to PEWTER. Most dealers used to think that it *was* pewter and would sell it as such when in its original form. But when it is electro-plated–as it was in later years, you might have easily mistaken it for Sheffield plate, though the initials E.P.B.M. (electro-plated Britannia metal) should give the game away.

Shellwork

People in eighteenth-century England loved the many exotic things which came from the East. Among these were shells, of all kinds, sizes and shapes.

Apart from the large cameo shells extensively used in JEWELLERY, smaller ones were used for decoration, while much use was made of pieces of the linings of shells. Fruit knives and forks, pocket knives, paper knives, the sticks of FANS, CARD CASES, trinket boxes and mirror frames were decorated with the nacreous lining of sea-shells, not all of which, by any means, could be described as MOTHER OF PEARL.

In the nineteenth century there was a craze for decorating small articles with tiny shells in a form of mosaic. This was yet another of these arts practised by love-lorn sailors whose shell VALENTINES are now much sought after. Shell mosaics may also be found on Victorian MUSICAL BOXES, table lamps, vases and the like.

Ships in Bottles

How does the ship, masts and sails trimmed for a fair wind, get through the narrow neck of the bottle? The answer is that it doesn't–at least not in sea-going order. First the sea itself is made up of cork, putty, sand and glue, painted realistically, poked in with a wire or needle, and glued in place. Then the hull is carved and masts and spars are cut and rigged, but packed flat for insertion through the neck, leaving thread lines for pulling up. The ship is stuck in position, the maker hauls away handsomely on the thread lines and drops a spot or two of glue here and there to make all secure.

These models were made all through the nineteenth century, and are priced according to the workmanship and whether they commemorate a particular ship. If you want to find your way among the named ones, there are plenty of reference books and histories. I have seen very few steamers, other than some very early hybrids; but most of the men who like doing these things were either brought up in sail or like to think they were.

Has anyone yet seen an aeroplane or a spacecraft in a bottle?

Shop Signs

A 19th-century locksmith's sign (The Museum of London)

Many are the covetous eyes which are lifted to the large old signs which still hang over tradesmen's or craftsmen's premises, or perhaps stand in their windows. Everyone over the age of sixty will remember when the kilted Highlander was as common in the doorway of a tobacconist as an Indian in an American cigar store. The story that he advertised Scottish snuff is a fallacy; such figures date from the time of the Jacobite Rebellion in 1745 and it is a curious psychological phenomenon that figures that were feared or hated–and this includes not only that cigar store Indian but Negroes, Blackamoors and Turks–were used at one time as tobacco advertisements; no one knows why.

An ironmonger's shop might hang out a huge padlock, presumably made of painted wood, and a sports outfitter's a tennis racket of dimensions which would add considerably, I am sure, to the interest of games on the Centre Court at Wimbledon. The huge coloured and gilded pots of the colourmen, the bottles with tinted glass in chemists' windows, the outsize hand and boot of the glovemaker and bootmaker respectively, the black and gilt canister of the grocer (or Italian warehouseman as he used to be called) are still to be seen occasionally, together with all the figures outside inns, such as Dun Cows, Bears with Ragged Staffs, White Swans, White Harts, Red Lions and the rest.

These items, as soon as they are prised away from their moorings through demolition or redevelopment, appear in the antique shops along with the ships' figureheads and are eagerly snapped up. There is one item being made again, and that is the large pig's head which once appeared in the windows of pork butchers. I know where you can buy a dozen of these new, all wrapped in nice tissue paper.

Silhouettes

Before the days of photography you could go to a painter for a portrait or a miniature, but it would cost you a tidy sum even in those days. If you wanted to be more economical you patronized a professional cutter-out of silhouettes, otherwise known as a shadowgrapher or silhouettist.

These little black-and-white pictures, which you now see framed on walls, are named after a French politician named Etienne de Silhouette–not, apparently, because he had anything to do with silhouettes (though some say that this was a hobby of his) but because he was a cheese-paring sort of minister who wanted to cut down on all expenditure he considered inessential. In his view, it seems, portraits were wild extravagances: much better save the money and go to one of these modern silhouettists.

The first of them appeared about 1750, and their real vogue lasted for about a century. Many of them were done free-hand, while others were made by means of a machine. The sitter was placed behind a light so that the shadow of the profile fell upon a sheet of oiled paper. A tracing was made of this and then reduced by means of a pantograph, a gadget which one still remembers as a childhood toy. You ran a point over a large tracing and simultaneously drew a smaller version of it with a connected pencil on another sheet.

A silhouette machine, designed by Johann Kaspar Lavater (1741–1801)

There were several types of silhouette. In its simplest form it was cut straight out of black paper, cloth or other material and pasted on to a white card, then framed. Others were painted by hand in various tones of black or grey so as to pick out features or details of clothes. Some of these are surrounded by gold and tinsel. In more expensive types the silhouette was painted on to the inside of a convex piece of glass in such a way that the image cast a shadow upon a white background, and so made the portrait stand out in relief.

Quite apart from the portraits of individuals there are the wonderful little family groups, also landscapes and sporting scenes, cut out freehand by famous people like Torond and Edouart and a host of lesser-known artists.

As well as the professionals there were, of course, the amateurs, for skill in this art was regarded as quite an accomplishment. It was even taught in schools. These hobbyists produced delightful little things for their scrapbooks, some of which occasionally come to light.

By about 1860, however, the professionals had been put out of business by the early photographers–or more probably had become photographers themselves. The scrapbook-fillers no doubt found it easier and more interesting to cut out the exciting new colour picture being published by the magazines.

Slagware

This sounds a dreadful name for a very much sought after and sometimes most attractive thing–although I suppose, as a name, it's no worse than Coalport. Other names include vitro-porcelain (not much better!), marble glass, purple slag and 'end-of-day' ware.

By way of identifying it, it may help if I say that you see vases of it in a very special and penetrating sort of blue, and they don't quite look like china or glass, but something in between. It also comes in a marbled form, either purple, turquoise, opal, green or other colours. You see it too, in something which looks like black, but when put up to the light shows deep amethyst.

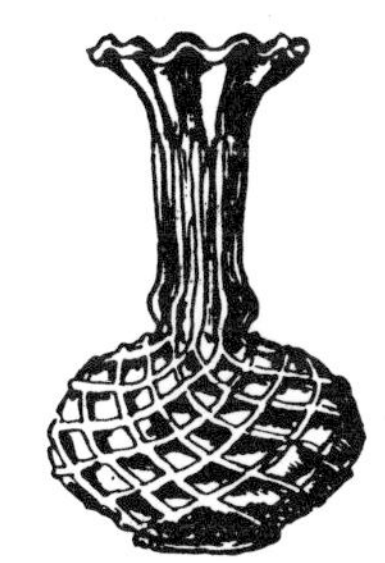
Blue slag vase

Slagware is really a cross between glass and stone, or at any rate crudities in iron ore. The name 'end-of-day' ware gives you the clue. It seems that where glassmakers found themselves near foundries they would buy up the waste or slag which floats upon the top of the molten metal, mix it with flint glass and so produced a tough opaque material which could be coloured and pressed into moulds, for both 'useful' and ornamental wares. It was called 'end-of-day' ware because this slag was taken off at the end of the day.

Cream slag basket

Though much of this material began life as something the workmen produced at the end of the day's normal operations, it soon developed into a speciality of some firms. Sowerby of Newcastle-upon-Tyne became the leading exponent of this trade, and vitro-porcelain was their own name for it, using a mark in the form of a peacock's head.

But there were other firms working in that locality, as I have discovered by looking up the registry mark on some of my own pieces. One day, I suppose, all these little firms will be as carefully documented as the eighteenth-century porcelain factories.

Apart from the purple and other marbled pieces, the blue vases and jugs, there are versions in dead white, such as a jug I have in the form of an up-ended trout. This was made by Heppell's of Newcastle. There is also a range of smaller cream-coloured pieces such as sugars, compotes, jugs, pretty little pinched-in baskets like the porcelain ones, tea canisters, butter dishes and so forth. Many of them can be identified and dated by the presence of a registry mark.

A more ambitious class of item in the blue variety included flat-faced PILGRIM BOTTLES impressed with nursery-rhyme pictures.

Delightful as many of these things are I have some misgiving about paying too much for them. It seems to me that since they are only moulded from materials which presumably still exist today there is nothing to stop their being made again, indistinguishably from the old, providing the price made it worthwhile. And the way prices are going they may very well be.

Snuff Boxes

French niello snuff box, c. 1840 (Aspreys)

Snuff boxes have probably been collected more than any other single thing. But I don't know that there's any more to say about them except that you find them in pretty well every sort of material from gold to PEWTER and from silver to HORN. They come from all countries, they show varying standards of workmanship, from the exquisite to the dull, and I can think of nothing more boring than the sight of a lot of them together.

Souvenir China

In the eighteenth century, when you went on a visit, you brought back with you a piece of porcelain marked 'A trifle from Lowestoft' or perhaps a piece of Bilston enamel with some more personal message on it.

In the nineteenth century people went to many more places than Lowestoft and, of course, in enormously increased numbers. The legacy of this is a huge quantity of souvenir china and glass of every sort and kind. It was also an age when people liked to pass on kind thoughts to their friends, relatives and lovers. So as well as the souvenirs of places there is a vast range of things inscribed 'Forget me not', 'Remember me' and so forth.

Much of this china is pretty hideous by any standards–or so it seems at first glance. Like so many other kinds of bygones these bits and pieces have now taken on a sort of period charm which makes us forgive things about them that we once thought crude, vulgar, brassy or mawkish.

Views, of course, were as popular on china as they were on postcards, and some of this work is very good. Much of it was printed in Britain on porcelain imported 'in the white' from Europe, chiefly from Saxony and Thuringia in Germany, and this fact is often proclaimed very prominently on the base. A great deal of this china, however, was latterly printed in the country of origin and the subject matter was by no means confined to British scenery and landmarks.

I have a plate which not only illustrates the Forth Bridge for me in charming colours, but proudly informs me that it cost over £3,500,000 and that 5,000 men worked day and night on it for seven years.

I have also, up to the time of writing, seven mugs all printed with views of English towns and villages–scenes which have now changed out of all recognition–and each mug is subtly different in shape and decoration although clearly of the same family. The differences in shape are probably due to different consignments or different makers.

Spinning Wheels

Pleasant to have an old 'cottage' type spinning wheel if you have an old cottage. Well, they are not all that difficult to find if you watch the sales carefully, and also look out for modern reproductions which wouldn't spin a yarn to convince anyone. It should be pointed out, however, that there *are* some excellent modern ones, constructed on traditional lines, which are not only fully operational but are the basic tool of the many people who have taken up spinning as a hobby or vocation.

The spinning wheel has a long history, and if you are really interested you will find it worthwhile learning a little about spinning. Originally the wool was spun in the fingers, using a weighted stick to set the yarn twisting and winding it into a thread; all you had was a DISTAFF carrying the yarn, and a spindle or weighted stick with which you wound it, thus producing the desired combination of twisting and winding. The spinning wheel as we know it today was the invention of a German woodcarver named Johann Jurgens, working in the fifteenth century, though it seems likely that he may only have improved an existing medieval pattern, which either wound or twisted but didn't do both at once.

A late 18th-century spinning wheel in mahogany with box and satinwood inlays (Aspreys)

Those made for cottages and farm houses were from hard woods like yew, box and oak, but without much trimming, except for the usual turning. Those do not cost a great deal even now. But there is another type which will cost you a considerable sum, since it was intended for the drawing-room and so had to look as handsome as the rest of things there. These elegant wheels are made of walnut and ebony, sometimes inlaid with ivory or mother of pearl, and were often most beautiful and intricate pieces of furniture.

Spoon Trays

If by any chance you should come across a little china tray shaped like the one in the drawing, don't write it off as just a dressing-table adjunct, or a crazy sort of saucer. It may well be a spoon tray.

Worcester spoon tray

In days when people drank tea out of little bowls, they usually poured the tea into the specially deep saucer and drank out of that (see CUP PLATES). This meant that you couldn't very well keep your spoon in the saucer, so when you'd used it you laid it delicately in just such a tray as this.

They were made by all the important factories, especially Worcester, quite early in their history, so they find themselves wherever such wares usually end up—in the very expensive shops. But you just might find one somewhere in that old pile of crockery I keep telling you to search untiringly!

Staffordshire Figures

No antique shop is complete without its quota of figures, priced at anything between a couple of pounds and a hundred, often more.

But those you see there nowadays in most of them are a late flowering: they come from the mantelpieces of the nineteenth century, and they owe very little to their predecessors, the elegant china figures of the eighteenth century or the ornaments in salt-glazed STONEWARE.

Staffordshire spaniels

They were, in fact, the ornament of the people, made in tiny back-street workshops in the Potteries, often by husband and wife working together, or by children on piecework rates, we are told, of about a penny a dozen.

It is easy to see why these colourful items were popular in their own day, whether they were the earlier figures for sideboard and cabinet made 'in the round', or those later ones which had a flattened back (hence the nickname 'flatbacks') so that they could stand on the mantelpiece.

As to their subjects, hardly any popular subject, person or idea of the day was ignored. Everyone will have seen the dogs, in their great variety–the sturdy poodles, the large and rather soppy-looking spaniels, the sleek greyhounds, the sporting dogs such as pointers, setters and foxhounds. Makers like Sampson Smith, James Dudson and William Kent were renowned for their dogs, and from their work you could almost trace the history of dogbreeding over the past century and a half–no doubt somebody has!

Then there are the cows, usually made as milk jugs with little lids on their backs and sometimes accompaned by a calf or a milkmaid. There are sheep, with their crinkly coats, sitting beside a tree-stump, the much rarer cats, horses and elephants. Strange that there should not be more horses in an age which depended so much upon that animal: but of course they do appear in equestrian groups like the circus pieces, or mounted characters such as Dick Turpin, Wellington, Napoleon and the champion jockeys of the day.

Potters also ranged over the whole of national life as if they were producing illustrated magazines. In fact it has now been proved that they were often inspired by particular magazine illustrations of the time, and also pictorial MUSIC COVERS. They depicted historical events like the death of Nelson and the assassination of Marat; they showed literary characters from Dickens and Shakespeare; they covered religious topics like the Widow of Zarepath, the Sacrifice of Isaac, Elijah fed by the Ravens, and the Return from Egypt. By the side of imposing statesmanlike figures of Gladstone and Pitt stood the effigies of boxers, cricketers, composers, writers, soldiers, sailors, thieves, murderers, parsons and the rest.

In this field the collector has to be on his guard against modern re-issues–pieces which are genuine enough in that they were made in Staffordshire and from the original moulds, but coming from there last month rather than last century. There is no difficulty about 'doctoring' these things to make them look a little more venerable than they really are.

Standishes

Standishes. Above, *globe and box.* Below: *tray*

The old name for an inkstand, especially those evolved for the Georgian writing table.

One type, of which one sees many examples today, is the 'Treasury'. It has in its day been called a 'pen and ink box', being oblong, with two covers hinged back to back. There might also be a little box filled with lead shot into which you could dig your quill point to clean off the rather muddy eighteenth-century ink; this same purpose was served by the holes round the rim of some free-standing inkwells, notably the capstan type–the shot also helps to give the inkwell stability. Here, too, one may meet for the first time the 'pen-knife', used for sharpening quills.

Most standishes, however, are variations on the open tray, with or without sockets or ring guards for boxes and bottles or long depressions for the pens. They echo all the favourite styles of the periods, sometimes with elaborate scrollwork and fret-cut decoration, or, in the late eighteenth and early nineteenth centuries, in streamlined Adam oval or boat-shaped forms. They are often associated with fine cut crystal glass, and in fact it seems to be the appearance of these types, with ink bottles rather than pots, which brought in the term 'inkstand'.

From Victorian times there are some fine examples in BRONZE and BRASS, and they were fair game for the ART NOUVEAU designer. Today, with ballpoints everywhere, the standish may still stand, but it serves only to please our eyes and senses.

Stirrup Cups

When every gentleman rode to hounds several days a week, he needed something to keep out the cold, so a stirrup cup was almost as great a necessity as a shaving mug. As the 'dram' was taken in the saddle, the cup did not have to be stood down anywhere, so it could be any shape you liked.

Usually it was fashioned in the shape of an animal's head, and these items have been collected for a very long time now. A gathering of them would cover a very wide range of materials, many of them in the rarer sorts of pottery and porcelain. There were also silver ones from Georgian times, inscribed with the name of the hunt.

Animal-lovers will find plenty to interest them here, for they included foxes and other quarry like hares and deer and even fish; among the dogs were foxhounds, greyhounds, bulldogs, setters, Dalmatians and terriers.

But look out for reproductions!

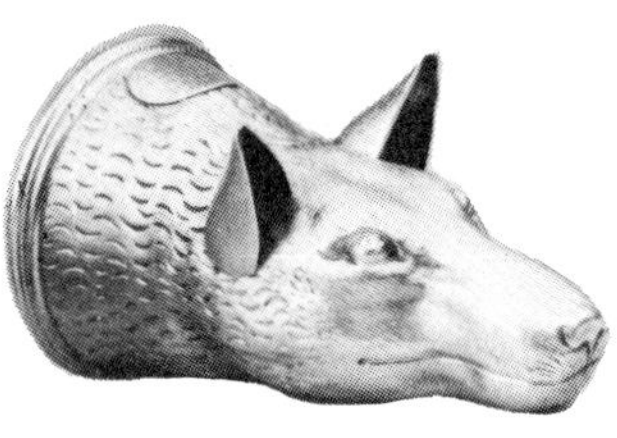

A silver and part-gilt stirrup cup (Christies)

Stoneware

If you go on baking a pot in the kiln to a higher temperature than is needed for earthenware it becomes stoneware, and will hold liquid, become immensely tough, and will open up all sorts of new possibilities in the way of decoration. You can, for example, polish it as if it were stone; you can stain it, as with jasperware; you can cut or scratch decorations in the ware itself, as Hannah Barlow did at DOULTON; or cut through a coloured glaze to the body beneath, in which case you have '*sgraffito* work.

To make stoneware even more durable, you can throw common salt into the hot kiln, and the fumes thus given off will settle on the piece and give you salt-glazed stoneware. In its earliest manifestations in eighteenth-century Staffordshire it is practically priceless, but see also the next paragraph.

A group of 20th-century stoneware containers (Doulton & Company Limited)

Stoneware Spirit Flasks

Few things could be better adapted to their purpose than the spirit flasks in salt-glazed stoneware which were to be found in inns and gin shops in Regency and early Victorian times.

You will see quite a lot of them about, for they suddenly dropped out of use, and being eminently tough many of them have survived to fill the cabinets of collectors. They are not particularly expensive; except for a few rarities they can be bought for a

Above left: *Three brown saltglaze stoneware spirit flasks* (from left): *man on barrel, Miss Prettyman, Mr and Mrs Caudle, c. 1846*. Above right: *A brown saltglaze stoneware 'Pistol spirit flask', early 19th century. All made by Doulton & Watts of Lambeth (Doulton & Company Limited)*

few pounds. Probably this is because they aren't regarded as particularly decorative and so *are* only of interest to collectors.

Like these colourful miniature bottles one sees on the shelves of modern pubs these buff and brown containers of whisky, brandy, rum and gin were designed to draw attention to themselves. They were made of this iron-hard stoneware, presumably because of the boisterous manners and the stone floors of the taverns in those days. They came in an enormous range of shapes–barrels, books, pigs, potatoes, pistols, clocks, policemen's truncheons (then a newish joke!). Others personified famous figures of the day–kings, queens, politicians and religious leaders, while others cracked jokes like 'Mrs Caudle's Bedtime Lectures' from *Punch*.

So far as materials go, there are two main types: those with a light buff and brown salt-glaze, and those covered with a shiny dark brown 'Rockingham' glaze. DOULTON of Lambeth were important makers, as were Bourne of Derby.

These flasks met their end quite suddenly about 1845, when the heavy glass excise was repealed, and the shelves of the inns became filled with labelled glass bottles which showed their contents. Except for a brief revival in Edwardian days they have not been seen since.

Straw Marquetry

Just occasionally one comes across an example of a kind of marquetry in which straw was used for decoration instead of wood. There are workboxes, TEA CADDIES, patch boxes, needle holders, FIRESCREENS, WATCH STANDS, picture frames and many other items.

Although some work of this kind was done in the straw plaiting areas around Luton, most of it was turned out by French prisoners of war during the Napoleonic period. Six thousand of them were housed in a great prison near Peterborough, and the museum there has a fine collection of the ware. Apparently the men went in for this particular use of straw because they were not allowed to compete with the local straw plaiting industry.

Pieces of straw were dyed in various colours, then split with a special tool, some examples of which survive. The pieces were glued on to a 'carcase', often supplied by the customer. There is a fine example of a straw marquetry picture, a stylized landscape, in the Victoria and Albert Museum. Quite large pictures of landmarks and scenery were also made in Europe, especially in Austria. A host of minor articles was decorated in this fashion as late as the 1920s.

Strike-a-lights

That race of people who can coax life out of the most ornate small piece of mechanism will delight in finding members of the varied clan of tinder boxes, strike-a-lights, fire steels and the rest.

A tinder box is essentially a receptacle for a piece of flint, a steel striker and tinder–a substance which will easily ignite, such as charred rag. When you get the tinder to smoulder by expertly dropping the spark on to it, you then have the problem of conveying this newly-created fire to whatever it was you wanted to set alight. This job is made easier if you have a sulphur match, which bursts into flame, lets off the most obnoxious smell, but lights your candle or fire. When one thinks what it must have been like to try to light a candle in the middle of a wet steamy night one cannot fail to be impressed by the fortitude of our ancestors.

Some tinder boxes are of wood, with a sliding lid, often very finely carved, especially in the case of the Dutch ones. Another type is a circular tin box with an inner compartment for the tinder, and a candle holder on the outside of the lid, so that the box then performs the office of a candlestick. These boxes come not only in tin but also in BRASS, COPPER and SHEFFIELD PLATE. As all nations were in the same boat as the British, so they all have their different sorts of boxes–or leather pouches and purses.

A tinder box with matching travelling case (S. H. Cole)

A more sophisticated means of making fire is the tinder pistol, or strike-a-light. This was obviously a development of the flintlock pistol, with tinder in a receptacle below the striker instead of gunpowder. This often had a little box at the side for the sulphur match and a candle holder as well. Some of the foreign examples are beautifully engraved or inlaid; others are simple brass or steel frames with a wooden stock and pistol grip. Fine examples in complete condition are now very scarce and highly priced, but incomplete specimens are still fairly plentiful at no great cost.

Tapersticks

You will sometimes come across short CANDLESTICKS with socket holes which are apparently much too small to take a candle.

They are, in fact, tapersticks–sometimes called Tea Candlesticks, because they formed part of the eighteenth-century tea equipage. Their purpose was only partly to act as candlesticks, for the tapers burnt in them, made of English beeswax, gave off a pleasant perfume–often much needed in Georgian interiors. They are also known as Tobacco Candlesticks, since they were apt to be kept at the elbows of gentlemen smoking their churchwarden pipes.

Most tapersticks are smaller versions of ordinary candlesticks and production went on just long enough to catch up with Victorian styles, when they became quite ornate. There is one type in which the bowl and drip tray are supported on the upward stretched arms of harlequins or other figures.

Tea Caddies

Otherwise known as tea canisters, tea chests and teapoys–though there seems to be some confusion over the exact meaning of these terms, partly, I think because they have been used in different ways at different times. Let's try and make some distinctions.

When tea first appeared in England in the seventeenth century it was kept in a *canister*, the word first being used in this sense about 1711. This receptacle could be in any number of different materials, all kinds of metals, ceramics and glass. These items come up frequently at sales and, of course, follow the price of the particular materials they were made in.

At first, canisters stood on their own, but as tea came into more general use these

An unusual pewter, china tea caddy (Mrs W. Bird)

containers would themselves be contained in a *tea-trunk* or *tea chest*, and locked away for safety, tea being extremely costly in those days. Then, somewhere towards the end of the eighteenth century, this chest, instead of being a container for canisters, acquired the tightly fitting boxes we know today and was called a *tea caddy*. The word comes from the Malay word *kati*, a measure equal to about half a kilogram.

As for the *teapoy* this is something different again. Many people believe–as I did for years–that a teapoy is simply a porcelain tea canister; I've certainly seen the word used in that sense. But this is a misleading use of the term, since the teapoy proper is a piece of furniture which is a sort of cross between a table and a tea caddy. The piece of furniture itself seems to have originated in the east, for the name comes from the Hindi for 'three' and the Persian for 'foot'; and somewhere along the line this three-footed table got itself translated from 'tinpae' into 'teapoy'–presumably under the influence of tea, as the *Shorter Oxford Dictionary* so nearly says. Later it became the table on which the tea caddy was kept, and then an actual caddy, mounted upon a three-legged pedestal foot. It is in this form that one sees it today, although very infrequently.

A tortoiseshell tea caddy (Christies, South Kensington)

Returning to caddies, here is a whole world for the collector. No doubt that the plain ones of standard size are cheap–quite exceptionally, I think, in view of the craftsmanship which has been put into them. On the other hand the small, individual ones, especially those shaped as fruits, pagodas and cottages, though eminently shelfworthy, are very expensive.

Caddies come in all various woods like mahogany, walnut, satinwood, harewood, maple and rosewood, in PONTYPOOL AND USK WARE, TUNBRIDGE WARE, PEWTER and so on. Some have rich carving, some are painted, others inlaid with materials like ebony, IVORY and MOTHER OF PEARL, or mounted with silver.

Every house should, I think, have at least *one* caddy, even if it is only a modest one, simply as a tribute to an age when craftsmen really put their hearts into quite everyday work.

Tea Caddy Spoons

On the shelves of silversmiths you will see small spoons or ladles, usually in some very attractive or interesting pattern.

These were once the inevitable accompaniment of the tea caddy, used to measure tea carefully in days when it was one of the dearest things on the shopping list.

These spoons come in a wide range of shapes, scallop shells being probably the most frequently met with, but there are others fashioned like shovels, acorns, vine-leaves, jockey caps, hearts and fishes.

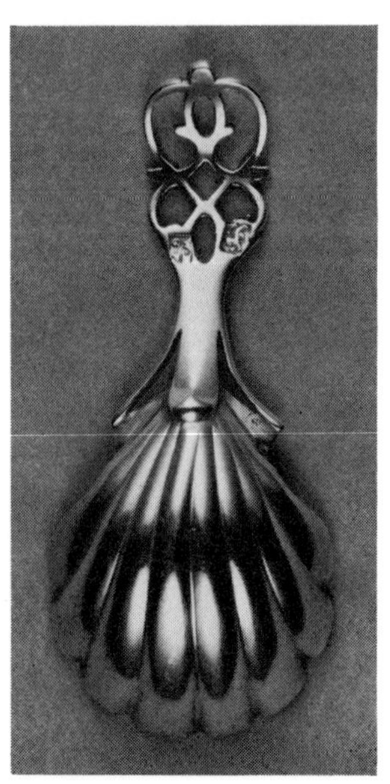

The back of a scallop-shell tea caddy spoon (Edward Kramer)

Terra Cotta

I would give the finest PARIAN figure there is for one in terra cotta, especially if it has been left 'in the rough' to show the true nature of the clay. Called the 'sculptors's delight', it is said that Michelangelo used this material to work out ideas which he afterwards executed in marble.

The Victorians loved it, like everyone else, and have left us TOBACCO JARS, vases, inkstands, mignonette boxes, ewers, garden pedestals, fountains and hanging baskets. Sometimes they painted it in enamels, sometimes inlaid it with mosaics, sometimes part-covered it with MAJOLICA glazes in rich colours.

Terra cotta simply means 'baked earth', and it is basic earthenware, varying in colour from ochre to pink or lobster red, but calling for a high degree of fineness; in ancient times it was used for PLAQUES, tomb figures, urns and pitchers, and was sometimes decorated with encaustic (baked on) colours.

Terra cotta TILES still grace many public buildings and as these relics come under the house-breaker's pick there will be many fine specimens offered to us in the junk shops. Our plaque is one of a set of twelve representing the months of the year, designed and modelled by W. J. Morris for M. H. Blanchard of Blackfriars, London.

If you want statuary in terra cotta the best, in my opinion, comes from France. The sculptor Jules Dalou has some touching maternal groups, some small, some almost life-size, in the Victoria and Albert Museum, and the handling shows a wonderful sense of the material. Small groups are to be found in the Marché aux Puces at no very great cost.

Terra-cotta wall tile

Theatre Bills and Programmes

For many years now our friends the breakers, have been pulling down theatres large and small, and this has yielded a crop of useful items. Many a pub I know has fitted itself out with a row of 'fauteuils' in which innumerable audiences once sat enthralled.

But the passing of all these Theatre Royals and Empires, Palaces of Variety and Music Halls has left another legacy to the collector. This is the theatre bill, copies of which were once carried on tour by 'artists', to be devoutly unfolded before your eyes so that you could see the steady progression of their names from the middle to the bottom and from the bottom to the top.

Such items have long been collected in America–the famous Harvard Theater Collection has no fewer than a million playbills. To some extent they have also been collected in Britain and there are now several specialist dealers, though it can still be most rewarding to hunt for these pieces of ephemera in the most unlikely places.

Prices have been rising steadily over the past few years and you would have to pay ten pounds or more for fine examples from the turn of the century, especially those with the names of famous music hall artists, but there are many others of more recent vintage that are still fairly cheap.

Theatre Royal Hay-Market

The New Serious Drama, called

A DUEL,

IN RICHELIEU'S TIME,

Having been received with a success the most decided, by a brilliant audience, will be repeated EVERY EVENING THIS WEEK.

This Evening, **WEDNESDAY, July 11, 1832.**

Will be performed, the Opera of The

Marriage of Figaro

Count Almaviva, - Mr. VINING,
Antonio, Mr. J. COOPER, Fiorello, Mr. YARNOLD,
Figaro, Mr. HARLEY,
Cherubino, (the Page,) Mrs. HUMBY,
Basil, Mr. HUCKEL, Notary, Mr. BISHOP, Sebastian, Mr. MOORE,
Countess Almaviva, Miss BELLCHAMBERS, (*from the King's Theatre, her First Appearance,*)
who will introduce the Grand Scena, "*AID ME, YE PITYING POWERS,*"
and the celebrated Melody of "*THE LAST ROSE OF SUMMER.*" (with Variations, arranged expressly for this occasion, by J. Augustine Wade.)
Susanna, Miss WILLIAMS, (*her First Appearance.*)
who will introduce "*THE KNIGHT WAS BRAVE.*"
Barbarina, Mrs. T. HILL, Marcellina, Mrs. COVENEY,
Incidental to the Opera, A PAS SEUL by Miss ROSE, (*Pupil of Miss Barnett.*)

After which, (THIRD TIME) a Serious Drama, in Three Acts, called

A DUEL,

IN RICHELIEU'S TIME,

Le Comte de Chalais, favourite of Louis XIII, Mr. VINING,
Le Duc de Chevreuse, Mr. COOPER,
Armand de Retz, Abbé de Gondi, Mr. WEBSTER,
De Fiesque, Captain of the Cardinals Guard, Mr. BRINDAL,
De Suze, Mr. BARTLETT, Balagnier, Mr. GALLOT,
Aubry, Secretary of Le Comte de Chalais, Mr. YOUNGE,
Soubise, Mr. W. JOHNSON, Officer of the King's Cabinet, Mr. EATON,
Marie de Rohan Monthazon, (Widow of the Constable de Luynes,) Miss TAYLOR.

To which will be added, a Comic Piece, (in One Act,) called

JOHN JONES.

Guy Goodluck, Esq. Mr. W. FARREN,
John Jones, (alias Mr. Henry Smith) Mr. VINING,
Mr. Milton, Mr. STRICKLAND, Cox, (Officer for Surrey) Mr. COVENEY,
Eliza Milton, Mrs. HUMBY, Jenny, Mrs. NEWCOMBE.

To conclude with (EIGHTH TIME) a Comic Piece, in One Act, called

The BOARDER.

Mr. Peregrine Plotwell, Mr. W. FARREN,
Mr. Pendleberry, Mr. STRICKLAND, Mr. Ferdinand Frampton, Mr. BRINDAL
Mrs. Pendleberry, Mrs. TAYLEURE, Sophia, Miss J. SCOTT,
Mrs. Tidmarsh, Mrs. COVENEY, Mary, Mrs. GALLOT.
Stage Manager, Mr. P. FARREN. VIVANT REX ET REGINA!

BOXES 5s.—PIT 3s.—FIRST GALLERY 2s.—SECOND GALLERY 1s.
The Doors to be opened at Half-past Six o'Clock, and the Performances to begin at Seven.
Places for the Boxes to be taken of Mr. Massingham, at the Theatre, Daily, from Ten till Five.
N. B. PRIVATE BOXES may be had Nightly, and Free Admissions for the Season, on application at the Box-Office.

A NEW COMIC DRAMA

is in preparation, and will be produced NEXT WEEK.

To-Morrow, THREE WEEKS AFTER MARRIAGE; Sir Charles Racket, Mr. Vining, Lady Racket, Miss Smithson, with The BUSY BODY; Sir Jealous Traffic, Mr. Strickland, Sir Francis Gripe, Mr. W. Farren, Sir George Airy, Mr. Cooper, Marplot, Mr. Harley, Charles, Mr. Brindal, Miranda, Miss Taylor, Patch, Mrs. Humby, A DUEL, in Richelieu's Time, and The WOLF AND THE LAMB.

On Friday, A DUEL, in Richelieu's Time, with SHE WOULD AND SHE WOULD NOT; Don Manuel, Mr. W. Farren, Don Philip, Mr. Cooper, Don Octavio, Mr. Vining, Don Lewis, Mr. Brindal, Trappanti, Mr. Harley, Hypolita, Miss Taylor, Flora, Mrs. T. Hill, Viletta, Mrs. Humby, Rosara, Mrs. Ashton, and The ILLUSTRIOUS STRANGER; Bowbell, Mr. Harley, Gimbo, Mr. Webster, Fatima, Mrs. Humby.

On Saturday, A DUEL, in Richelieu's Time, with JOHN JONES, and other Entertainments.

On Monday, SPEED THE PLOUGH, with A DUEL, in Richelieu's Time, & other Entertainments.

Printed by S. JOHNSON, 2, Herbert's Passage, Beaufort Buildings Strand.

Left: *Bill of the Theatre Royal, Haymarket, London, for July 11 1832.*

'Lion Rampant' tile panel by De Morgan (William Morris Gallery)

Programmes are so often carried home to remind one of an evening of delight, but usually kept for no more than a few weeks. These, too, are now sought. Nineteenth-century examples are now decidedly elusive, but there are many kinds of programme still available from the early years of this century.

Tiles

Delftware tile

Tiles fascinate me almost as much as PLAQUES, probably for the same sort of reasons, namely that they come in endless variety, that they're done in many kinds of ceramics, and that with them you can cover a very wide range of periods and styles at a not very outrageously high cost.

Looking round at some I have accumulated almost casually in the last few years, I find I have three Dutch DELFTWARE ones, showing biblical scenes like Tobias and the Angel; two which I feel sure are Bristol delftware, with waterside scenes of ships and houses; and a pair of Victorian glazed earthenware ones which were evidently part of a 'Country Scenes' series; one of them had a youthful fishing party and the other a shepherd's boy. All of these seem to have cost me no more than a few shillings each, but they were purchased in the 1950s and now they would probably cost as many pounds.

Then there is a very handsome one, much larger, in a mixture of relief and tone, a charming picture of two little Victorian girls playing on a drum and a tambourine. I suspect they are Minton MAJOLICA but it is not easy to identify such things–which, I think makes collecting them even more fun. I would dearly love to find a specimen of Bristol *bianco sopra bianco*, but I'm afraid that so far the dealers have always been ahead of me.

Tiles can be framed, and in fact you often come across sets of them in threes and sixes. They can also be laid round a fireplace, and if you have one of these modern monstrosities of made-up 'surrounds' in a pinky buff, with one square missing at each end for subtle decoration, I would recommend you to strip the whole thing down and have your local builder put some old tiles round it.

Tinsel Pictures

Difficult to run to earth now anywhere but in the specialist shops but worth knowing about all the same are these engaging little pictures decorated with tinsel. They usually depict some famous actor of the early Victorian era in a preposterously heroic attitude, with scenes from the play going on in the background.

These things were originally sold as prints, and you could buy your tinsel decoration–stars, dots, helmets, swords and so forth–and do your own brightening up. Only a few years ago they could be found quite cheaply but lately I have only seen them in the theatrical districts of London, such as St Martin's Lane and Charing Cross Road.

They derive from the 'penny plain, tuppence coloured' figures of the toy theatres which were put out by publishers of the juvenile drama like J. K. Green.

Many famous actors and actresses of the day are shown in their favourite roles–the villains are always especially fine. But apart from stage figures, royalty and other celebrities appear in these prints. There was some attempt in the 1920s to revive this art, primarily for theatrical pictures, but latterly degenerating into *genre* scenes and figures. There were even tinsel pictures of the *Queen Mary*, done presumably at the time of her launching in 1934, and one still comes across pretty little pictures of ladies in crinolines and gentlemen in top hats and frock coats.

Tobacco Jars and Boxes

You may sometimes come across a battered lead box with relief decoration, perhaps traces of colour, and a little figure on the lid. Inside–if you are lucky–is a flat sheet of lead used for pressing down the tobacco which this article contained.

This is only one of the types of tobacco boxes one sees about. Often the relief decoration shows a landscape or even a battle scene. I recently saw one depicting the battle of Sevastopol in the Crimean War. With the earlier ones this decoration was cast as part of the main piece, but later it was applied to a plain box. Tobacco jars may also be found in other metals, and in various forms of pottery and glass.

George II silver tobacco box, 1745 (Aspreys)

One interesting family, evidently an early version of the vending machine, were the brass ones with a ha'penny-in-the-slot arrangement used in coaching inns. On putting in a coin a lock was released and you helped yourself to a 'twist'. But apparently there weren't any means of seeing that you didn't take more than your share, for an inscription on one of them reads:

'Gentlemen, it's for your pleasure
I wait here from day to day
To supply you (when at leisure)
With the weed, who puff must pay.
For half a penny a pipeful take
And pay regard to what I say
Having that, for credit's sake,
Close the lid, or sixpence pay'.

A penny-in-the-slot tobacco box, c. 1840–1880 (S. H. Cole)

Another smoker's item well worth looking at now are those small round brass and copper boxes used as pouches. They often have interesting pictures or crests on them, with much social and general history: many of them have regimental or club crests.

Toby Jugs

Real old Toby jugs are now as highly priced as any other early Staffordshire ware, but if you simply want a Toby there is nothing to stop you buying him brand-new from your local china shop.

His full name is Toby Fillpot, and some say the character was based on a famous toper named Harry Elwes, who is reputed to have put away 2,000 gallons of beer in his lifetime. Others favour Paul Parnell, a Yorkshire farmer and grazier who in *his* lifetime drank nine thousand pounds worth of Yorkshire stingo.

But these are evidently cases of tying up a well-known personage with something that was already there, for the real Toby seems to have originated in, of all places, Italy. We owe the design of the jug to a popular engraving published about 1761 to illustrate a song translated from the Italian by a clergyman named Francis Fawkes. The reverend gentleman's rendering was as follows:

'Dear Tom, this brown Jug that now foams with mild Ale,
In which I will drink to sweet Nan of the Vale,
Was one Toby Fillpot, a thirsty old Soul,
As e'er drank a Bottle or fathom'd a Bowl.
In boozing about 'twas his praise to excel,
And among Jolly Topers he bore off the Bell.

It chanc'd as in Dog-days he sat at his Ease,
In his Flow'r woven Arbour as gay as you please,
With a Friend and a Pipe, puffing Sorrow away,
And with honest old Stingo was soaking his Clay.
His breath Doors of life on a sudden were shut
And he died full as big as a Dorchester Butt.

His body, when long in the ground it had lain,
And time into Clay had resolv'd it again
A potter found out in its Covert so snug
And with part of fat Toby he form'd this brown Jug
Now sacred to Friendship and Mirth and Mild Ale.
So here's to my lovely sweet Nan of the Vale.'

Many Tobies carry inscriptions, most of them jovial or provocative. 'It is all out, then fill it again' strikes a typical note, and so does 'Drink your Ale up, cock your Tail up'; while 'Not for you, Boney' cocks a snook at Napoleon across the Channel.

Toby himself appears in all sorts of guises–as a sailor, a parson, a night watchman, planter, fiddler, as Punch (with his Judy), John Bull, the Woodman, Silly Billy and so on. There are also female Tobies, like Martha Gunn and the Gin woman.

As to cost, Toby has been made in almost every kind of ware, from the celebrated Ralph Wood's early work in coloured glazes down to modern pottery; so obviously his price will go according to the rarity of the ware his is made in. Some of the rarer figures, like Prince Hal and Martha Gunn, have been known to fetch many hundreds of pounds at auction.

In view of this, our helpful friends the fakers have been at it, and if you want rare old Tobies they can be made for you without any trouble at all.

Below left: *Saltglaze slip-cast Doulton Ware Toby jug, designed c. 1925 (Doulton & Company Limited).*

Above right: *'The Anxious Bride'. A German clockwork toy, c. 1900 (Christies, South Kensington)*

Toiles de Jouy

These famous French expressions of the printed calicoes we call CHINTZ owe their origin to Philip Oberkampf, a native of Weisenbach, whose father set up as a textile printer in Basle.

Like other skilled craftsmen, Oberkampf moved to Paris, where such works were in great demand, and from about 1758 started to print in fast colours, like those of the original *indiennes* or *toiles peintes*.

In 1760 after the French government, despairing of enforcing their regulations, had removed their total prohibition on calico printing, Oberkampf set up in a very small way at the village of Jouy, near Versailles. The stamp of the firm from 1767 onwards was *Manufacture de toiles peintes et imprimées de Sarrasin-Demaraise et Oberkampf, a*

Jouy près Versailles. It was designated *Manufacture Royale* in 1783, thus adding the royal arms up to the Revolution in 1792.

By Oberkampf's method a black outline was printed, 'filling' was carried out with colour blocks, and colours which were difficult to print were applied by hand. Louis XVI's Swiss Guard were called in to watch over the printed calico as it lay bleaching in the surrounding fields. Oberkampf continued at work until his death in 1815, the year of Waterloo.

Perhaps the best-known edition of the *toiles de Jouy* are those printed in red, either from blocks or in picotage. At first the patterns used were mainly the contemporary *chinoiseries* followed by landscapes and pastoral scenes, but later there was a much greater range of pictorial chintzes in various single colours which suited the prevailing furniture styles admirably and were exported in huge quantities to Britain and other countries.

Best known of the designers was Jean Baptiste Huet; but it should be borne in mind that there were many other centres of production of *toiles*, even in France, and the English chintz industry was well-established before Oberkampf ever set up shop at Jouy.

Tôle Peinte

While the tin-platers of South Wales and Wolverhampton were offering their gaily-painted PONTYPOOL AND USK WARE the same kind of thing was going on in France under this name, which means 'painted tinware'. A difference was, however, that–as with the Dutch variety–it was PEWTER *(étain)* which was painted and not iron plate: something that English pewterers had ensured would not be allowed to happen in their country.

French tôle peinte tobacco jar

A great variety of articles appear in tôle peinte, especially vases, chestnut jars, samovars and urns, candlesticks and sconces. Since it flourished during the Empire period, many of them take on the kind of classical forms you see here, often with classical decoration as well. Colours include a green, a mustard yellow and (especially in Italy) a rich cream.

Some very attractive lamps were also made in tôle peinte, especially in Italy and Spain–in the latter country there is a spectacular kind of hanging lamp or lantern painted in colours and gilt and called a *farol*.

Toys

There is a certain sort of shop which is not exactly a junk shop in the sense that you look there for things which are, or might have once been, considered attractive to look at, but all the same it has its customers. The stock includes old boxing gloves, door handles, cricket bats, golf clubs, empty oil drums, field glasses, pram wheels (in great demand for go-carts), cameras, drain pipes, cigarette cards, bird cages, guns and old electric light fittings. Women fly from these places in horror: but men love them, and spend hours considering how they might make striking use of something which can be acquired for a few pence. It is an excellent place, by the way, to replace those brand new tools left to rust in the garden–at a fraction of their original cost.

Mid 19th-century pedestal stereoscope (Christies, South Kensington)

Boys and small children also like them, one of the reasons being that they often have a stock of old toys, battered, but often quite serviceable. I wonder that no Victorian genre painter has ever given us a picture of father and son in one of these shops speculatively turning over an old gipsy van or coal trolley and wondering if it could be knocked into shape again.

These old toys have a really surprising survival rate considering the rough handling they have had: one can only conclude that the best are still first-hand, and have been in a box in a cupboard ever since.

Automaton monkeys: right, *violinist and cellist,* left, *a boot black (Christies, South Kensington)*

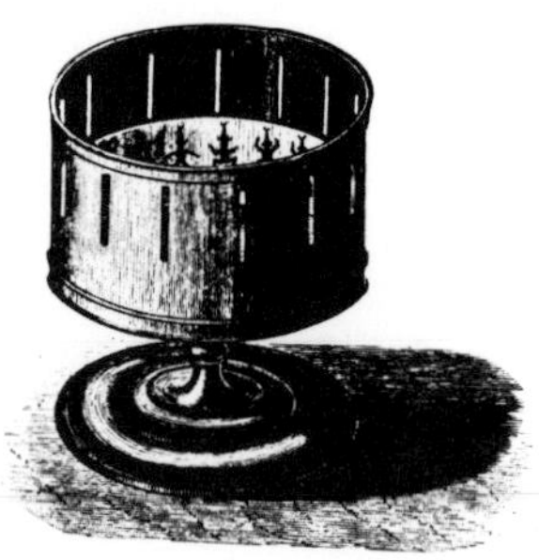

A zoetrope, early 19th century (Pollock's Toy Museum)

Anyway, there they are, if you look hard for them, the funny little 'penny toys' of all sorts. Those were the days of many sorts of children's cars, and they appeared in their miniature form, sometimes with horses galloping up and down on the wheel axles. Buses, hansom cabs, taxis, cars and even locomotives look pleasantly out of date. Allied to these are the pull-along toys–animals and human figures which dance about in an entrancing way when you trail them on the end of a string.

Cardboard boxes sometimes contain the melancholy remains of a board game, but usually the board has been lost; jigsaws might tempt one but for the fear of missing pieces, and anyway the subjects are often rather solemn and religious. Early examples of building bricks also tend to be rather didactic.

If we are going mechanical there is sometimes one of those tin Highlanders or guardsmen which, on being wound up, move around sideways like Mr Jingle's horse, frantically saluting everyone in sight. There are mechanical barrel organs playing unrecognizable tunes and Indian jugglers performing tricks with snakes.

If instead of a hard-up-looking father and son, you see a smartly-dressed business man hanging around one of these shops, be sure he is looking for one of those steam or petrol engines we had bought for us away back in the 'twenties. I suppose these could be called models rather than toys, but the businessman wants to be in the fashion and put one on his office window-sill, so that he can remind himself that if his firm hasn't made any progress at least they're now using electricity instead of steam.

Then there are the old magic lanterns, the kaleidoscopes and stereoscopes and a whole host of optical toys with fantastic Greek names like phenakistiscope, zoetrope,

A model swing plough, made by a Cumbrian blacksmith in 1911, the date when most hill farms gave up using the swing plough (S. H. Cole)

Above: *A toy flatiron and stand ('At the Sign of the Sad Iron' Limited)*. Left: *A carved and painted German Noah's Ark, c. 1850 (The Museum of London)*

thaumatrope and zograscope. Many of them operated on the principle known as persistence of vision, and they may be regarded as the ancestors of motion pictures.

Just occasionally you will see one of those marvellous butcher's shops with all those ribs of beef and sides of mutton hanging outside, and the butcher in his blue apron. (I never had one of these myself: is it true for everyone that the toys one liked best were those one was never bought?)

Lastly there are the soldiers, now no longer in those fine big boxes with cavalry and infantry, tents and stamped-out bushes and trees, but chucked in a box and probably covered with chalk. I pick them up occasionally and contrast their leaden heaviness with the lightweight, unbreakable ones of today: no boy would ever want them, but for all I know I may be handling some great rarity of a hussar from Germany, wanted by collectors all over the world. A good Noah's Ark I have not seen for a long time, but there are plenty of crude home-made ones.

As for the great rocking horse, with their studded saddles and flowing manes, these move quickly into the better-class shops for they make their money as decoration.

A 'Safety' rocking horse of 1900

Truncheons

Now and then you will see one of the old painted police truncheons. A collection of forty-odd came up for sale in 1960 and included about twenty painted ones, five showing the arms of George IV and one those of George III.

When people collect truncheons their earliest specimens are usually those of what you might call the opposition; being used by bad men, however, they are called cudgels or bludgeons. Some of these were pretty murderous things–there is one of twisted

A mid-Victorian painted police truncheon (Metropolitan Police)

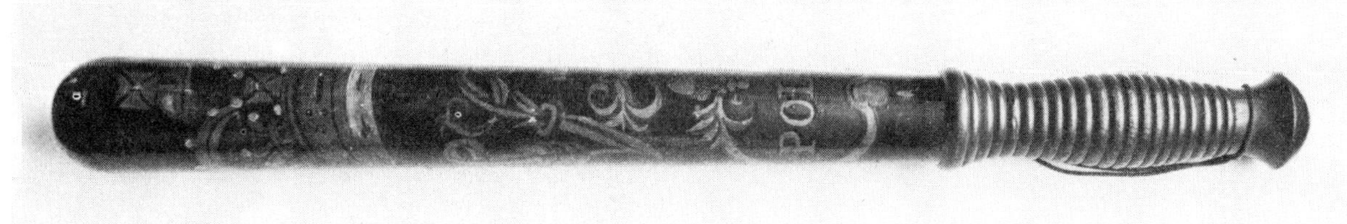

whalebone with a leaden head–so it is not surprising that the early watchman's staff was a very hefty affair, at least twice the size of a modern policeman's baton (the change in terminology is again instructive). The Bow Street Runner's weapon, the tipstaff, was a badge of authority as well, and anyone who received it on the head got a right royal bruise the exact shape of the crown with which the staff was capped.

But people in those days had also to look after themselves, so you will come across truncheons which are nothing to do with the police. Private citizens carried them; inns kept them in case it became necessary to keep customers in order. Civic dignitaries, magistrates, sherriff-officers and bailiffs are among those who had truncheons and tipstaves, often ornately decorated with coats of arms and cyphers. Many societies and organizations also had ceremonial tipstaves with handsome painted and gilded emblems and inscriptions.

Tunbridge Ware

Or wood mosaic, as it is sometimes called. The Victorians loved anything that called for enormous pains in the making. You can take an ordinary wooden box and paint or print a picture on it; but in their view it was much more interesting if the picture, instead of being painted, was made up from the tiny *ends* of hundreds, or even thousands, of little sticks of different coloured woods.

That roughly, is how Tunbridge ware is made. Slips of different coloured woods, each about half the size of a school ruler, were glued together in blocks so as to give a pattern or picture. Then these blocks were sawn across the end to provide veneer sheets, which were mounted on the article to be decorated.

Over 150 British and American woods were used, and it was apparently a point of honour not to use any colouring matter, although staining effects could be obtained by soaking some of the woods in the famous local spring water.

The craft was carried on all through the nineteenth century in and around Tunbridge Wells in Kent; not so long ago you could still buy small articles decorated in this fashion for no great sum, but, like everything else that was decorative in the Victorian era, Tunbridge ware has shot up enormously in price these past few years, and really intricately decorated items have become exceedingly scarce.

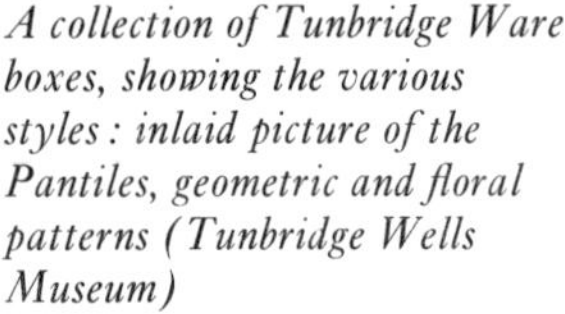

A collection of Tunbridge Ware boxes, showing the various styles: inlaid picture of the Pantiles, geometric and floral patterns (Tunbridge Wells Museum)

Urns

The classical urn was a round or oval bowl standing on a pedestal, used by the ancient Greeks and Romans and others, to preserve the ashes of their dead.

If we no longer have such a vessel in our houses we may have one in the garden, bought either from country antique shops which get them from big houses when they are demolished, or perhaps in cement from a contemporary manufacturer.

Some of the most pleasant ones to have are those in Victorian TERRA COTTA and MAJOLICA. Urns were also put on the top of pedestals in Adam dining-room suites, and used to carry the water for washing up when you dared not trust the servants with the cutlery. From that time they seem to have travelled along to the sitting-room or the boudoir, where they appear as tea and coffee urns: and it is here that we shall find them in many shapes, forms and materials.

There are those tall cylindrical ones in PONTYPOOL WARE and TÔLE PEINTE, there are COPPER ones, sometimes now ELECTRO-PLATED, perhaps with brass or silver mounts. If you want the exotic look, seek a Russian samovar. Many of these urns derived their heat from a spirit lamp, but there are also those with the sort of iron heaters used in taverns.

When you change the shape a little, give them a handle, and put urns on hinges, they become swinging kettles–just as useful and often more decorative. There is a kind of table with a narrow top and a metal gallery running round it which was specially designed to carry the urn: and nowadays it does equally good service for a CACHEPOT carrying a potted plant.

Valentines

'Tomorrow is St Valentine's Day
All in the morning betime,
And I am a maid at your window
To be your valentine.'

Those romantic, playful, usually anonymous missives, got up in their pierced hearts, lacing and pink silk, which once appeared in their hundreds of thousands on St Valentine's Day, have enjoyed a tremendous revival since the Second World War. This makes one interested in all the old ones, which can sometimes be found in those inexhaustible boxes and albums in the back of junk shops.

A Victorian valentine (S. H. Cole)

Nobody seems to know which of the various St Valentines is the one celebrated on February 14, nor what connection he has with

'Unnumbered lasses, young and fair,
From Bethnal Green to Belgrave Square
With cheeks high flushed and hearts loud beating
Await the tender annual greeting.'

As will be seen by our quotations (from Shakespeare and Macaulay respectively) the tender traffic was a two-way one, this being the day when an approach was permissible not only from the man, but also from the maid–though Ophelia's lady perhaps went a little too far. It is probably no accident that the day coincides with the Roman feast of the *Lupercalia*, in honour of the great god Pan.

There always seems to have been some element of chance, or mystery, about the greetings and when, in the eighteenth century, the first cards were sent, it was generally anonymously. The idea seems to have been that you were suddenly made aware of being adored by someone: who could it possibly be (as if you didn't know!).

From the first hand-written cards (words culled from textbooks) one moves to the first printed cards, appearing early in the nineteenth century, and decked out in embossed paper, velvet, lace, shells, leaves and even spun glass: and then to cards with scented sachets, edged with swansdown, cheques drawn on the 'Bank of Love' and parodies of banknotes in the same vein.

Two factors seem to have contributed to the decline of the Valentine in Britain at the turn of the century: one, the emergence in the late nineteenth century of the mocking ones, sent with deadly effect to those who had scorned you, or merely as crude (and often cruel) jokes. The other was the fact that it paid manufacturers to concentrate on the CHRISTMAS CARDS which were used by everyone, not only lovers and haters.

Vase-in-Hand

Vase-in-hand

Vases are usually bought individually, but sometimes they fall into a pattern or type which seems to call for putting together and seeing what they look like.

In an antique shop in Sussex some years ago I saw about a dozen of the sort which consists of a small vase held in a hand, usually a lady's. They are being made again today, of course, but that's no reason why one shouldn't seek out those made in the past.

I have seen it stated that the idea originated at Worcester in the Kerr and Binns era, but I can hardly believe that it came as late as that, especially when you find specimens in PARIAN WARE. Those in bone china are very attractive indeed, and will probably take some finding nowadays.

Vinaigrettes

You will have seen in the better sort of shops tiny boxes of silver, perhaps no larger than a postage stamp, having a fretted grille inside. These are called vinaigrettes and their purpose was to revive ladies in days when a timely fainting fit was one of the few remedies they had against an obdurate male world. It was also a help in an age when bad smells could be found without any trouble at all.

The aromatic 'vinegar' was really acetic acid combined with some essential oil like cinnamon, lavender or mint, and a little sponge soaked in it was kept under the grille. If

Below: *A Victorian silver vinaigrette in the form of a hunting horn, c. 1870 (Aspreys)*

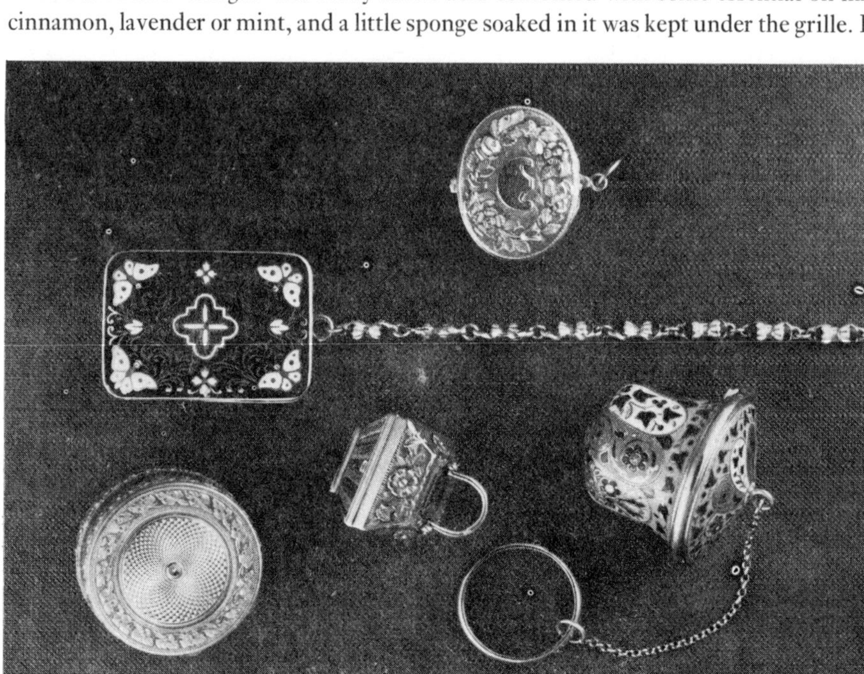

Right: *A selection of early 19th-century gold and enamel vinaigrettes. (Aspreys)*

you are very lucky, you may find one with the sponge still there. As this 'vinegar' was highly corrosive, most silver vinaigrettes have a gold or gilt lining, but they were also made in semi-precious stones, glass and MOTHER OF PEARL. Apart from the boxes, they came in many shapes: as books, purses, shells, acorns and nuts. Silver-gilt and PINCHBECK were also used.

Of course you will not expect to find these often exquisitely made little things in heaps of junk. They are usually to be sought in silversmith's shops. But they have been noted in jumble sales, and if you come across one in an inherited jewel box it may well set you off on a collection of them.

Wallpaper

Is it possible to collect wallpaper, that highly perishable form of decorative art? Can it be done without actually carrying a paperhanger's stripping knife under one's coat when visiting a friend's old house.

In his *Literary History of Wallpaper* (1960), E. A. Entwhistle very properly reminds us of the habit our forebears had (as many today) of using wallpaper for the linings of cupboards, drawers, boxes and travelling trunks. It has been used (especially in America) to cover bandboxes and books. Furthermore the house-breaker or knacker to whom we look for our DECORATIVE IRONWORK and other items is much more alive to the fact that old wallpaper can be of as much interest as old wood, iron or stone; wallpaper has even been found occasionally *under* old wood panelling.

What kind of wallpapers are worth collecting? First there are the hand-painted or hand-printed variety made down to about 1840. The earliest of the latter were printed in plain black from woodblocks. Then there are the early flock papers in which the minute shearings of waste wool were used to simulate the rich cut velvet hangings of the seventeenth and early eighteenth centuries.

Chinese papers came in the East Indiamen along with the porcelain and the Indian CHINTZES, using very much the same kind of patterns. They were very different designs, of course, from the *chinoiseries* made in the West, having been developed for the tastes of the Chinese–there are in fact echoes here of the great K'ang Hsi porcelains.

Then there are the French scenic wallpapers of the early nineteenth century, which sometimes appear at auction in 'sets' of rolls; but it should be noted that many of them have been reprinted. A duty stamp appeared on papers between 1712 and 1836.

In Britain there are 'embossed' finishes designed to give the effect of leather or textiles, while 'stucco' papers try to look like stone or plaster–and *moiré* papers show

From left: *Two C.F.A. Voysey designs currently in production: 'Savaric' and 'Aldworth' (Sanderson & Sons Limited); 'Indian' wallpaper by Morris (William Morris Gallery)*

watered silk effects. There were 'pilaster' papers in sets to contain panelling schemes.

With the coming of printing we have the fine floral designs of mid-Victorian times, elaborate panels setting off pictures as though they were oil paintings hanging in a room–the subjects range from battle scenes in the Crimean War to hunting scenes and curious *trompe l'oeil* effects which create an optical illusion. There was also a rich ecclesiastical 'Gothic' style–in startling contrast with the frivolous 'Gothick' or Horace Walpole. Christopher Dresser and C. F. A. Voysey designed wallpapers for Liberty, but the leading figure in revolutionizing the design of English wallpaper was William Morris; his patterns were considered the ultimate in good taste at the turn of the century and these are now the ones most sought after–but many patterns have been revived and are in current production. Other designers from the ARTS AND CRAFTS MOVEMENT include Kate Greenaway and Lewis F. Day.

In France you ask for *papier peinte*; in Germany (where you should visit the Wallpaper Museum in Kassel) for *Tapeten*; and in Italy for *carta di parati.*

Warming Pans

18th-century warming pan, shown with an early copper bed bottle (S. H. Cole)

These once useful objects, perhaps the first of the household items to become a wall decoration while still in daily use, have become so closely identified with the world of antiques that one almost forgets that they have their range and varieties like any other piece. This is emphasized by the fact that so many of those you see about are either modern reproductions, or very late and entirely practical affairs intended for use rather than ornament.

But if you really want to go to town on your warming pan, you ought to travel back to the seventeenth century and find a silver one engraved with the crest of the nobleman in whose bed it was introduced while he sat drinking in the dining-room. No need to worry about damaging the silver if you should happen to want to put it to use: it should have inside an ember pan, for carrying glowing charcoal or wood *embers–not* blazing coals, please.

If this sounds ambitious, try to get a BRASS one, finely punched with a simple design, or perhaps with heraldic designs and a date. It will, of course, still cost you dear, but at least it will probably be genuine. The modern forger would surely find it heavy going to get *exactly* the right style of old punched design, whereas anyone can manage some sort of pressed pattern.

Watch Keys

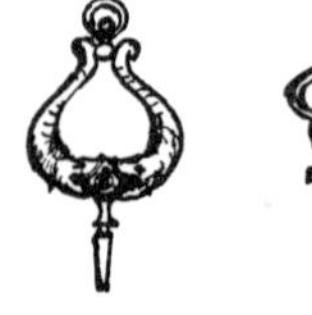

Watch keys

Those who like to collect in miniature might have a look at the watch key from before the days of the self-winding watch. Surprising though it may seem to those who have seen only one or two, these come in enormous variety, and many of them are quite beautifully designed.

In the early days of watches, the patterns of the watch keys followed those of clocks, but later they became very much more elaborate. Many reflect the beautiful work that went into the watches themselves, being engraved, enamelled and often set with semi-precious or precious stones and Wedgwood cameos. Cut and polished steel, BRASS, PINCHBECK, silver and gold were used, and some bear the emblems of different trades, or heraldic motifs of one kind or another.

Watch Stands

Among the many small items which reflect in miniature the tastes of their time, and also the many sorts of material in which these were expressed, is the bedside watch stand.

Now that we wear wrist-watches one presumes that these things are no longer made;

Victorian watch-stands

but once upon a time they were necessities. Upon retiring, you detached your gold hunter from its chain and hung it on one of these little stands which stood upon the bedside table; it could then serve as a clock.

Some of these stands in fact are so large and elaborate that one wonders if they did actually serve as clock-mounts: perhaps housing a second watch, or one too large for the pocket, like a carriage clock. Most sought after, perhaps, are the elaborately carved rococo ones in soft pearwood, many of them from France, which show workmanship equal to anything else in the furniture of that time. These often have a figure of Father Time bearing the clock on his shoulders.

Towards the end of the eighteenth century, as one might expect, they take on the more austere lines of Adam, some in the form of grandfather or longcase clocks, or miniature swinging mirrors. These are attractive and so also are those in the form of well-heads or garden temples, where the watch hangs from a hook in the centre of an arch. Sometimes you get a combined watch and trinket stand, or folding ones for travelling, or others carved in the form of houses and castles.

Apart from wood, polished or painted or perhaps with brass inlay, there are Regency examples in bronzed BRASS and other metals. In the same family, of course, are those watch pockets in BEADWORK, for hanging on the curtains or headboard, presumably for those who had no bedside table.

For those who hadn't a watch anyway there was always the STAFFORDSHIRE FIGURE in the form of a sham clock with the painted or gilded hands perpetually at half-past one.

Wax Fruit and Flowers

Not so long ago we were scornful about those 'shades' of fruit and flowers made in wax or other materials which our Victorian grandparents loved to collect in their crowded rooms. I suppose they liked them because the more colourful and exotic fruits and flowers weren't so often to be seen; and in any case they always admired anything which was ingeniously made to look like something else.

Nowadays we are filling up our rooms again, and these 'shades' are keenly sought after.

A few years ago you could still pick up these ornaments for a pound or two–the glass-domed mounts must have been worth more. Nowadays, however, they have become quite elusive in fine condition, though examples with cloth or cut-paper work decoration are much more plentiful. Examples decorated with SHELLWORK are becoming rare and those PLAQUES with relief profiles and figure groups are now much sought after.

White Metal Goods

There are shops tucked away in back lanes where you will find, standing in serried rows and sometimes a little battered by time, the Apollos, the Mercuries (standing on one leg) the rearing Marly horses, the sou'westered grizzled fisherman and buxom fishermaids, the Cupids, the Castors and Polluxes: in fact, all those classical, sentimental or comical figures which were the household gods of the Victorians.

These actual items have been made in a wide range of materials, but I would like to draw your attention to a range of similar cheap figures which were produced at one time for the less well-off homes, where even ELECTRO-PLATE, let alone silver, was too expensive.

These figures were made in a cheap alloy known as white metal. The makers claimed that it was 'untarnishable', and this has proved, even many decades later, to be true; but naturally they did not mean that these pieces would stay bright. As a result, they resemble unpolished pewter–which I think is one of the nicer metal colours anyway.

There are small trinket and jewel boxes, sometimes in the shape of hearts, hairpin boxes, stud-boxes and cases, CANDLESTICKS, calendars and date-stands. The same metal was used for the mounting of hand mirrors, STANDISHES and a great variety of PINCUSHIONS with velvet tops.

These items were stamped out in thousands by the whitesmiths of Birmingham and other industrial towns, but they have attractive designs of flowers, foliage and all kinds of borders and bandings which workers in more valuable metals have been using since the days of Greece and Rome.

So if you want a small inexpensive collection showing most of these decorative motifs, keep a keen eye open for these things–and there are probably just as many still on dressing tables as there are (so far) in the junk shops.

'Comb back'

Windsor Chairs

I suppose we all know a Windsor chair when we see one: if not, there are drawings of some of the more distinctive patterns shown here.

But the odd thing is that nobody seems to know why it is so called. There is the old legend that King George IV, when hunting in Windsor Forest, was caught in a shower of rain, and took refuge in a cottage. A chair with spindles and a bow back was brought to him and he liked it so much that he ordered some to be made for Windsor Castle.

The only trouble with this story is that the Windsor chair was thus named in print long before 'Prinny' was born. Moreover, so far from being a product of Berkshire it appeared everywhere from Lancashire to Somerset at about the same period.

What appears to have happened, in fact, is that somewhere in Stuart times there

Fan back

Gothic

Child's

Smoker's bow

Bow back

arose a reaction against the heavy oak settles and stools of Elizabeth's reign and people began to buy from their local craftsmen much lighter affairs, made up of sticks and spindles instead of great hunks of wood.

There are endless variations in design, and woods used include beech, ash, willow, yew and elm. But to try to sort all of them out into any sort of chronological or geographical order would be practically impossible, for the amateur craftsmen in one part of the country went on copying styles long after they had gone out of fashion elsewhere. Experts do find some sort of progression but except in the few cases where a maker has left his name or a number on the back of a chair, it's difficult to trace their origin.

There are, however, recognized terms for the different features of the chairs, which enable the various types to be put into categories. Some of these are shown in the drawings.

Wicker Ware

Everyone surely remembers the comfortable creak with which one sank into a wicker chair or settee; and how cool they could be in summer, and cushionly comforting in winter. Here they are, both of them dating around 1900.

When was basketwork first used for these comfortable fat affairs? Some say about 1880 or 1890, but the experts help us little with such humble things. Perhaps their history goes back a very long way indeed, like that of the wicker or basketwork cradles which one can see in prints of the seventeenth century.

Today one sees the plain ones lingering in junk shops; but those gaily painted ones, or those with different coloured osiers interwoven to make patterns, have they all gone to the bonfire on Guy Fawkes night?

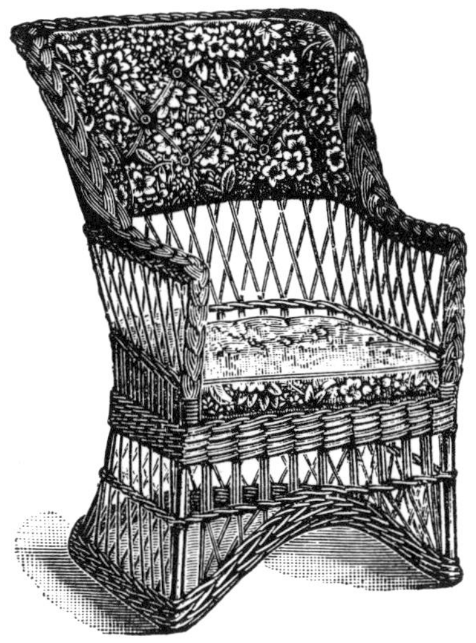

Wicker chair and settee, 1900

Wine Coasters and Wagons

If you get worried about your wine bottles making a mark on the table, you can buy one of those handled basket things in which the bottle reclines. But I have always felt that these are clumsy things which can make the wine slop up and down in the bottle, and even all over the tablecloth.

I much prefer the coaster or stand, an item of tableware with a long and respectable history. Bottles in the eighteenth and nineteenth centuries, especially the heavy 'sealed' ones, had rough bottoms, and if anyone asked you to slide it along the table the chances were that you would score the wood. Hence the round or octagonal stand usually of wood with a silver rail, though occasionally found entirely in silver or SHEFFIELD PLATE, with a pad of felt or baize underneath to protect the surface of the table. Decanter stands of the nineteenth century were generally wider and shallower than those for bottles.

After the stands, the wagons and carriages. It evidently occurred to somebody that a more elegant way of sending round the wine than shoving it along would be to put it on wheels; so you have that pleasant thing, the wine wagon, complete with shafts, and compartments for two bottles–of port and madeira, perhaps. Those who still prefer shoving can buy a coaster in the shape of a boat.

Mahogany wine coaster (Christies, South Kensington)

Wine Coolers

This can still be a useful article about the house, and so many people have discovered this that they are no longer cheap to buy.

This is a pity, for I personally detest what happens to a bottle of Pilsner or white wine when it is kept in a refrigerator as though it were milk. These drinks need to be cold but not frozen, and our Georgian and Victorian ancestors knew better than to invent something which made it necessary for them to wait for their drinks to become drinkable.

A Regency mahogany wine cooler (Christies, South Kensington)

These wine coolers, with their iced water, are just the job. What is more, they look well in any company of furniture. I like the brassbound ones, used in taverns, with their capacious depth in which you can submerge the bottle completely. The early eighteenth-century ones were rather shallower, being designed for the 'dumpies' of the time.

Those who like to do their drinking in an outhouse, away from all the female clatter, might like to know that William Kent, the great architect of the English baroque, provided his house with stone ones: they used much less ice. Which brings up a point that people are sometimes curious about: how did they produce ice in the eighteenth century? The answer is that they collected ice in the winter months and stored it in ice-houses underground.

Wine and Sauce Labels

Wine labels, or bottle tickets, as they used to be called, still offer a happy hunting-ground for the collector who doesn't mind spending a few pounds at a time. They look attractive, they have a family likeness, and they come in a great many different styles and materials. A group of them mounted in a case can look most decorative.

A selection of 19th-century silver wine labels showing a variety of vine, scallop, crescent and other shapes (The Museum of London)

Experts believe that they have their origin in the pieces of parchment which were once attached by string round the neck of bottles of port and other wines. As more modern forms of decanter were evolved, however, such parchment or vellum tickets were no longer practical and a more substantial ticket, of metal suspended on a tiny chain, was produced instead. As these labels would be displayed prominently on the sideboard, it was natural to make them in the same styles and qualities as the other thing in the dining-room, so that, apart from the interest of their names, they provide quite a miniature museum of decorative themes.

Every kind of drink, both known and long-forgotten, seems to have had its label, a collection of which would also serve as a history of conviviality over the years, representing such drinks as shrub, sack, arrack, constantia, mountain, Old Tom, Ay Mousseux and Bucellas, sitting alongside the more familiar madeira, hollands, sherry, whisky and port.

Materials include silver, enamels, porcelain and SHEFFIELD PLATE, and there is usually a little silver chain for attachment. The shapes are most varied, ranging from simple crescents and chamfered oblongs to tiger's claws, shells, vine-leaves and animal forms.

As the title of this paragraph indicates, there were, apart from wine labels, others which attract the lady collector. These were labels for sauces, essences and perfumes. N. M. Penzer's *Book of the Wine Label* (1949) also deals with labels for cordials, sauces and perfumes like Bergamot, Frangipani, Hungary Water, Golden Trasser, Quin Sauce, Nepaul, Poverade and Milk of Roses.

Wooden Spoons

To talk of 'spooning' dates us rather–although, according to the *Oxford English Dictionary* only as far back as about 1831. But it must be much further back than this that a wooden spoon, elaborately carved, became associated with courtship: a man became 'spoons with' a girl.

Best known of the British examples, of course, are the famous Welsh love spoons. The genuine, old hand-made article is now quite rare, but they have been produced by mechanical means as a tourist souvenir in recent years.

Once upon a time these spoons were carved personally by a young man and presented to the lady of his choice as an indication that he wished, if she were agreeable, to start the courtship 'bundling'–i.e. lying together on her bed fully dressed so that

A wooden love spoon, with the bowls and chain carved from the one piece of wood. The key of the house and love birds were also a love gift (S. H. Cole)

they could discourse on various matters away from the ears of other members of her family.

Most of the spoons which have survived, however, show such expertise and elaboration in the carving that (as with so many other love tokens) many of them must have been made by professionals and bought at markets and fairs. This seems to be the case with Welsh love spoons after about 1820; later on–and down to the present time–they could be bought from fancy goods shops.

There is the greatest interest in the many different kinds of motifs carved into the handles. As one might expect there are a great many hearts, but also wheels, six-rayed stars, anchors (on spoons carved by sailors), cups and keyholes, and even whole houses (of their dreams, perhaps). The 'Indian pine' motif of the Paisley shawl found its way on to them; and some incorporate a ship's bottle screw. Variations in treatment can be

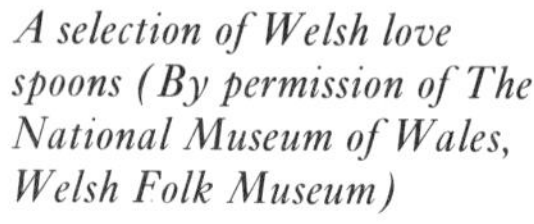

A selection of Welsh love spoons (By permission of The National Museum of Wales, Welsh Folk Museum)

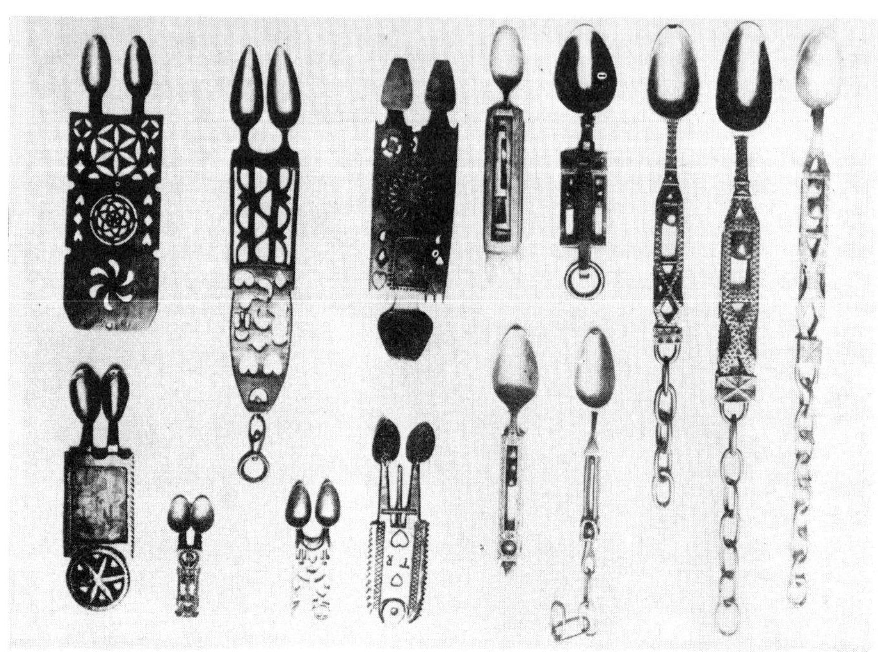

traced to particular localities.

The European continent offers some fine carved spoons, some of them still being made in their original districts. The spoons of Brittany are interesting in that they were worn by the male on his waistcoat button; they could be carved or inlaid with coloured wax and shells. In some districts of Zamora in Spain there are spoons with very long handles, decorated with geometric patterns, and other shorter ones with figures such as Adam and Eve. From Alentejo comes another kind of spoon with an oval handle carved in exquisite detail and foliate and other designs decorated with pierced work. Geometrical piercing is also seen in spoons from the villages of the southern Alps.

Workboxes

Few things bring back one's childhood so vividly as the rosewood workbox, perhaps inlaid with IVORY OR MOTHER OF PEARL, with a silk-lined tray inside the lid. You see these about, of course, but usually needing repair, for they were for use rather than ornament. PAPIER MÂCHÉ ones are very often seen and even these can be repaired. Sometimes the workbox shades off into a 'pouch' table with legs, or even into a full-blown compendium, with room for games as well.

If you are lucky you will find inside them some of the fascinating things described under NEEDLE AND THREAD.

A mid 19th-century workbox with inlaid decoration and fitted compartments for cottons, silks, scissors, needles, bodkins etc. (The Museum of London)

SELECT READING LIST

General

AMAYA, Mario, *Art Nouveau*, London, 1966.
ANGUS, Ian, *Collecting Antiques*, London, 1972.
BATTERSBY, Martin, *The World of Art Nouveau*, London, 1968.
Art Nouveau, London, 1969.
The Decorative Twenties, London, 1969.
The Decorative Thirties, London, 1971.
BEDFORD, John, *The Collecting Man*, London, 1968.
CAMERON, Ian and KINGSLEY-ROWE, Elizabeth (eds.), *Collins Encyclopedia of Antiques*, London, 1973.
COYSH, A. W. and KING, J., *The Buying Antiques Reference Book*, Newton Abbott, 1974.
GARNER, Philippe, *The World of Edwardiana*, London, 1974.
HILLIER, Bevis, *Art Deco*, London, 1968.
HUGHES, G. Bernard, *The Country Life Collector's Pocket Book*, London, 1963.
HUGHES, Therle, *Small Antiques for the Collector*, London, 1964.
Cottage Antiques, London, 1967.
LATHAM, Jean, *Miniature Antiques*, London, 1972.
LAVER, James, *Victoriana*, London, 1966.
MACDONALD-TAYLOR, Margaret, *A Dictionary of Marks*, London, 1962.
MACKAY, James A., *An Introduction to Small Antiques*, London, 1970.
Dictionary of Turn of the Century Antiques, London, 1974.
An Encyclopedia of Small Antiques, London, 1975.
Price Guide to Collectable Antiques, Woodbridge, Suffolk, 1975.
MADSEN, Tschudi, *Art Nouveau*, London, 1967.
NORWAK, Mary, *Kitchen Antiques*, London, 1975.
PETER, M., *Collecting Victoriana*, London, 1965.
RAMSAY, L. G. C. (ed.), *The Concise Encyclopedia of Antiques* (5 vols), London, 1955–60.
The Complete Encyclopedia of Antiques, London, 1975.
SAVAGE, George, *Dictionary of Antiques*, London, 1970.
SPECK, G. E. and SUTHERLAND, Euan, *English Antiques*, London, 1969.
TOLLER, Jane, *Regency and Victorian Crafts*, London, 1969.
WHITTINGTON, Peter, *Undiscovered Antiques*, London, 1972.
WILSON, Peter, *Antiques International*, London, 1966.
WOOD, Violet, *Victoriana: A Collector's Guide*, London, 1968.

Clocks, Watches and Instruments

BAILLIE, G. H., *Watches*, London, 1929.
BELL, G. H. and E. F., *Old English Barometers*, London, 1970.
BRUTON, Eric, *Clocks and Watches, 1400–1900*, London, 1967.
Clocks and Watches, London, 1968.
CHAPUIS, Alfred and DROZ, E., *Automata*, London, 1960.
CLARKE, J. E. T., *Musical Boxes*, London, 1961.
DAUMAS, M., *Scientific Instruments of the 17th and 18th Centuries*, London and Paris, 1972.
GOAMAN, Muriel, *English Clocks*, London, 1967.
GOODISON, N., *English Barometers, 1680–1860*, London, 1969.
JOY, Edward T., *The Country Life Book of Clocks*, London, 1967.

LLOYD, H. Alan, *Old Clocks*, London, 1970.
MICHEL, H. *Scientific Instruments in Art and History*, London, 1967.
TYLER, E. J., *European Clocks*, London, 1968.
ULYETT, Kenneth, *In Quest of Clocks*, London, 1969.
WENHAM, Edward, *Old Clocks*, London, 1965.

Glassware

BARRINGTON-HAYNES, E., *Glass through the Ages*, London, 1959.
BEDFORD, John, *Bristol and Other Coloured Glass*, London, 1964.
Paperweights, London, 1968.
CHARLESTON, R. J., *English Opaque White Glass*, London, 1962.
CROMPTON, Sidney, *English Glass*, London, 1967.
DAVIS, Derek C., *English and Irish Antique Glass*, London, 1965.
English Bottles and Decanters, London, 1972.
DAVIS, Frank, *The Country Life Book of Glass*, London, 1966.
ELVILLE, E. M., *Collector's Dictionary of Glass*, London, 1961.
FLETCHER, Edward, *Bottle Collecting*, London, 1972.
GROS-GALLINER, Gabriella, *Glass: A Guide for Collectors*, London, 1970.
HUGHES, G. Bernard, *English Glass for the Collector*, London, 1967.
MACKAY, James A., *Glass Paperweights*, London, 1973.
MIDDLEMAS, Keith, *Continental Coloured Glass*, London, 1971.
ROBERTSON, R. A., *Chats on Old Glass*, London, 1969.
WARREN, P., *Irish Glass*, London, 1970.
WEBBER, Norman, *Collecting Glass*, London, 1972.
WEISS, Gustav, *The Book of Glass*, London, 1971.
WILLS, Geoffrey, *English Looking-Glasses*, London, 1965.
English and Irish Glass, London, 1968.
Antique Glass, London, 1971.

Metalwork

BURY, Shirley, *Victorian Electroplate*, London, 1971.
COOPER, Jeremy, *Nineteenth-Century Romantic Bronzes*, London, 1974.
ERAS, Vincent, *Locks and Keys Throughout the Ages*, London, 1957.
FROST, T. W., *Price Guide to Old Sheffield Plate*, Woolbridge, Suffolk, 1971.
HARTFIELD, G., *Horse Brasses*, London, 1965.
HAYWARD, John F., *English Cutlery*, London, 1956.
HUGHES, G. Bernard, *Antique Sheffield Plate*, London, 1970.
MACKAY, James A., *The Animaliers*, London, 1973.
MICHAELIS, Ronald, *British Pewter*, London, 1969.
PEAL, C. A., *British Pewter and Britannia Metal*, London, 1971.
PERRY, Evan, *Collecting Antique Metalware*, London, 1974.
SAVAGE, George, *A Concise History of Bronzes*, London, 1968.
WILLS, Geoffrey, *Collecting Copper and Brass*, London, 1962.
The Book of Copper and Brass, London, 1969.
Candlesticks, London, 1974.

Militaria

CLARK, E. F., *Truncheons, Their Romance and Reality*, London, 1935.
DICKEN, E. R. H., *Truncheons, Their History*, London, 1952.
RILING, R., *The Powder Flask Book*, London, 1953.

Models, Games and Toys

BELL, R. C., *Board and Table Games* (2 vols), London, 1960–69.
BLUM, Peter, *Model Soldiers*, London, 1971.
DAIKEN, Leslie, *Children's Toys Throughout the Ages*, London, 1953.
FRASER, Lady Antonia, *A History of Toys*, London, 1966.
GARRATT, John, *Model Soldiers: A Collector's Guide*, London, 1961.
GREENE, V., *English Dolls' Houses*, London, 1967.
HARRIS, H., *How to Go Collecting Model Soldiers*, London, 1969.
HILLIER, Mary, *A Pageant of Toys*, London, 1965.
LATHAM, Jean, *Dolls' Houses*, London, 1969.
MACKAY, James A., *Nursery Antiques*, London, 1976.
NICOLLIER, J., *Collecting Toy Soldiers*, London, 1967.
SPEAIGHT, George, *A History of the English Toy Theatre*, London, 1969.

Objects of Vertu, Jewellery and Accessories

ARMSTRONG, Nancy, *A Collector's History of Fans*, London, 1974.
BEDFORD, John, *Small Boxes of All Kinds*, London.
BRADFORD, Ernle, *English Victorian Jewellery*, London, 1967.
BUCK, A., *Victorian Costume and Costume Accessories*, London, 1961.
COOPER, Diana and BATTERSHILL, Norman, *Victorian Sentimental Jewellery*, London, 1972.
DELIEB, Eric, *Silver Boxes*, London, 1968.
ELLENBOGEN, Eileen, *English Vinaigrettes*, London, 1956.
EPSTEIN, Diana, *Buttons*, London, 1968.
FLOWER, Margaret, *Victorian Jewellery*, London, 1967.
Jewellery, 1837–1901, London, 1968.
FOSTER, Kate, *Scent Bottles*, London, 1966.
GERE, Charlotte, *Victorian Jewellery Design*, London, 1972.
HICKMAN, Peggy, *Silhouettes*, London, 1968.
HUGHES, G. Bernard, *English Snuff-Boxes*, London, 1971.
LAUNERT, Edmond, *Scent and Scent Bottles*, London, 1974.
LEWIS, M. D. S., *Antique Paste Jewellery*, London, 1970.
LUSCOMB, Sally C., *The Collector's Encyclopedia of Buttons*, London, 1967.
PEACOCK, Primrose, *Buttons for Collectors*, London, 1974.
PETER, M., *Collecting Victorian Jewellery*, London, 1970.
WOODIWISS, John, *British Silhouettes*, London, 1966.

Pottery and Porcelain

ALDRIDGE, Eileen, *Porcelain*, London, 1969.
BACCI, Mina, *European Porcelain*, London, 1969.
BARNARD, Julian, *Victorian Ceramic Tiles*, London, 1972.
BEDFORD, John, *Wedgwood Jasper Ware*, London, 1964.
Toby Jugs, London, 1968.
BUTTERWORTH, A., *Pottery and Porcelain*, London, 1964.
CHARLESTON, R. J. (ed.), *English Porcelain (1745–1850)*, London, 1965.
World Ceramics, London, 1968.
CLARK, Harold, *The Pictorial Pot Lid Book*, London, 1955.
COOPER, Ronald G., *English Slipware Dishes*, 1968.
COYSH, A. W., *Blue and White Transfer Ware*, Newton Abbott, 1970.
CUSHION, John P., *English China Collecting for Amateurs*, London, 1967.
Continental China Collecting for Amateurs, London, 1970.

CUSHION, John P. *(continued)*, *Pottery and Porcelain*, London, 1972.
CUSHION, W. John P. and HONEY, W. B., *Handbook of Pottery and Porcelain Marks*, London, 1965.
FISHER, Stanley, *British Pottery and Porcelain*, London, 1962.
GARNER, F. H., *English Ceramics*, London, 1966.
English Delftware, London, 1972.
GODDEN, Geoffrey A., *Encyclopedia of British Pottery and Porcelain Marks*, London, 1965.
An Illustrated Encyclopedia of British Pottery and Porcelain, London, 1966.
Jewitt's Ceramic Art of Great Britain, London, 1972.
British Porcelain: An Illustrated Guide, London, 1974.
British Pottery: An Illustrated Guide, London, 1974.
GRANT, M. H., *The Makers of Black Basaltes*, London, 1967.
HILLIER, Bevis, *Pottery and Porcelain, 1700–1914*, London, 1968.
HUGHES, G. B. and Therle, *English Porcelain and Bone China*, London, 1955.
IMBER, Diana, *Collecting Delft*, London, 1968.
JOHN, W. D. and BAKER, Warren, *Old English Lustre Pottery*, London, 1951.
LEWIS, Griselda, *A Collector's History of English Pottery*, London, 1969.
MACKAY, James A., *Commemorative Pottery and Porcelain*, London, 1971.
MANKOWITZ, Wolf and HAGGAR, Reginald, *Concise Encyclopedia of English Pottery and Porcelain*, London, 1957.
MOUNTFORD, Arnold R., *Staffordshire Salt-glazed Stoneware*, London, 1971.
OLIVER, Anthony, *The Victorian Staffordshire Figures, A Guide for Collectors*, London, 1971.
PUGH, P. D. Gordon, *Staffordshire Portrait Figures and Allied Subjects of the Victorian Era*, London, 1971.
RHODES, Daniel, *Porcelain and Stoneware*, London, 1960.
RUST, Gordon A., *Collector's Guide to Antique Pottery*, London, 1973.
SAVAGE, George, *Pottery Through the Ages*, London, 1958.
Porcelain Through the Ages, London, 1961.
SAVAGE, George and NEWMAN, Harold, *An Illustrated Dictionary of Ceramics*, London, 1974.
SHINN, Charles and Dorrie, *Victorian Parian China*, London, 1971.
TILLEY, Frank, *Teapots and Tea*, London, 1957.
WAKEFIELD, Hugh, *Victorian Pottery*, London, 1962.
WILLIAMS-WOOD, Cyril, *Staffordshire Pot Lids and their Potters*, London, 1972.

Printed Ephemera

BARNICOAT, John, *A Concise History of Posters*, London, 1972.
BUDAY, George, *The History of the Christmas Card*, London, 1965.
HILLIER, Bevis, *Posters*, 1968.
HOLLAND, Vyvyan, *Hand Coloured Fashion Plates*, London, 1955.
LANGLEY-MOORE, Doris, *Fashion Through Fashion Plates*, London, 1971.
LEE, Ruth W., *A History of Valentines*, London, 1953.
LEWIS, John, *Printed Ephemera*, London, 1962.
Collecting Printed Ephemera, London, 1976.
RICKARDS, Maurice, *Posters of the First World War*, London, 1968.
Posters of the Nineteen-Twenties, London, 1968.
Posters of the Turn of the Century, London, 1968.
SPELLMAN, Doreen and Sidney, *Victorian Music Covers*, London, 1969.
STAFF, Frank, *The Valentine and its Origins*, London, 1969.

Silverware

BANISTER, Judith, *English Silver*, London, 1969.
Late Georgian and Regency Silver, London, 1971.
Collecting Antique Silver, London, 1972.
BRADBURY, Frederick, *Guide to the Marks of Origin on British and Irish Silver*, London, 1968.
CAME, Richard, *Silver*, London, 1972.
CHAFFERS, W., *Handbook to Hallmarks on Gold and Silver Plate,* London, 1971.
DELIEB, Eric, *Investing in Silver*, London, 1967.
DENNIS, Jessie M., *English Silver*, London, 1970.
FINLAY, Ian, *Scottish Gold and Silver Work*, London, 1956.
HOLLAND, Margaret, *Old Country Silver*.
HUGHES, G. B., *Small Antique Silverware,* London, 1957.
HUGHES, G. B. and Therle, *Three Centuries of English Domestic Silver, 1500–1820*, London, 1968.
MILES, E. B., *Antique English Pocket Nutmeg Graters*, London, 1967.
PENZER, N. M., *The Book of the Wine Label*, London, 1949.
TAYLOR, Gerald, *Silver*, London, 1965.
WARDLE, Patricia, *Victorian Silver and Silver-plate*, London, 1963.
WHITWORTH, R. W., *Wine Labels*, London, 1966.

Textiles

CHURCHILL-BATH, Virginia, *Lace*, London, 1974.
KENDRICK, A. F., *English Needlework*, London, 1967.
KING, D., *Samplers*, London, 1960.
MORRIS, B., *History of English Embroidery*, London, 1954.
Victorian Embroidery, London, 1962.
POND, Gabrielle, *An Introduction to Lace*, London, 1968.
WARDLE, Patricia, *Victorian Lace*, London, 1968.

Wood, Ivory and Furniture

ARONSON, Joseph, *Encyclopedia of Furniture*, London, 1938.
BEIGBEDER, O., *Ivory*, London, 1965.
BUIST, John S., *Mauchline Ware*, Edinburgh, 1974.
DAVIS, Frank, *A Picture History of Furniture*, London, 1958.
DEVOE, Shirley S., *English Papier Mâché*, London, 1971.
FASTNEDGE, Ralph, *English Furniture Styles from 1500 to 1830*, London, 1955.
GLOAG, John, *Victorian Comfort*, London, 1961.
JONES, Barbara, *English Furniture at a Glance*, London, 1954.
PINTO, Edward H., *Encyclopaedia and Social History of Treen and other Wooden Bygones,* London 1969.
Tunbridge and Scottish Souvenir Woodware, London, 1970.
ROE, F. Gordon, *English Cottage Furniture; Victorian Furniture; Windsor Chairs,* London, 1950–53.
TOLLER, Jane, *Antique Papier Mâché in Great Britain and America*, London, 1962.
WILLS, Geoffrey, *Ivory*, London, 1968.

ACKNOWLEDGEMENTS

The publishers are grateful to the following for allowing us to use material:

Aspreys; Associated Biscuits Limited; Mrs W. Bird; Christie's; Christie's, South Kensington Limited; S. H. Cole; Colman Foods; Coty; *Country Life;* J. Denton Robinson; Mrs D. Dey; Doulton & Company Limited; The Dyson Perrins Museum of Royal Worcester Porcelain; Rodney Engen; Francis, Day & Hunter Limited; Derek Hill; Edward Kramer; Metropolitan Police; William Morris Gallery; Museum of London; National Museum of Wales; National Museum of Wales (Welsh Folk Museum); Pan Books Limited; R. J. Phillips; Phoenix Assurance Company Limited; Pilkington Glass Museum; Pollock's Toy Museum; A. Sanderson & Sons Limited; 'At the Sign of the Sad Iron' Limited; City Museum & Art Gallery, Stoke-on-Trent; Sun Alliance & London Insurance Group; Tunbridge Wells Museum; Josiah Wedgwood & Sons Limited; The Tiffany Shop; Christopher Wray's Lighting Emporium; Donald Wright; Young and Company.

Line illustrations by Susan Holland

Picture research by Susan Fleming and Viola Wylam

Book design by Paul Minns